The Room and the World

Sculpture: *The Invitation* by Terry Bachman. Owned by Stephen Dunn.
Photograph courtesy of Dave Romero/vibrantimage.com.

The Room and the World

Essays on the Poet Stephen Dunn

Edited by Laura McCullough

SYRACUSE UNIVERSITY PRESS

First Edition 2013

13 14 15 16 17 18 6 5 4 3 2 1

∞ The paper used in this publication meets the minimum requirements of the American National Standard for Information Sciences—Permanence of Paper for Printed Library Materials, ANSI Z39.48-1992.

For a listing of books published and distributed by Syracuse University Press, visit our website at SyracuseUniversityPress.syr.edu.

ISBN: 978-0-8156-3335-8

Library of Congress Cataloging-in-Publication Data

Available upon request from publisher.

Manufactured in the United States of America

To our friend

Kurt Brown

(1944–2013)

Contents

Intraview and Interview

Foreword

Dave Smith

A Twinship with Stephen Dunn

American poets, with the possible exceptions of Whitman, Dickinson, and Frost, have never been household names. Stephen Dunn stands, all the same, as a remarkable example of the American poet: once a superior basketball player at Hofstra University under the coaching of the great Butch van Breda Kolff, long a tennis player of such deft and heady strategies he was more fun to watch than to play, a poker player of such prowess even friends learned to avoid his table. My point, however, is not biographical exposition but that play, for Dunn, is synonymous with intellectual challenge, a kind of thinking that cognitive scientists find present in innovators, tinkerers, and dreamers, and, in writers, people who enact and study life-lesson moments as if they were clinical experimenters. Dunn's history as an athlete parallels a similar evolution as a poet: a book-by-book history of learning, adopting, trying out, discarding, consolidating, and simply owning a way of expression, a poetry whose idiosyncratic sound is the avuncular, whimsical narrating of a man who appears never so interested in the story he tells as in the reverberations of language, the ripplings of nuanced phrase, the placement and setting off of little bombs of discovery. The present collection of essays sets itself the task of introducing and identifying exactly what poetry is in Dunn's eighteen award-winning collections, and why it matters.

The task of a foreword is to provide a glimpse of terrain provided by one close to it, with some experience thereof, leading to a sort of scouting report, even a snapshot, however slippery its defining details. "Slippery" is about how I'd define Mr. Dunn, as I like to call him when the will is upon me to tease a little. Yet the honorific "Mr." properly recognizes a democratic citizen in American letters whose uncommon and multiple accomplishments, if not so gauded up with fame, are yet so known his name means poetry to many readers. When poets talk about who matters, the talk touches Mr. Dunn sooner or later; few colleges or universities have not offered him stage and crowd; prestigious journals now devote special issues to his poetry; like a be-medaled, general he wears the weight of awards, including the Pulitzer prize. Yet for all the glitter, he has for forty years remained utterly, daily, a practicing servant of the art. No poet I know is more devoted to the labor of writing poems before and beyond all else. This defines integrity that might evoke anyone's "Mr." in his presence but I use it also to express my admiration for Stephen Dunn, my dear friend since the Bread Loaf Writers' Conference in the summer of 1975.

Fellows at Bread Loaf used to be selected if they had published first books good enough to make them viewed as "comers." I had done my due diligence, had read the books by fellow fellows, before I arrived on the Vermont hilltop, and Mr. Dunn's *Looking for Holes in the Ceiling* seemed to me ordinary stuff, softly surreal, in the image manner then de rigueur. Yet it was memorable. Perhaps I sensed in the poems a pre-poetry life not unlike my own. Steve and I came from blue-collar families that were hardly nuclear, split by circumstances fateful and economic; our people were not bookish and none before us had known the experience of college life or the intellectual world it promoted. Like many young Americans, we grew up aware of a difference, in ourselves, that became a kind of diffidence, a mask, when we felt ourselves to be misfits. We wouldn't have called it a *je ne sais quoi* exactly. The way to compete in the society of success around us, among those who had that *quoi*, or at least the wherewithal to know what *quoi* was, was by default in athletic endeavor. We played. We sensed, as brutes do, we didn't possess what success meant, a finer harmony. Voices in our heads might say so, but we, being outsiders, had only speechlessness. We had to learn how to play with language.

The ways we were drawn to the power and grace of language would not then have seemed to us eloquence in fiction or poetry. We had to learn how writing is play, we who were committed to the play of bodies on courts and on playing fields, where the language is bluntly countable, win or lose. What did count was deeper, grayer, more changeable and rarely evident in a final score. Any good athlete learns that how you play matters the most, and how you feel about yourself in that playing, and how you are both respected and tasked by the best with whom you compete. The language of competition is, I believe, the language of nuance, as metaphoric as it is physical. Writing novels, poems, plays, criticism, is the play of discovery that affirms what matters to the one writing; and what that individual configures, we readers take up, consider, and either set aside or keep as worthy. Time changes what we value, as T. S. Eliot reminds us in "Tradition and the Individual Talent," and yet there is a changeless core, an obdurate, veining character as singular in a man's or a woman's writing as in any opponent one might face. Some, in games as in writing, never show that character. In others, it is immediately present; over years it may shape, fade, or shade otherwise, and then, again, there it is. No full-fitting word exists for what I mean. I call it character and I mean a presence that is language inside language, knowing and doing and being that exude what a poem of James Dickey's calls "the little more" that makes every difference.

The poems in *Looking for Holes in the Ceiling* were, however, cut-to-fit suits of the age. They spliced Dunn's New York youth and life to the flirty and half-leaping image portraits touted in the early 1970s by Robert Bly as "new thinking." Bly, James Wright, and John Haines, mainly, made poetry as a quasi-therapeutic dig into the self for repressed experiences that, drawn to daylight and juxtaposed with the unpredictable, could affirm that life hymned in the Age of Aquarius, the bolt to California, the long-hair-smoke-'em-let-it-all-hang-out, the times they were a-changin' days. Young poets mimicked their teachers. Donald Justice, Mark Strand, Philip Levine were relentlessly replicated. Stephen Dunn worked hard in poems to enter the charmed circle of the art's insiders. The early books of poets are commonly imitative issue of what bends and stamps their society. Among we pretenders in those days there was character already shining, undeniable. Dunn's first book had it.

I still see myself in the sweet late sunlight of Vermont when Steve Dunn asked me what I thought of *Looking for Holes in the Ceiling.* I had had some drink; maybe that released me. I said "not much." In my mind there is a puzzled expression on his face and I am feeling, oh Lord, I will have to explain myself and all I can say is it seems like the pseudo-mysterious stuff you read in the magazines where we are all trying to reside. Maybe I have angered him? I knew little of the bureaucracies and politicizing and back-alley decisions the poetry world stood on, but I knew enough to know I risked a long-term animosity no one needs. Thirty years later, Donald Justice took an occasion to write that he had overheard me say at that same Bread Loaf dance I didn't like his poems and he knew it must be still so—despite actual evidence to the contrary. All Steve Dunn did was hand me the manuscript of his second book, *Full of Lust and Good Usage*, and say, no tongue in cheek, "See if you like this one better."

That book and each subsequent book I have liked better. The essays here attend to Dunn's now venerated collections. They adduce compelling reasons for how play became the matured enactments of character tested, threatened, responding—in one of America's most dicey periods of cultural and historical change. It's contemplative, really. What a big word for dudes like us, I want to snicker. Still, Dunn's poetry, as these essayists make clear, has always been dominantly philosophical, working to and through verbal snares, obstacles, oppositions, playing paradoxes, complexities—examining the life moments trapped, angled, pressured, conflicted, and thereby defined, or at least in hand, a poetry that resists the unresisted, the unseen, the unheard. A poetry of quiet courage—not a declaration of character, but a sewing together of a fabric that might hold the shape of character, its actioning.

Courage is a glib word. To us, in the 1960s and '70s, courage was measurable by what you did in military service or what you did against military service, even perhaps poems you wrote. Some senior poets curried public approval for antiwar poems, most self-serving and unworthy. Because James Wright then seemed to me as formidable and conscionable a poet as any, I asked him about a poem's moral role, mentioning his poem "The Morality of Poetry." He said, his sigh a measure of the tedium he felt for a question he had so struggled with, that the poet's only moral obligation is to write well and that, he argued, required courage. We had grown up in the last shadows of the New Critical era, which metaphorically asked us to dress uniformly, respect tradition, not laugh too much, and keep our personal stories to ourselves. The progress of poetry for the next four decades was to resist in some measure in every respect. Almost any form exploration required a moral decision. Young poets easily found themselves, as Richard Hugo once had, "a wrong thing in a right place," and there was much confusion over the inner fortitude our grandmothers praised—who had it and who did not—to choose to join up, to hang out, or to make it new. The fundamental difficulty would be to enact not what ought to be truth but what was *true*, obliging language that escaped glibness and indulgence, an idiom as alive with personality as with the smell and feel of what we lived. To demand that poems speak in a particular mechanistic way, carry a particular progressive vision, or articulate a definitive agenda seemed intellectually immature—a matter of faith, not the aesthetic accomplishment by which a writer ought to be measured. Yet poems must have durable weight; they must presume and cast light upon the causes and effects which shape us; they must entertain us; they must risk their own demand for time and trust in boldness that cannot ever be gainsaid. Those who skate near the thinnest ice, who chill us with the feel of threat, whose art has the daring of potential and the artifice that renews us come with character, or courage, beyond mere lineation skills.

As Mr. Auden told us, in our time poetry makes nothing happen. It doesn't win or lose; it doesn't yield measurable production; it evades meaning though it comes stuffed with the porridge and pieties and piglet truths of our experience. Yet more of us seek to be, and may be, poets than at any time in recorded history. More books, more journals, more gill-bursting MFA programs, more boomers with gray locks shaking at poetry readings. Our poetry is ubiquitously small stuff, yet we can't get enough of it or of the search for something only true poetry has. And what is that? Strip away the costumes of posture and ego-tremble, and behold the poet: man or woman who, in words, enacts and struggles and competes for what we think we want, at least temporarily, an identifiable, responsible self. I daresay it is meaning we want. We don't have it often, maybe we can't imagine it often, but when we recognize it, and we sometimes do, we grow with a feeling of gratitude, even of purpose glimpsed in the ways of things. We are grateful to see, we believe in the poet's courage, in his competition for what words envision, and we want to do and say as he has done. So we learn in Stephen Dunn's poems a gratitude for language that is plain and simple and also inherently self-competitive, complex, a kind of lens held this way and that until it becomes a prism giving the most extraordinary delights, though it shows little in the ordinary way we expect, a throughway for the uncommon happening that is knowledge, a magnifier altogether. Have I contradicted Mr. Auden? Well, he did not say poetry has not, and cannot achieve, meaning.

The expression of meaning teases us all but no one more than the private woman or man who wants to be what Dunn, in a recent poem, called "the real deal." He referred, albeit tongue in cheek, to Jesus, but he might have as easily mentioned Popeye, famous for declaiming "I yam what I yam," as I once heard I. M. Pei remark playfully. Dunn, an assiduously private person, could not, in poems, be more charming, social, erudite, one of the folk who covets vignettes of off-balance behavior, life lessons of hypothesis, occlusion, paradox. Dunn writes convinced that in his words nothing is what it is until it is bent by a tale. Though by tale's end it might not be. His dodgy, off-balancing act is fuel for fable and playground for parable, his soft, wry voice saying whatever is necessary to bump readers against the unexpected. Then it's game on, ethical, aesthetic, theosophical, historic, whatever suits his cagey wandering. He seems a man troubled by a contentious world, a sometimes grim living, but he likes things to work out for the best; he's a comic writer, encouraging but rarely ameliorative. His gentle judgments can be as strict as a Fahrenheit thermometer but uncertainty is his human path where forgiveness and duplicity are both directions to hope, where knowing and saying seem unrecognizable identical twins.

Some years ago, I introduced Stephen for his reading at the Catskill Poetry Conference. I noted how odd life had been for me, his twin brother, though four years younger and born to a different mother in a different state. He won awards I didn't win; he wrote poems I thought of writing, beautifully too. I worked up a pretty good steam assaying how both men and women, many of the latter, found his poems endearing and exciting, especially his bad-boy confessions, which left me the role of the invisibly good and pure. He's better than he'll admit, I'd say. Knowing and saying are almost the same, right? I can still see Steve in the front row, that instant of recognition in his eyes, before delight wells up all over him, and laughter, and the gift passes between us, as it had almost four decades earlier, as it does between him and his readers. I mean the gift of knowing language played with for all marbles at stake. Recognition and declaration mark the true poet's unrefusable calling. But to what? To life's isness, to measuring the sacred, always slippery and troublesome and run together with the profane, to sorting out joy from mere contentment. To Dunn, the poet's task is superior observation and speculation that prompts what can be called the best *possibles*. That's why, in the recent poem, "If the Poet," he asks, "Would the real and the imagined fuse, / become something new?" Well, what else explains the twinship of strangers? Or the strangeness of the ordinary so often twinned with the sacred? I said to the conferees that all my brother does is ask questions, wander through puzzles, say memorable things we might say for ourselves, if we were good enough. Dunn, after all, isn't so bad. As "If the Poet" tells us, the good and the bad are mirror images competing in the imagination for the final word. No matter what he says, I'd say, it's the play of an athlete with ideas, a brother challenging you.

And what if the poet and priest were one,
each invoking the other as the crops grew
and rain was steady in rainy season, or,
just as confusing, things got worse
and prayer proved useless, and poems
merely decorated the debris where a house

once was? Would it be time for the priest
to admit he'd only really known one book? For the poet
to say he'd read many, and look, it hasn't helped?
Or has the issue from the start been a great need
that can't be fully met, only made bearable
and sometimes served by those who try? (*Parnassus*, Spring 2013)

Acknowledgments

The editor wishes to acknowledge the following journals in which some of these essays, most written for this project, and interviews first appeared and for those editors' support. Further, grateful thanks go to Kurt Brown, without whom this project would not have come to pass, to Megan Cushing, intern extraordinaire, and finally, to Michael Broek, for more than can be said.

David Jauss, *Shenandoah* (Fall 2011)
Alicia Ostriker, *Green Mountains Review* (Fall 2010/Winter 2011)
Gregory Djanikian, *Cortland Review* (Fall 2010)
Kathleen Graber, *Georgia Review* (Summer 2011)
George Looney, *Georgia Review* (Summer 2011)
BJ Ward, *Journal of NJ Poets* (Spring 2012)
Philip Dacey, *Two Cities* (Winter 1997)
Larry Raab, *New Ohio Review* (Spring 2012); a substantial part of the essay appeared originally as "Where the Path Leads: Collaboration, Revision, and Friendship"
Pam Houston, *Gulf Coast* (Fall 2013)
Andrea Hollander, *Writers Chronicle* (Fall 2013)

Stephen's Essays and Talks

"Forms and Structures" originally as a talk to the architecture students and faculty at Pratt Institute. *Georgia Review* (Fall 2008)
"Solstice Talk" was the first "The State of the Union: Diversity and Poetic Craft" keynote reading at Pine Manor College, *Georgia Review* (Fall 2012)
"Intra-view," *Georgia Review* (Summer 2011)

Interview

"Relentlessly Interesting, Interview," by Laura McCullough, *Georgia Review* (Summer 2011)

On the Cover

The Invitation is a sculpture by Terry Bachman based on Stephen Dunn's poem "The Stairway." The sculpture is owned by Stephen Dunn. The cover is a detail of a photograph taken by David Romero.

Introduction

Once, in a workshop Stephen Dunn was leading, I heard him say that James Dickey's poem "The Sheep Child" had given him great permission as a young poet. First, he talked about the image central to the poem—the glass jar in a shadowy museum back corner holding the thing alluded to in the poem's title "that's only half / Sheep . . . like a woolly baby" (Dickey, 248)—and having gotten our attention with this perverse and sad creature, read us the poem, Dunn's sonorous voice shifting just so in tone when the narration gave way to what the sheep-child might be saying with its sad and fathomless eyes. We understood that the poem was a permission for us as well. When Stephen said this poem had made all subjects possible in poetry for him, we understood he was passing this permission on to us but also offering a warning. Above all else, one must be "interesting," he said, but daring would never be sufficient; we had to be precise, as well, a thing the Dickey poem delivers.

Dunn writes eloquently in his essay "The Good, the Not So Good" about the relationship between precision and passion. The essay appeared in his collection *Walking Light: Essays and Memoirs* (*WLN*, 37–45), the entirety of which makes clear that the line between the life and the work is anything but distinct; orchestration is central to meaning making but also to the lived life, the gestures, the moves, the strategies, the *storification*—a word Stephen used to explain the transmuting of mere fact into meaningful artifact, the act of composing making the life of the mind visible, apprehendable to the *other.* As Dave Smith's foreword suggests, there is a gift in this, a kind of serve—in friendship, in sports, and poetry—that has both an inevitability about it and an expectation of a return, but also a sense of boundaries. The court, manners, where to start a story, when to leave a poem.

Dickey's sheep-child poem is where the sacred and profane collude, but it knows when to end. Like Dunn's "The Routine Things around the House" (*ND*, 39–40) a poem much admired by his readers and referenced in more than one of the essays that follow, it doesn't dwell on the details that represent the taboo; rather it points to deeper matters such as shame, alienation from the self, repression, the hidden life, and more, things hard to talk about, not the ordinary fare of poetry, and Dunn's poem says this clearly, the knowing when to stop a crucial move, maybe more so than the many moves that get made in the forward rush of a poem's creation, the accumulation of moves accruing to the artifact. Dunn's poems embody the act of choosing, and in this way, the poems, besides their subject or concern—usually though not always domestic—are ars poetica and are always ruled by aesthetic decorum.

Decorum, in rhetoric, is the rightness, the appropriateness of a subject to its form as well as its likely meeting of the audience's expectation. In general usage, it is what we don't break in social contracts. Dickey's poem broke expectation, as did modernist thought about decorum, and this can be seen, too, in Dunn's delightful and mischievous poem titled simply "Decorum" (*NS*, 24–25), where he is the teacher and a student poem is under discussion that uses some version of the word "fuck" multiple times, giving rise to great laughter from some audiences when it is read and slow, low chuckles from those stunned by new knowledge of poetry's range, often students new to poetry. But the poem does more than examine the nature of vulgarity; it is about revision, about choosing the right word, "the proper fit / of word with act" (ibid., 24). The end of the poem has the poet-speaker enacting the role of poet-teacher, wondering which word would be better, "gymnasium" or "boat house," sure the former was the wrong choice. The poem, funny as it is, is quite serious, serious about language and the choices to be made with it, the ways it can be employed with a sense of rightness—not socially, not in terms of idea, but in terms of the "beingness" of the world enacted and manifested in the poem, that being the only decorum the poet has any obligation to maintain, and the vulgarity, not for its own sake, but for the foil it offers.

In "What Men Want" (*WG*, 192–95) the final poem in *What Goes On: Selected and New Poems, 1995–2009*, the history of the men in Dunn's family is explored—his father, brother, himself in relation to work life, in relation to what they wanted and what they had. The closing four lines are instructive:

> I've always needed paper and pencil
> in order to speak as little as I should.
> After the power to choose
> a man wants to the power to erase. (195)

Erasure is the revisionist's power, a weapon, a tool, what forgives or indicts; what is left out as important, sometimes, as what is kept, and here in "What Men Want," the poem that takes as its subject the role of gender expectation in the lives of men in Dunn's immediate life is also a poem about composing and about writing as another way to be a man.

Many of the essays that follow will talk about the internal landscape deemed Dunnian, of his famous quarreling with himself on the page, his contrarian strategies in composition, his exfoliation of the secret life, which is also the title of one of his mid-career poems. In "The Secret Life," we are told:

> Even when you speak to your best friend,
> the one who'll never betray you,
> you always leave out one thing;
> a secret life is that important. (*LE*, 72)

Whatever we have pickled in a jar in the somewhere of our psyches, however ugly or trivial or even in some way sublime, we sense that Dunn understands our need to protect it but would also be very interested in hearing the story of it, the story of it that has found its own music, and that it, the poem, would matter more to him than whatever shame or reticence we had to burn off to hold this one thing to the light. He is above all an "ice traveler" as he writes in his essay, "Alert Lovers, Hidden Sides, and Ice Travelers: Notes on Poetic Form and Energy" (*WLN*, 144–56), someone who goes out on the thin ice, taking risks. Of them, he writes, "Their goal is to disappear while leaving evidence of their journey. It's to make a livable environment for what's hidden, rearrange what's already known" (ibid., 152). But he also speaks of the "alert lover," meaning the one not so self-absorbed as to miss discovery or surprise, and that we are often "some composite of ice traveler and alert lover" as writers (ibid.).

In his book that won the Pulitzer Prize, *Different Hours*, his poem "A Postmortem Guide" (119–21) speaks to those who might speak of him after his death. It's a funny poem, wry, but not too funny; it's sly in its gestures of self-knowledge versus admission, even indictments, small ones, the tonal juxtapositions part of the poem's pleasure, and it's useful here at the start of this gathering of poets and writers, fellow ice travelers, who have also been "burned by books early / and [keep] sidling up to the flame" (ibid., 120). The job of these essayists has been to consider how "we go on" (*LE*, "Loves," 94), determining the rhetoric of his decorum, to unmask, not the man, but the character of the man on the page, who as alert lover and ice traveler tells his eulogist,

> say that I loved
> my companions most of all.
> In all sincerity, say that they provided
> a better way to be alone. (ibid., 121)

The writers in this anthology have been some of his companions: former students, friends, colleagues, fellow poets, older, contemporary, younger. Some know him personally; others do not, but still, they are his companions.

Many of these essays involve close readings of certain poems, certain books. Most address issues, themes, strategies, gestures, and effects that have become and accrue to the signature authorial voice that is Stephen Dunn on the page and that has earned him a wide and dedicated audience. Further study will include an overview of the oeuvre, the way the work began in the poems in fashion when Dunn was studying at Syracuse University with W. D. Snodgrass, Philip Booth, and Donald Justice. The newest book, *Lines of Defense* (in manuscript form as this anthology was being assembled) includes a poem titled, "Out of Respect" for and dedicated to Justice, a poem much different than those he would have been turning in to workshop with any of those three great poets or in the first books. Dunn's lines have tightened, relinquishing homage to the cri de coeur of mid–twentieth century poetry—"no ideas but in things"—and owing a great deal to the cerebral nature of Wallace Stevens's poetry, instead becoming driven by lean and sinuous lines built on the rebar of rhetorical strategies and prosody. His earlier tendency to a sliding tercet, for example, gave way over time to an allegiance to the pleasures of interestingly resonant enjambment. The speaker's tone in the books published by Norton, beginning with the much beloved *Between Angels* through the Pulitzer Prize–winning *Different Hours*, changes significantly with the publication of *The Insistence of Beauty*, which occurred following a major change in Dunn's personal life, relationships, and residence, something a literary biographer may take up some day.

Since then, the poems have become increasingly more musical, more sonically compact and controlled, while still maintaining the music of syntax and rhetorical strategy, and their lens and focus have widened: more political poems coinciding with poems addressing the aging of the body and the fact of mortality, and poems of the spiritual residing with the philosophical quarrels that had always been part of the work, more things for the literary biographer to consider that are not taken on by the contributors to this project. The tendency to quarrel on the page will be noted by several contributors here, but the ways in which declaration and interrogation balance over the course of the work is significant, including, and maybe even more so in the most recent book, *Lines of Defense.*

For anyone uncertain that Stephen Dunn is an expert sentence wright, the 1998 book of what Dunn called prose pairs, *Riffs and Reciprocities*, is a must-read and an important book for understanding more fully—in terms of his control of line and stanza against the sentence—the lineated poems that comprise the bulk of his creative work. *Walking Light: Essays and Memoirs*, published first by Norton and then in expanded form by BOA, is, as the essays in this project will suggest, a crucial text for understanding Dunn's attitude toward his writing life, practicably, in terms of composition on one end, and perhaps most engagingly, in terms of world view and aesthetic architecture on the other.

In addition to the foreword by the masterful essayist, poet, and longtime friend of Dunn's Dave Smith, this anthology includes selected essays by Stephen Dunn himself and one of the interviews that I conducted with Stephen Dunn during the last decade. Additionally, there is an "intra-view," meaning an essay Stephen wrote comprising the answers to an imagined series of questions from an imagined interviewer. The bulk of the project includes twenty-eight essays by writers and scholars, many of which appeared in journals and magazines. It is worth particular note that a significant number appeared in the *Georgia Review*, which has been a major champion of Stephen Dunn's work throughout his career. Indeed, one of the essays in this anthology is by the editor of the *Georgia Review*, Stephen Corey, and one is by one of its poetry reviewers, Judith Kitchen.

The contributed essays offer fascinating perspectives on Dunn's work, some more sweeping, others on a smaller sometimes acute scale, but whether an overview or a thin slice of the work, all convey a sense of the passion and precision, as Dunn explores in his essay "The Good, the Not So Good," that have been the hallmarks of his own poems, riding the necessary balance between the two. This collusion of effects—between what precision and passion bring to the page—has been part of what has made Dunn's work respected by so many. The admiration for Dunn and his work that each of these writers feels is palpable; there is a sense of cherishment in these essays, and this is married inextricably with their discussions of craft, form, aesthetics, and world view in Dunn's poems and books.

While each essay stands alone as one lens into Dunn's body of work, they have been organized into nine sections of two to four essays that reside together, either in terms of form, structure, subject, or concern, and that would make for interesting dialogue in relation to each other.

Fred Marchant's "Beyond Words" follows a number of Dunn's books and the changes over them and considers isolation and loneliness, words and verbs, and a Melvillian aspect to Dunn. George Looney's and James May's essays enter the work at radically different points on the arc of Dunn's work over time. Looney's essay concerns itself largely with the early book *Not Dancing*, while Dunn's latest collection, published at the same time as this anthology, is the subject of James May's essay "Against Satisfaction" (for which a prepublication manuscript was used).

In the second part, Gregory Djanikian and David Jauss scrutinize Dunn's strategies on the page, his tendency to reverse and take back, for quarreling with his own assertions, his tendency to parry and thrust. BJ Ward's essay, "A Certain Capaciousness and 'The Routine Things around the House'" concerns itself with a more microscopic view, considering tension and word choice in the poem of the title.

David Rigsbee, Kathleen Graber, and Michael Broek, in part 3, all circle the ideas of ambivalence and ambiguity: Rigsbee considers what he calls Dunn's and "double-seeing," Graber examines Dunn's poems as "glass-bottomed boats," and Broek views the work in terms of its subtle political arguments. The essayists in this part call upon thinkers such as Hegel, Heidegger, and Berlin, and Graber's essay uses as a fulcrum the morality play of the TV show *Deadwood*.

An interesting paring is Philip Dacey's essay considering Dunn as a poet of consciousness against the backdrop of modernism and Tony Hoagland's, whose essay "Claustrophobia, Decency, Truth: One Speaker's Civil War" exfoliates in detail the notions of character, self, and oppositions and preservations of selfhood in Dunn's poems. Together these essays bounce off each other in interesting ways.

The realm of the sacred and the spiritual are mined in the essays in part 5. Ilyse Kusnetz closely reads Dunn's essay "Poets, Poetry, and the Spiritual" in the BOA edition of *Walking Light*, as well as in his poems. The Jungian scholar and longtime friend of Dunn, James Hollis, explores myth and man in his essay "The Poet as Theoginist," while the student Timothy Leyrson, in his essay, "Facing Masks and Masking Faces," considers what Dunn's poems reveal about the act of becoming.

Part 6 concerns gender—men and women and the lives of men—and is led by Alicia Ostriker's aptly titled, "The Poet's Women and the Ordinary Mysteries," in which generosity of spirit plays a large role. Jason Schneiderman explores the two important poems, "What Goes On" and "What Men Want," finding in them contradictions, mercy, forgiveness, and the answer to the latter poem's implied question, that revision of Freud's famous quote. Finally, R. Dwayne Betts explores love and relationship in one poem of Dunn's, "The Affair."

Wendy Canella, Andrea Hollander, and Judith Kitchen offer very different essays in part 7, in which extraterrestrials, aliens, desire and duty, self and other, ice travelers, and point of view all come into consideration. Canella ruminates on the sociopolitical and the historical in Dunn's work, especially since 9/11, and ponders, too, on the role of angels in the poems. Dunn's essay, "Alert Lovers, Hidden Sides, and Ice Travelers: Notes on Poetic Form and Energy" is key to Andrea Hollander's essay, while Judith Kitchen reprises parts of a number of her reviews on Dunn's work from the *Georgia Review*, assembled into a pastiche that includes, among other things, a close read of Dunn's important poem "Loves," which closes his book *Landscape at the End of the Century*.

The longtime editor of the *Georgia Review*, Stephen Corey, opens part 8 with his essay, "Double-Teaming." A lover of both basketball and poetry, Corey explores the analogue between sports and poetry, strategies and maneuvers on the court and the page, necessarily touching on the personal as Dunn was, famously, a college basketball player, and the subsequent essays in this part are personal, as well. In "Mount Holyoke, 1992," the novelist and short story writer Pam Houston offers us a memoir about family, writing community, and personal kindness. Following this is the essay "In a Different Hour: Collaboration, Revision, and Friendship" by Lawrence Raab, Dunn's longtime friend, collaborator, and first reader. Closing this part is an essay by Lisa Honaker, "'Let Things Darken as They Will': the Revision Process." Honaker is a professor at the Richard Stockton College of New Jersey where Dunn spent most of his teaching career, and she staged a Stephen Dunn Retrospective and Revision Process Exhibit, which informs her essay.

The final part includes four essays, one that transitions from the previous part on more personal approaches and three with more lyric qualities. A fixture in the southern New Jersey writing scene, Peter Murphy, writes a humorous essay on the relationship been God and dogs in Dunn's work. Kurt Brown's "Scattered Notes on a Coherent Poet" includes sixteen micro-essays on aspects of Dunn's style, aesthetics, or world view. In "Five Sketches of 'Tenderness,'" Brian Turner rotates one poem in his mind, viewing it through different imagined lenses. Gerald Stern's essay, "The Quarrel," is the final one of the contributed essays, and it explores one of Dunn's dog poems, the funny "Don't Do That," and harkens back to the essay by Murphy to pose in the end, a most serious question about Dunn as poet, one with crucial ramifications for considering the poet's oeuvre and, indeed, the poet himself.

▸ ▸ ▸

Who is Stephen Dunn? This anthology is not a literary biography, though necessarily it touches upon the man while trying to understand the work of the poet. There is a relationship, of course, but what is the line, what is useful to know, to talk about, to reveal?

A few years ago, in conversation, Stephen mentioned that Robert Bringhurst's book, *Everywhere Being Is Dancing*, was very important to him; in fact, he said, it had changed him. Stephen rarely makes such unequivocal statements, a fact many of these essays will make clear; Stephen's bent toward questioning and reversals is a signature element of both the mind and the work on the page. Yet here he was making a claim.

Even before I'd gotten past page 1, I knew Stephen hadn't been lying. Bringhurst writes that "poetry is one among many forms of knowing, and maybe knowing in the purest form we know. [. . . This] knowing in the sense of stepping in tune with being, hearing and echoing the music and heartbeat of being—is what we mean by poetry" (15). Stephen was interested early on by the metaphoric resonance of "stepping," "walking," and indeed, "being," each alone, but also in their relationship to each other. The notion of "walking light" forms the title of his book of memoir and essays, of which "Stepping Out" is the first in the collection (*WLN*, 3–14).

"Stepping Out" is a memoir, one that establishes for the reader the *who* of Stephen, bringing together the boy he was with the writer he became, the development of both the thinker and the *be*-er, and he writes, prefiguring the Bringhurst he would read years after writing his own essay, that "you have to know where you are, but that's just the beginning of useful consciousness. Then you have to go where you can't" (*WLN*, 13) because to *be* one has to go through the process of *becoming.* To do that, Dunn had to learn to "walk light," a phrase he borrowed from a William Meredith poem, "Crossing Over," that Dunn discusses in two of the essays in *Walking Light.* The paradox, Dunn writes in "Stepping Out," is that "you must walk wrong in order to walk right" (ibid., 13), and walking lightly, being aware of one's surroundings, the landscape, if you will, is crucial.

For Stephen, awareness started in silence, which began early and is the subject of "A History of My Silence" (*WLN*, 107–23). He writes about his relationship to silence, the dual nature of it:

> Silence was my tactic, my bane. Occasionally it still is. Whatever quality presently exists in my silence has arisen partly out of fear, partly out of a need to fill up that storehouse which I knew didn't belong to me yet. Often it is locked. I keep on finding and misplacing the key. (ibid., 123)

Of silence, Dunn jokes in his prose pair, "Silence" (*RR*, 71), and here in full, that "over the years, I've spoken too much about it," yet in "The Secret Life" (*LE*, 72), he writes "that silence is a kind of truth." In the early book, *Work and Love*, Dunn writes in "Meditation on Two Themes" about making "a new kind of silence" (30). The poem is delightfully about one of the things two people might do in bed, but it is also about what Dunn has done himself, walking or stepping out from the silence of his youth to become the public poet. The way he has done that is to build, line by line, poem by poem, book by book, a body of work, and like an architect of poetry, he has built the house he now lives in.

I mean this both literally and figuratively, as the tropes of the architect and architecture have been a part of many of Stephen's poems. In his long series of linked poems, "The Snowmass Cycle" (*NS*, 3–10), he writes that he thinks he "learned something / about architecture from a swallow" (ibid., 9). Yet often the notion of architecture appears in his work in terms of the relationship between the small and the large, a room, say, and everything else (and his essay in this volume, "Form and Structure" will offer additional ways to consider this).

In the book that may be considered the start of his middle period, *Not Dancing*, in the poem "The Room and the World," he writes, about the key he was misplacing and re-finding, the key that unlocked his silence, which may be the key, to the house in which his poems dwell. In its entirety:

> The room was room enough for one
> or maybe two if the two had just
> discovered each other and were one.
> Outside of the room was the world
> which had a key to the room, and knowing
> a little about the world he knew
> how pointless it was to change the lock.
> He knew the world could enter the room
> anytime it wanted, but for the present
> the world was content to do its damage

elsewhere, which the television recorded.
Always, he kept in his mind the story of the man
hanging from a cliff, how the wildflowers
growing there looked lovelier than ever.
That was how he felt about his one chair
and the geometry of the hangers in his closet
and the bed that fit him like a body shirt.
Sometimes the world would breathe heavily
outside the door because it was obscene
and could not help itself. It was this
that led him eventually to love the world
for its pressure and essential sadness.
One day he just found himself opening
the door, allowing the inevitable.
The world came in and filled the room.
It seemed so familiar with everything. (*ND*, 34)

The metaphor of the room appears in others of Stephen's poems, including "Leaving the Empty Room" in the recent *Here and Now*, in which he writes, "The door had a double lock, / and the joke was on me" (25). He says, "it was an empty room," and how he wished for "a secret tunnel, perhaps / a winding path" out of the room. The idea of leaving or staying, what courage or magic one might need to negotiate between worlds, the inner room, the outer, and what happens when the man will, as we all do, finally leave, are central to the poem's concerns.

. . . Maybe I needed
a certain romance of departure
to kick in, as if I were waiting
for magic instead of courage,
or something else
I didn't have. (ibid.)

And when the speaker does leave, the idea of how to do so, how to step out, how to walk light is reprised:

. . . I just followed
my body out the door,
one quick step after another,
even as the room started to fill
with what I'd been sure wasn't there. (ibid., 26)

The poem "The Stairway" in *The Insistence of Beauty* is instructive in synthesizing these poems—"The Room and the World" and "Leaving the Empty Room"—and establishing a link between them. Stephen writes of an architect who negotiates what the world wants—utility—and what he, the architect wants, which is beauty for its own sake. The contributors to this anthology are certainly those "to whom nothing / about it need be explained" (ibid., 14), ones who would love the stairway for its own sake, and who champion the beauty of the stairway that is not about where it leads but its essential beingness, but I will also note that this collection is not exhaustive and that Stephen is decidedly not, as he wrote in the poem "Connubial" (*HN*, 89) "in danger / of being terribly understood." Humorous as that is, it is simply true as Stephen has written more than eighteen books, an astonishing body of work, and many of the contributors talk about the same poems, a fact in itself that is interesting to note: certain poems have become emblematic, have and retain a certain power drawing Stephen's most avid and dear readers to them again and again. Of the many poems touched on in the essays, four emerge as having singular importance. In order of the most mentioned, they are "The Reverse Side" (73) from the Pulitzer Prize–winning *Different Hours*; the late poem that closed *What Goes On: Selected and New Poems, 1995–2009*, "What Men Want" (192–95); the long poem, "Loves" at the end of *Landscape at the End of the Century* (81–94); and the early, tender poem that dips into the territory of the unspoken from *Not Dancing*, "The Routine Things around the House" (39–40).

The poem "Sweetness" from *Between Angels* (a book that a number of these essays touch on and that firmly marks Dunn's ascendancy to the American poetry scene) render precisely Dunn's world view: the idea of travel, of having to figure out not just how to get somewhere, but how to arrive and do so in the right way, the relationship between a small "sweetness" and the long

> . . . bitter road
> it's traveled
> to come so far, to taste so good. (44)

The end provides us, his companions and his readers, permission to travel between the bitter and the sublime. Somewhere in the borders, the interstices, is how we find the means "to go on," a notion Dunn loves, as he writes in the closing line of "Loves" (*LE*, 94), and since all of the contributors are writers (most, but not all, poets), he gave us permission to write from our own borders, our own rooms in this world.

A recent, uncollected poem, "Their Architecture" (*Hampden-Sydney Poetry Review*, winter 2012) has two people in the "room" in the "house," and it explores the ways marriage is a series of accommodations and, too, how the living is itself an accommodation:

> All he wanted was to lie down with her
> on a real bed in a house in which all the terms
> were theirs, something he thought reasonable
> because nothing else made sense or felt as good.
> He had constructed the house as the world
> seemed to allow, blueprints true to code,
> six steps to the front door, a solid railing
> to grip if you might find yourself on some verge,
> and a foyer that led to stairs at the top of which
> was their bed, a king-size and queen-making
> downy bed with pillows monogrammed
> Lucky and Hers.
>
> He wished for desire
> and deep sleep, and thought the world would comply
> because, after all, he was only wishing
> for what had been granted to others with lives
> like theirs, but the world had a stake

in everything under roof and sun, and an affinity
for the real. It seemed to be waiting for doubts
to arise—a few *maybes* to lodge in the man's mind.

Their lovemaking was wild and inconsiderate,
windows open, un-neighborly—wonderful,
in other words. When they woke, they were
on the floor, naked and cold. They hadn't fallen,
it was just that the real bed in the real world
had cast them out. Crumpled and stained,
its covers roughly pulled back, hospital corners
loose, it was as if a general lack of respect
had been shown (the man could see that now).

It was uncomfortable on the floor,
and the man hated discomfort. The woman
had prior experience with positions like this.
This is what happens, she told the man,
when someone wants too much what he wants.
But while the woman was desiring
something that felt more like home, the man
was thinking doors and ways out,
an architecture of escape.

The floor
started to creak, complain. He began
to understand that even the most perfect house,
built with sweat and dreams, would never
wholly be theirs. She suggested they build
a smaller house, a house that could
be better controlled, perhaps with a cot
instead of a bed in a tiny room,
and on it quiet love-making the night long.
If the world could smile, it would have.
If the real could speak, it would have said—
perhaps through its teeth—*Yes, good,*
in time they all settle, come around.

This is a poem only the mature poet could write, and Dunn's years and many books are its architecture, and in its particularities and specificities—a couple, their life, *their* architecture—it is also an ars poetica in the sense that he has always written about a room, he has been the architect of his own becoming, the stepping out of silence into being, by being the architect of words, and he has resisted, by walking light, every step of the way.

In the poem "The Room," he writes that "the room has no choice. / Everything that's spoken in it / it absorbs" (*WG*, 176). Stephen knows that "the room" like the larger world "plays no favorites" and that when everyone leaves, the room goes on. It "will need to be imagined / by someone." The someone is himself, of course, but it is also all of us in the rooms of our own making and being. The room, when empty, the poem continues, will not be empty. The speaker knows "from experience how deceptive / silence can be." This is the world within this one, as Eluard wrote, and as Stephen has revealed, a place upon whose chairs we sit temporarily. Bathed in the room's "shades / of light and dark," we lucky ones become ourselves, perhaps have friends and companions—something Stephen has written of often—or teachers along the way who help us "go on," and when we leave,

> . . . This is when the walls
> start to breathe as if reclaiming the air,
> when the withheld spills forth,
> when even the chairs begin to talk. (ibid., 177)

Works Cited

Bringhurst, Robert. 2008. "Everywhere Being Is Dancing, Knowing Is Known." In *Everywhere Being Is Dancing*. Berkley, CA: Counterpoint Press. 15–32.

Dickey, James. 1992. "The Sheep Child." In *The Whole Motion: Collected Poems, 1945–1992*. Hanover, NH: Wesleyan University Press. 248–49.

Abbreviations

BA	*Between Angels*. New York: Norton, 1989.
CN	*A Circus of Needs*. Pittsburg: Carnegie-Mellon University Press, 1978.
DH	*Different Hours*. New York: Norton, 2000.
EE	*Everything Else in the World*. New York: Norton, 2006.
FL	*Full of Lust and Good Usage*. Pittsburg: Carnegie-Mellon University Press, 1976.
HN	*Here and Now*. New York: Norton, 2011.
IB	*The Insistence of Beauty*. New York: Norton, 2004.
L	*Loosestrife*. New York: Norton, 1996.
LE	*Landscape at the End of the Century*. New York: Norton, 1991.
LH	*Looking for Holes in the Ceiling*. Amherst: University of Massachusetts Press, 1974.
LT	*Local Time*. New York: William Morrow, 1986.
LV	*Local Visitations*. New York: Norton, 2003.
ND	*Not Dancing*. Pittsburg: Carnegie-Mellon University Press, 1984.
NS	*New and Selected Poems, 1974–1994*. New York: Norton, 1994.
RR	*Riffs and Reciprocities: Prose Pairs*. New York: Norton, 1998.
WG	*What Goes On: Selected and New Poems, 1995–2009*: New York: Norton, 2009.
WL	*Work and Love*. Pittsburg: Carnegie-Mellon University Press, 1981.
WLB	*Walking Light: Memoirs and Essays on Poetry* (expanded edition). Rochester, NY: BOA, 2001.
WLN	*Walking Light: Essays and Memoirs*. New York: Norton, 1993.

Part One

Essays

Beyond Words

Fred Marchant

In 1991, the poet Chris Merrill edited *The Forgotten Language: Contemporary Poets and Nature* and included "From Underneath," a poem Stephen Dunn had published a few years before in *Local Time* (1986). Around that time I was writing a pair of essays on nature poetry for the *Harvard Review*, and I felt that Dunn's poem spoke to some of the predicaments raised by the ecological crisis of our time. The poem was based on a newspaper story in the *Syracuse Post-Standard*, where it was reported that "a giant sea turtle had saved the life of a 52-year-old woman lost at sea for two days after a shipwreck in the Southern Philippines" (*LT*, 74). The woman apparently rode on the turtle's back until she was rescued by a fishing boat, and in his poem Dunn imagines the turtle rising from the depths, coming up under the woman between her legs. She is terrified, thinks this creature is sent from hell, but she is also all alone on the open sea and there is nothing else to hold on to. So she clings to the sea turtle as if it were a life raft. Eventually she faints. When she wakes, the turtle is still swimming, seemingly with a purpose. As she lays across its back, she admires the beautiful pattern of the shell and begins to talk to the turtle as if it were a pet, eventually speaking in what Dunn calls "the jibberish of the lost" (ibid., 75). This jibberish culminates with an unstoppable, hysterical laughter rising out of the core of her being. Then, in the poem's last stanza, the turtle and its human cargo come to the fishermen who hoist her off the turtle's back. The creature circles the boat three times before diving back into the ocean depths. As for the woman, Dunn says,

> The woman was beyond all language,
> the captain reported;

the crew was afraid of her
for a long, long time. (ibid.)

When I first read this poem, I knew that "nature poet" would not be the first thing I would think of when I thought of Stephen Dunn. Still, I was taken by the nearly mythological dimensions of the story, and I thought that for a tough-minded realist such as Dunn to imagine his way into this story must somehow be significant. Even for Dunn, the web of our interconnectedness with the natural world had surfaced, and perhaps too the degree of our alienation from it had made itself known. This poem was a parable of just how profound and frightening a mystery it was for us to be in nature but not of nature.

This is of course only one possible reading of the poem, and it was mine some twenty years ago. Now, however, I read the poem through darker lenses and attend to Dunn's more ominous notes. In the beginning of the encounter, Dunn tells us the woman soils herself in fear. By the end she is out of her mind, and though rescued, she is "beyond all language." I now see the insistent and truly terrible word *all*! I note how the working crewmen shy away from her. My initially sunny, or at least mostly affirmative, reading has given way to a sense of this person's unwilled fate. This woman—and perhaps she is just like the rest of us—has seen and experienced something miraculous and monstrous. She may have been rescued, and she may feel "safe" on a boat destined for shore and home and the rest of life, but she is now so marked that she might be forever beyond language. In this predicament, we can hear a few notes of Dunn's deep core of insight and feeling throughout the body of his work. Beyond language, this woman is likely to be more truly alone than she could ever have imagined.

Dunn's parable now reminds me of something out of Melville. I am thinking not so much of the white whale as much as of Pip, the African American cabin boy who jumps from a whaleboat while a hunt is underway. The whaleboat cannot and will not stop to pick him up. With an understanding that once the whale is harpooned, they will come back for him, Pip floats on the ocean vastness and waits, as Melville says, in the center of such immensity that he loses his mind. Ishmael thinks Pip alone on the ocean has been carried down to wondrous depths and has there seen into the heart of existence. Pip, according to Ishmael and Melville, "saw God's foot on the treadle of the loom, and spoke it, and therefore his shipmates called him mad" (2002, 322). These depths that Ishmael imagines are a metaphor for the vast, empty, indifferent universe wherein we are just lonely specks. Our fate is of no concern or meaning to anyone. At the edge of the abyss, reason and language are fragile and limited resources. Jibberish becomes the language of the lost and the mad and those who bear witness to this essential loneliness. As it is for Melville, so too for Dunn. Although under a less heroic and romantic proscenium, for Stephen Dunn too there is something in existence that is beyond all, is in fact an unsayable and perhaps unbearable glimpse of our final and ultimate isolation.

This unsayable dimension of our experience—be it a glimpse of, or a swerve into, or a collision with it—has been a central concern of Stephen Dunn's poetry. Yes, we can speak about his realism, his ironies, the woes of love and domestic, middle-class life, the South Jersey landscape, his religious perplexities, our American social violence, the psychological wounds we all endure. All these are a part of his panorama. But underneath any given predicament in Dunn, I sense a nagging awareness on his part that there is always something near but just beyond our grasp, something so terrible that we almost want it to elude our words. It is that sense of just how finally and fundamentally alone we are that haunts his poetry, and calls him and us to try again and again to find the words that might catch even a glimpse of it. Language, even if torqued to the highest poetic intensities, cannot in the end ever be adequate to the task of saying what Dunn senses somehow must be said. It is not just the failure of words but the appalling discovery that our language is both inadequate to our experience *and* is all we have. As Dunn says in "What Men Want," the last poem in *What Goes On* (2009), it is the "chosen, happy torment / of words" (192) that is and always has been his one true subject and muse.

If we go back to his earliest work, the predicament we find in "One Side of the Story," from *Full of Lust and Good Usage* (1976) is about the failure of language. Dunn opens this poem with a dour prediction about words:

> I was thinking of
> the candle and the candle's end
> when you took your place at the table.
> Of what to do when the words fail
> As they most surely will. (53)

Or consider "Those of Us Who Think We Know," in the same book, a poem that ends with

> And the words we find
> are always insufficient, like love,
> though they are often lovely
> and all we have. (49)

Lest we think that language fails us only in matters of the heart, consider "Letter about Myself to You," a meditation on mortality addressed to a dying friend. Here Dunn says, "I used to believe in words, how they could / come together happily, and change. / Now I pray they don't distort" (*WL*, 42).

And he ends the poem on the following question and a not very comforting answer:

> What good are words?
> I'm feeling that impotence that wants
> a Lazarus to rise
> everytime someone loved is sinking.
> *Rise. Miracle. Heaven.*
> There, I've said them, sadly,
> to make you laugh. (ibid., 43)

Over his forty years of writing poems, Dunn returns time and again to a skeptical questioning of language itself. He questions its utility, its reliability, and its consolations. It is adequate neither to ecstasy nor agony truly encountered, and yet it is all we have. It keeps calling the poet back to his lifelong project of finding or inventing the right words, the right order, and neither are never quite right enough.

Interlude: Some of Dunn's Favorite Verbs

say	said	tell	told
call	write	describe	ask
answer	declare	rant	apologize
scream	recite	shout	mention
yell	praise	bark	come back
talk	talked	talking	listen

I wish I had an electronic version of Dunn's entire body of work so I could be precise in tracking how many times Dunn uses words that indicate a conversation ongoing, recalled, thwarted, or otherwise damaged. But to anyone who reads Dunn's poetry with an ear for his conversational elements, then the above matrix of verbs will glow with resonance and meaning. This is the motherboard of his art, the key operations and actions in Dunn's aesthetic vocabulary. Stephen Dunn's poems talk about talking. His narratives often pivot around a recollected conversation, often a shred of a quarrel or a quick interchange that the poet then begins to turn over in his mind.

Consider "He/She," another poem in *Local Time* (1986). A domestic quarrel leads the poet into a memory of schoolyard fights, which is where the speaker says he learned that words matter, where "one word too many meant / broken fingers, missing teeth" (26). *Between Angels* (1989), Dunn's next book, offers us "Sweetness," a poem built around a friend's late-night phone call. The friend has called to say his beloved has been killed in a car accident. Stunned, almost speechless, the friend, says Dunn, repeats the words "he needed / to repeat" (43). In turn Dunn "repeated / the one or two words we have for such grief // until we were speaking only in tones" (43–44). And again one senses the desire to find language that would bridge the gap between us, yet all we are able to do is repeat words that are woefully inadequate.

Such recalled conversations are also crucial in "Loosestrife," the culminating poem in the 1996 book by the same name. Here in the last of ten sections, the poet recollects a student asking him why he stayed in South Jersey. Dunn replies, "'Because it hasn't been imagined yet'" (96). The wisecrack, however, now gives way to a deeper reflection.

> So hard not to lie.
> I should have said this landscape,
> lush and empty and so undreamed,
> is the party to which we bring our own.
> I should have kept talking until I'd gotten it true.
> Something about what the mouse doesn't know
> and the owl does. Something intolerable
> like that, with which we live. (ibid.)

In this poem Dunn hints, I think, at his own aesthetic hope or faith: his poems keep talking until he's gotten the story to be as "true" as his language will allow, which is never quite true enough. In "Loosestrife," for instance, we glimpse something intolerable, something with which we live, something unnamed that the bird of prey knows and that its favorite meal does not. It is that final and terrible isolation under the ocean sky that Pip knew, that the woman on the turtle's back knew too, and it is beyond words.

To keep talking until he gets it true is echoed a few years later in "Sixty," a poem from *Different Hours* (2000) wherein he says he'll "keep on describing things / to ensure that they really happened" (22). In "Story," from the same book, he recalls listening to his wife tell a story about a dog hit by a car. He says he knew he'd take the story from her, and would retell it

every which way until it had an order
and a deceptive period at the end. That's what
I always do in the face of helplessness,
make some arrangements if I can. (90)

Poems such as "Loosestrife" and "Sixty" put me in mind of the thoughts of another New Jerseyite, the critic Richard Poirier in his landmark book *Poetry and Pragmatism* (1992). Poirier argues that philosophical pragmatism is a doorway into understanding what is both great and unique in American poetry from the mid–nineteenth century onward. It is a philosophical "line of force" (5), a tradition that begins with Emerson and passes through William James onto John Dewey and Richard Rorty, among other thinkers. It is also a poetic line of force, a tradition that traces its roots to Emersonian self-reliance—the injunction to speak today's truth in hard words, and to speak tomorrow's truth in equally hard words, even if they will contradict one another. The pragmatist poetic tradition, argues Poirier, comes to flower in twentieth-century modernists as different as Frost, Stein, and Stevens. Stephen Dunn's poetry is, I think, in this pragmatist tradition.

At the core of Jamesian pragmatism is a sense that truths are multiple, variable, and evolving over time. There is no essential truth with a capital T, but instead there is a process of adjusting our sense of the truth as the facts of life and experience. James argued that the pragmatist measured truth by the degree to which there was any practical consequence to the idea under consideration. Pragmatism is vigilantly empirical, distrustful of overarching abstractions that would in effect remove us from the world or filter what experience has to teach us. Pragmatism is thus a response to the world as it is rather than as one thought it to be, and as our instruments are always faulty, the response to the world will shift, maybe even progress in time. Richard Poirier argues that language is one of those instruments by which we measure the world, and that pragmatism is "a form of linguistic skepticism" that allows for a "liberating and creative suspicion as to the dependability of words and syntax, especially as it relates to matters of belief" (5).

Viewed from this angle, Dunn's project—intuitive as it may be—has been to discover and rediscover the limits of language in the face of experience, a discovery that prompts a renewed effort at finding words that will try to suffice. We see in several places in his later poems a kind of happiness in the idea of erasing the board, wiping the slate clean of words, starting over again with the dance of words. It is not out of a sense that words will finally ease the existential terror but that the labor of language is itself its own end and has an essential worth. That is the culminating gesture of "What Men Want," in *What Goes On*. The poem ends on this:

> I've always needed paper and pencil
> In order to speak as little as I should.
> After the power to choose
> a man wants the power to erase. (195)

Erasure and starting over again, these experiments in language are acts of the pragmatist imagination. Stephen Dunn's sense of the inadequacy of language to console or alter our existential loneliness is less a lamentation than it is a description of poetic inspiration. To find oneself beyond words is not just the predicament Dunn outlined way back in "From Underneath," nor is it the problem that his poems return to again and again. For this poet, discovering again that he is beyond words is what makes him erase what he has written and try again.

Works Cited

Melville, Herman. 2002. *Moby Dick; or, The Whale*. Second critical edition. Ed. Parker and Hayford. New York: W. W. Norton.

Merrill, Christopher, ed. 1991. *The Forgotten Language: Contemporary Poets and Nature*. Salt Lake City: Peregrine Smith Books.

Poirier, Richard. 1992. *Poetry and Pragmatism*. Cambridge, MA: Harvard University Press.

The Desire to Keep Saying Yes

George Looney

Stephen Dunn's poetry—from his first book, *Looking for Holes in the Ceiling* (1974) to *What Goes On: Selected and New Poems 1995–2009*—has been filled with and driven by a longing for wisdom, for getting the world right and in so doing consoling all of us who stumble through trying to understand both it and ourselves. In his fifth book, *Not Dancing* (1984), Dunn's maturing voice hit its stride in a remarkable construct of grace.

The cover photograph of John T. Young's granite and steel sculpture *The Climber* is an appropriate portico for this remarkable collection of poems. The stark, gray construct—pillars and cables around a lone figure held static in the act of climbing—calls to my mind two famous poetic ladders: Robert Frost's long one "sticking through a tree / Toward heaven still" in "After Apple-Picking" (1975, 68), which explores how strong a hold on meaning the form of a poem can have, and William Butler Yeats's absent one in "The Circus Animals' Desertion," that marvelous late-career ars poetica in which the speaker accepts that all of us must, in the end as in the beginning, "lie down where all the ladders start / In the foul rag and bone shop of the heart" (1996, 213).

Ladders link that which is below to that which is above, the most famous in western literature perhaps being Jacob's, that dream ladder on which angels ascend to and descend from heaven. To suggest that ladders—literal *and* metaphoric—link two very different states is to recognize, as Dunn does in "Climbing Ladders Anyway," that their use always includes risk. Dunn's poetry not only takes those risks but has always been at least in part *about* the nature and significance of the uncertainties a poet takes on in the lifelong endeavor both to experience this world and to try to come to an understanding of the difficult terrain of the human heart.

The speaker of "Climbing Ladders Anyway" recalls steadying a dangerous ladder while his father climbed it. The boy "learned // to be afraid of ladders and to climb them / anyway" (*ND*, 46). This brief passage offers an excellent example of the precise collusion of form and passion in Dunn's work. The scalpel edge of the break after "them" does two things: it creates a unit of meaning, as any line in a good poem must, by conflating the fear and the necessity of taking risks to move from one state to another—from being a son to being a father, for instance; and it also creates a wonderful, exacting pause between "to climb them" and "anyway."

Dunn's best poems have an exactness of tone which can be both exhilarating and devastating, and many in *Not Dancing* carry us rung by rung up what could be Jacob's ladder leading to some heaven; but, even as they invite us to ascend, they will not let us forget that every ladder—in order to take us anywhere—must be grounded in *this* world. In "Bringing the Strange Home," an essay from his collection *Walking Light*, Dunn argues that it is "amazing when someone gets the world right" (*WLN*, 18). But to say a poem gets the world right is to speak of more than just precise description, although accuracy of depiction is in any art a rare achievement. However, as Dunn points out, art is "the orchestrating and shaping of experience" (ibid.). A poem cannot ever *give* us the world, but it can be a meditative act that reveals some wisdom or achieves some understanding of our experience in the world. The importance of such a presentation, such a gift, should be evident to anyone who longs to encounter authentic responses. As Dunn puts it, good poems

> must make available the strangeness that is our lives. By this I mean not much more than how most of us find ourselves at odds with official versions of things, with images that, say, come from TV, from advertisements, from the daily language used to describe us. We can go months, even years, without ever being crucially spoken to. The

simplest good poem is a small correction of that, and may seem difficult or strange because of what regularly passes for the truth. (ibid.)

Near the middle of *Not Dancing* is a poem all about being crucially spoken to, both in the event being recollected and in the way the poet "orchestrates and shapes" that experience. "The Routine Things around the House" (*ND*, 39–40) doesn't shirk its dual responsibilities to make us see anew something so familiar, so mundane, that we tend not to notice the strangeness of it, and on the other hand to enable us to live with something that might initially strike us as so strange it doesn't seem familiar at all. This poem sets out to bring the strange home and, in accomplishing this, becomes one of the most authentic poems I know about the love between a mother and a son.

In the second tercet, the speaker separates from the reader by acknowledging he has been able to forgive himself because he is a son who has been loved by his mother. And it is within this context—in the effort to provide an example of, to prove, this love—that he presents his strange and perhaps disturbing memory. In framing the narrative of the mother showing her curious young son her breasts "without embarrassment or coyness" (*ND*, 39), the poet provides us the way to understand, to *accept*, this strange gesture so that it becomes neither prurient nor perverse but one more proof of a mother's love for her son.

The son later realizes, as he stares into the mother's coffin, "how many lifetimes there are // in the sweet revisions of memory" (ibid.). This gives those of us who might need it another out, another way to accept the strangeness of the event, by intimating that the poem might be a *revision* of experience. However we may choose to think of this narrative, the speaker's meditation has an impact on how we understand "the routine things / around the house" (ibid., 40) when the phrase closes the poem. Art, which provides a frame and the possibility of meaning, has changed the fundamental nature of the experience, and this poem challenges the way we think of ourselves. As Dunn says in "Bringing the Strange Home," poetry "should offer us something we can believe about ourselves and the world, or it should offer us something that will provoke or suggest contemplation about ourselves and this world" (*WLN*, 17).

A poem is, after all, language that listens to itself as well as the world, which means that in a good poem, words achieve what should be our highest aspiration for them—genuine and authentic significance. The form of a poem serves a function similar to the one suggested by Dunn's "In Defense of Blowfish," where the awareness of the creature's poison, and the real possibility of death it presents, changes the way the diners use their words:

> Imagine how fine the conversation must be!
> Imagine, when the effect sets in,
> the immense feeling of love for one another,
> how whatever could be slipping away
> must be spoken and held. (*ND*, 61)

Here, set in one of those routine experiences we often let go by without being fully aware of it or ourselves in it, is a concise expression of the effect of our awareness of mortality that Rilke spoke about so passionately and compellingly in his *Duino Elegies*. Such awareness is what Dunn gives us again and again in his poems: moments in which we are allowed, via the poet's act of noticing and his commentary *on* such noticing, to know the world and ourselves better by knowing the moment more fully.

"Always," the speaker in Dunn's poem "Essay on the Personal" tells us, "it's a matter of precision, / what it feels like" (ibid., 31). In these two seemingly innocuous lines, the precision of Dunn's articulation of the quotidian allows us to recognize the shimmer of the mysterious; his poems repeatedly form moments of such precise and authentic expression that they convince us, if only *for* a moment, that someone has in fact gotten the world right.

Donald Barthelme says in his essay "Not Knowing" that art "is not difficult because it wishes to be difficult, but because it wishes to be art" (1997, 15). A typical poem by Stephen Dunn may have a surface so apparently direct and uncluttered that one would hardly label it *difficult*, but the truth is that Dunn has so mastered his craft that he is able to help *us* master the difficult. He wields the techniques of his art with such a deft and precise hand that, as "Essay on the Personal" puts it, "Loss seems so common / it belongs to the air, / to breath itself, anyone's" (*ND*, 31).

This is what we might call the magic (the sleight of hand?) of his poetry, this ability he has to use form (which means, in part, syntax and grammar) to lead us to a moment of enlightenment with such agility and grace that we follow without being fully aware we are being led. Dunn crafts a voice of sincerity and authenticity that compels us to experience the mundane as anything but mundane, to experience the complex world in all its strangeness and familiarity.

This is why "Traveling to Nova Scotia," on its surface the story of a father's boat ride from Bar Harbor with his two daughters, can become an experience of the fragility of our lives. The daughters are young enough that the trip is a thrill, so they ride "the wave / between nausea and excitement" (*ND*, 50). For the father, this excursion calls to mind other kinds of journeys and the difficulty of coordinating the directions anyone ends up taking in life. With his daughters getting older and one about to become a teenager, the father feels the fear that comes from recognizing impending change. "Soon," he thinks, "the passage / into other waters" (ibid.). What those other waters may be, how turbulent or calm, is unknowable until the passage is completed. So when the daughters hear a foghorn and imagine disasters like those they've seen in movies and on television, the father realizes they wouldn't understand if he tried to tell them about the real perils they must face. He is left with only the immediate moment and a gesture of protectiveness—putting his arms around them as if to prevent any tragedy from taking them away. "When we don't die," the father realizes,

> it's a small triumph
>
> for this kind of loving,
> another stay

against what's out there,
what they suspected all along. (ibid., 51)

I am reminded of Robert Frost's definition of the poem as a tiny bit of order, a "momentary stay against confusion," a hesitation or pause within a particular now. Dunn's poems provide us with such stays again and again.

Such work is rare enough, but a poem that can also praise the world we share and the ways we share it, that can praise even our foolhardiness, is a true joy, and Dunn has repeatedly given us poems over his long career that do just that. One such poem in *Not Dancing* is "Desire," a work that has many wonderful moments, including its first line—"I remember how it used to be"—which seems mundane, even clichéd, but proves to be anything but by the time we reach the end of the poem's first sentence seven lines later (59). That opening line turns out to express not nostalgia for the past but rather the speaker's distress about an earlier time and outlook, a time when desire seemed absent, when all that was left was "the clarity / the cynical survive with, / their world so safely small" (ibid.). However, that time is sublimated here to the desire evident in every line and sentence of this poem, a desire for immersion in "the interesting, the various, / the conjured life suggested by a glance"—with the imaginative life of the artist being one possible source of such immersion (ibid.).

The power of imagination, wielded by one who does not close out the richness of experience, allows the speaker to exclaim, "I praise how the body heals itself. / I praise how, finally, it never learns" (ibid.). Often what we mean when we tell a child to "grow up" is *Give up your dreams, your imagination.* "Be realistic," we are told more and more the older we get, though the admonition starts in childhood. Dunn's poetry is imbued with the wisdom of the child, who knows intuitively that what we can see and taste and touch and feel and hear is only part of it, and that this part is connected somehow to that mysterious realm Paul Éluard referred to as "another world," saying that, if it exists, "It is in this one."

Such openness to the richness and complexity of experience allows Dunn to write "The Wild," in which a wasp refusing to fly out an open window into the cold air of October makes the speaker think of his dog, who knew when his time had come and so wandered off to "die next to / something wild, in the wild" (*ND*, 76). The man regrets how he brought the dog back and took it to the vet, who ended up putting it down; this "stupid human hanging-on" (ibid.) seems almost a sin to the speaker now, certainly a selfish act, and, like any such act, shortsighted. Now, even though the speaker wants the wasp to die in the wild the way his dog tried to, he realizes

> . . . wasps weren't meant
> to have choices or, like us,
> make the short-range choice
> their bodies want. (ibid.)

This leads him into a memory of a time when the speaker almost froze to death and when, as his body was telling him to give up, he saw a farmhouse that became a sort of promise and a source of strength. In remembering that moment, he is able to say that "something beyond choice / got me there"—and, with the wisdom that memory has provided, he closes by saying,

> I want that wasp out in the air
> obeying whatever it is
> the species obeys when winter comes;
> when it can't, but does, live on. (ibid., 77)

One thing that poetry, and all art, can provide for us is the ability to keep going when our bodies, and our spirits, might want to give up, lie down, and close ourselves off from the sometimes overwhelming heaviness of existence.

In this way a poem can be a kind of prayer. The close of Dunn's "In the Blowdown Zone"—the term for the area of devastation around

Mt. St. Helens—is set a year after the volcano's 1980 eruption, and the poem proclaims

> this broken syllogism
>
> like a prayer: There's no nitrogen in ash.
> No plant can live without nitrogen.
> The fireweed is coming up. (*ND*, 16)

To utter this prayer is to praise, cherish, and love this world and all that it brings us: all the pleasure *and* all the pain; all the joy and all the sorrow; all the hope and all the despair. To keep saying yes. To know that, as "Climbing Ladders Anyway" puts it,

> the roof, maybe the sky,
>
> would someday ask me of something simple
> and terrifying, and I wanted
> to be ready. (*ND*, 46)

And there it is again—evidence of Stephen Dunn's craftsmanship as he breaks the line to emphasize how, even terrified, the speaker is still filled with desire. And yes, he wants "to be ready," to be able to climb the ladder that connects the "foul rag and bone shop of the heart" with the vast possibilities of what can be made out of the refuse and shattered remnants of what was—the ladder that is always a prayer, against all evidence to the contrary, for possibility. This is the psalm Dunn's poems have continued to sing: the healing and consoling power of the imagination.

Works Cited

Barthelme, Donald. 1997. "Not Knowing." In *Not Knowing: The Essays and Interviews of Donald Barthelme*, edited by Kim Herzinger. New York: Random House. 11–24.

Frost, Robert. 1975. "After Apple Picking." In *The Poetry of Robert Frost*. New York: Holt, Rinehart, and Winston. 68–69.

Yeats, William Butler. 1996. "The Circus Animals' Desertion." In *Selected Poems and Four Plays*, edited by M. L. Rossenthal. New York: Scribner. 212–13.

Against Satisfaction

James Davis May

(Editor's note: This essay was written using an early manuscript of Dunn's newest book, *Lines of Defense.)*

Stephen Dunn, especially in his recent works, reminds me of Wallace Stevens's "The Well Dressed Man with a Beard," you know, the guy who says, "It can never be satisfied, the mind, never" (1990, 247). At first glance, this seems like a pessimistic conclusion, one that diagnoses the mind with a tantalizing thirst. Satisfaction, though, is not the same thing as peace, and it definitely isn't the same thing as understanding. Consider the roots of the word: "to discharge fully," "comply with," or "to have enough" (OED). If that's what satisfaction is, Stephen Dunn's latest work wants nothing to do with it. The mind, after all, isn't all that different from the body's other organs whose collapse—the stilled heart, the failing liver—will shut the entire system down. The same holds true for the mind: once the mind stops thinking, it's no longer functional. To put it another way, for the mind, satisfaction means death; to stay alive, it has to keep thinking. This means it must reject its past conclusions in order to find new ones. In his latest works, Dunn champions this vetoing power of the poet's mind, the way it discriminates, rejects, and even rebels (especially when it rebels against its past beliefs). "After the power to choose," Dunn writes in "What Men Want," "a man wants the power to erase" (*WG*, 195).

In the title poem of his previous collection, *Here and Now*, we see Dunn describing this process of rejection:

> I learned, in time, to let heaven
> go its mythy way, to never again

be supplicant
of any single idea. (42)

Having turned aside heaven as an answer (I'm tempted to add the adverb "officially"), Dunn in this poem settles—to use an odd phrase—for the moment on the present. It's a mature version of a carpe diem poem that argues, as the title suggests, that Dunn will think only of "*here and now* from here on in" (ibid.). Though a powerful and convincing poem, it can't be the final answer. At the end of the poem, Dunn invites the night, saying that he will "let things darken / as they will" (ibid.) There's an evening coming in, after all, and Dunn has to describe that, too.

In "Nothing to Hold Onto," one of the first poems in his forthcoming manuscript, *Lines of Defense*, Dunn sees himself on the edge of the unknown, right before he's about "to enter the great waters." The poem addresses a "you," but as is the case with most directive poems written in second person, it's clear the advice the poet gives is to himself (I should note, too, that in this essay I will commit the sin of equating the speaker with the poet—the subject, the poet's mind, seems to justify such a transgression). "It might be the right time to cultivate / disbelief, which can make certain angels / disappear," he writes, and adds that "disbelief is always useful, / helps the discriminate discriminate." This is where "Here and Now" left him, but the finality that poem argues for has to be abandoned if for no other reason than the fact that finality is, well, a dead end:

Still, there'll be turbulence as you enter
the great waters. Love alone can't save you,
and disbelief only frees you long enough
to see clearly where you're going.

Dunn enters those waters, imaginatively at least, in this manuscript. Disbelief has helped him get here, helped him to find the way, but he now sees its limited uses. To keep moving, he has to disbelieve disbelief. He advises not to worry "if you can't tell the angelic // from the hellbent, or the exact meaning of guidance." "Confusion," he says, "won't hurt you." And what is confusion other than an opportunity for the mind to work?

Never in this collection does Stephen Dunn conclude; he makes statements, but they're all qualified by subtle moves that opt for the subjunctive and the hypothetical instead of the certain and the determined. So many of these poems begin with or are propelled by phrases like "Let's say," "I imagine," or that word that Dunn uses better than any other poet: "If." These phrases are conversational, as is Dunn's impulse to investigate his theories, and like a good conversation with friends, each poem offers a sort of test chamber for these theories, hunches, and desires.

In "The Widening," for example, Dunn is, fittingly enough, "holding forth at the dinner table." It's worth noting that this is his dinner party, and so he feels an obligation "to fill" a silence that he views a "void." Obviously, the "void" on the literal level is those awkward lulls in conversation that worry any attentive host. Nearly as obvious, though, is the existential "void" Dunn has railed against throughout his career. The small talk Dunn uses to fill this gap in conversation comments on silence itself:

> I had just read a book on music,
> about which I know very little,
> and, anticipating being corrected, was saying
> something about the courage to break off,
> the breaking of rhythmic obligations. (ibid.)

I want to note how Dunn has, in an unassuming yet elegant way, set up the poetic situation to serve as both an ars poetica and a career retrospective. It's a rare species of poem; the ones that immediately come to mind are Yeats's "The Circus Animals' Desertion" and Lowell's "Epilogue." This is a poem about endings and what comes after them. Dunn puts forth a theory, positing that sudden endings, like those that tempted him in *Here and Now*, take "courage." As he suspects, he will be corrected. But that correction comes later in the poem. First, Dunn gets an opportunity to test this "break off" theory when his daughter calls to tell him her "lost cat / had been found." It's a mini narrative within the poem: the cat was lost, but now it's found. His audience is delighted with the story, and, as he notes, "the void / seemed to fill with good cheer, / like vodka at the bottom of the glass."

Pleased by their pleasure, he tells another story, one that seems less likely than his daughter's news:

> So I told them that the baby crow
> a hawk had tried to kill this morning
> was still alive—three birds of different species
> standing around it as if on guard.
>
> The hawk was up on a nearby branch,
> frowning, I said.

There's something suspicious about this story. The audience, perhaps sensing that Dunn is imitating his earlier success, isn't convinced. "No one smiled or laughed," the poet reports. This is really interesting: in this poem, Dunn has effectively created a situation in which imitating his past success will not be successful. For what it's worth, this sort of self-effacement seems to be rare in American poetry. Think of how many times you've felt a renowned poet is simply imitating his or her previous successes. Dunn's suspicion of self-imitation is nothing if not admirable.

The second story having failed, the dinner guests turn cynical and begin questioning Dunn. One guest, a scientist, asks his host to name the species of birds in his story. Dunn doesn't know—or doesn't know enough to lie plausibly—and he grows defensive, naming the birds "Nutfinch, plutarch, free-to-be." Then, another friend, a clarinetist, discredits his first theory about endings:

> And by the way, he added,
> there's no such thing as a full stop

> in music—silence is a sound, an afterlife
> for anyone with an ear.

The void returns, and it's wider now, Dunn tells us. Here, halfway through the poem, we see a crisis. The poet's stories have been dismissed and the silence—which, as we've been told, is not an ending—leers over him. To make matters worse, escape isn't an option either: "I wanted to go home," Dunn tells us, "but I was home." Dunn could have ended on the line I just quoted or even on the lines about how silence is an afterlife and the poem still would have been pretty good, even by his standards. But to end either way would have been to end with disbelief; in other words, the cynicism of the dinner guests and the speaker's despair would have prevailed. Dunn doesn't give in, though. His mind keeps thinking, taking us through a series of options of what he could have done but didn't. Three of the last four sentences in the poem end with some form of the construction "I wanted to." Here's the last of that series, the penultimate sentence in the poem: "I wanted to tell them that in my ignorance / I was serious, and that when things get lost / or are about to die all kinds of thoughts are legitimate." This is not an ending that suggests resolution; rather, it picks up where the confusion of "Nothing to Hold Onto" left off by justifying—apologizing for?—multiplicity and the exploration of manifold endings. To put it simply, "The Widening" ends by suggesting there's more to say.

Having more to say is the last line of defense. "Trudge on," Dunn writes in "Before We Leave," adding that "In the higher regions, / where the footing is unsure, / to trudge is to survive." And when we get to that steep, precarious edge, "That won't be / the abyss" below us. "The abyss," he writes, "is usually nearer than that." Immediately I think of Frost's "Desert Places," the way that that poem argues that even the vastness of outer space can't terrify us as effectively as the loneliness within (1979, 296). The abyss in "Before We Leave," though, differs—this abyss may be terrifying, but it's "at the bottom of something / you've *yet* to resolve" (emphasis mine), suggesting that it can, in fact, be resolved. At the very least, that abyss gives the mind something to keep thinking about.

In this book, Dunn makes the abyss seem less abysmal, but he doesn't accomplish this through escapism or lying. Instead, he thinks, acknowledging, as he does in "The Proliferation," that darkness, which he calls a "take-over artist," informs us. If darkness informs us, then it doesn't simply just take from us, as we often think it does—it gives something back, as it does in "Out of Respect," Dunn's elegy for Donald Justice. At the end of the poem, which is addressed to Justice, Dunn describes the day he got word of Justice's death and how, after receiving the news, he went to his friend's poems:

> . . . and there you were
> again, master of the stilled life
> and its tones, and everywhere the tact
> of those rich refusals—what you held back,
> no doubt out of respect for us.

As with most elegies, especially those written by poets in their seventies, this poem is as much about the living poet's mortality as it is about the deceased. Through Justice's death, Dunn is able to see finality, to see that even in death the mind, at least the mind on the page, is still able to make its "refusals."

And though this collection does celebrate the mind's refusals and rejections, it also praises the mind's considerations. In "Feathers," for example, Dunn presents us with a hypothetical situation, one that starts innocently enough:

> If a lone feather fell from the sky,
> like a paper plane wafting down
> from a tree house where a quiet boy
> has been known to hide,
> you might think message or perhaps
> mischief, not some mid-air
> molting of a bird.

As the poem continues, though, the vividness of Dunn's imagery leaves us wondering whether the situation it describes actually happened, unlikely though it may seem. "But what if many feathers fell," Dunn asks and then, further along in the poem, asks us what we'd think if the "feathers were large / and grayish, some of them bloody, / with signs of tendon and muscle." Would we think the government was exterminating "enormous raptors"? Then the poem grows even stranger:

> For years now you'd heard rumors
> of homeless gods in the vast emptiness.
> And if they'd appear in your dreams,
> as they sometimes did,
> begging to be believed in once again,
> you'd feel this icy refusal hardening in you.

The gods "begging to be believed in once again" may seem cynical, if not frightening; but because he believes in not believing, Dunn seeks to disbelieve disbelief, as we can see in the final two sentences of the poem, which, appropriately, are questions:

> . . . Was the world,
> as you knew it, simply over, no more
> rain or snow? Would there always be
> just this strange heaviness coming down,
> covering what used to be the ground?

While the questions may suggest doubt, sadness, or despair, they don't yet confirm it. Ending with questions leaves the mind still pondering—it has not concluded, and so it is still active, still unsatisfied.

The collection ends with "Sea Level," a "Tintern Abbey"-esque poem, where Dunn revisits his old haunts and "the friends who've stayed / casualty's course." Everywhere he turns, he sees "the visages of ghosts." "There's the house I left for good," he writes, "(if forever can ever be good)." Indeed, as we've seen, this collection resists forever and finality. But still, there's the impulse to conclude, to say something to his friends:

> I pull into their driveway, wanting
> to tell them how it feels to have
> —for the first time—an undivided heart,
> a sudden purity of motive,
> but when I begin to speak I realize
> I don't. I say it anyway, won't take it
> back.

After so much negation and rejection, the mind's at risk: yes, it doesn't want to conclude, if concluding means to stop, but it does want a conclusion, something to show for all its effort. Fickleness isn't what Dunn's after, although as he observes his friends' cat, he realizes he may be guilty of it:

> When their outside cat wants in,
> they let him in. Then he wants out.
> They accommodate. That cat
> is almost as lucky as I.

This passage is half temptation, half confession. In identifying himself with his friends' well-obliged feline, Dunn constructs an image of satisfaction, but even though he calls both himself and the cat "lucky," the image, if read metaphorically, works as a sort of self-accusation, or at least the consideration of a charge: Are the poet's poems just elaborate ways for him to "accommodate" his mind, letting it wander and return as it pleases? The next image is one of finality, yet another evening coming, this one at the end of the book:

> . . . No mountains
> here, I can see the afternoon sun
> on the horizon hanging on,
> about to dip and be gone. Their yard

is a dusty orange. I love the truth,
I swear I do.

That last sentence, nearly a non sequitur, paradoxically dripping with both sincerity and irony, verifies and undermines itself as it simultaneously reaffirms and repeals the poems that precede it in the collection. So the poem, and thus the book, finds a way to end without concluding. Where "What Men Want" ends with celebrating "the power to erase," "Sea Level" seems to celebrate the power to not erase. At least not right away, anyway.

Works Cited

Frost, Robert. 1979. "Desert Places." In *The Poetry of Robert Frost*. New York: Holt. 296.

"Satisfy, v." OED Online. September 2012. Oxford University Press. http://www.oed.com/view/Entry/171239 (accessed October 28, 2012).

Stevens, Wallace. 1990. "The Well Dressed Man with a Beard." In *The Collected Poems of Wallace Stevens*. New York: Vintage. 247.

Part Two

Compositional Strategies

Verse and Reverse

Gregory Djanikian

In his essay "The Good, the Not So Good," Stephen Dunn describes the process by which we come to new ways of seeing and saying:

> Not only must poets turn away from the tired or dead language, they must be wary of their best ideas and all the language that was available to them before the poem began.
>
> That is, all language that hasn't been found by the language in the poem. And then even that new language should be doubted and resisted. Resistance leads to discovery. No, no, no, no, and then yes. The good poem offers us a compelling, vibrant replacement for what, in our complacency, we allowed ourselves to believe we knew and felt. (*WLN*, 42)

I've always admired this notion of resistance because it's too easy to surrender, not only to bad language, but also to resolutions of conflicts and paradoxes that might seem initially gratifying but, later, appear too neatly contrived to sustain any lasting resonances. And yes, the paradox disappears in a false reconciliation, but no one is happy. "When the compulsion of speech is to find and say the truth . . . all utterance must be tormented by doubt," Louise Glück advises us in her essay on T. S. Eliot (1994, 21): if we are preoccupied with truths, then we should also keep in mind their durable antitheses; too often, we are drawn toward the merely synthetic amalgamation.

In a general sense, we might say that Dunn's poetic preoccupation has been with oppositional forces and their effects on our lives. In much of his earlier work, his strategy has been to find compromises between antithetical impulses and beliefs, even if they turn out to be temporary. For instance, in "Waiting with Two Members of a Motorcycle Gang for My Child to Be Born," (*FL*, 54), the impending birth of his daughter about to refresh the world is set against the violence and danger that two gang members in the same hospital waiting room represent, though Dunn has a hope that one force will overcome the other:

> I expected "The Eliminators" to
>   disappear, snuffed out
> by a stronger force, a white tornado
>   of my own.
> That's not what happens, though
>   in life
> as you will learn.

The life force and the destructive force remain at odds, but there is here a curious rapprochement between the two: "They smiled when / they heard of you / and shook my hand. At another time / it might / have been my head" (ibid., 54). We note a give and take, a coming together of sorts, however short-lived, symbolized by the handshake. Tolerance and human kinship win out for the time being.

Similarly, in "At the Smithville Methodist Church" (*LT*, 53–55), there's a spirit of accommodation when the speaker's daughter comes home during a week of arts and crafts at the church singing "Jesus loves me, / the Bible tells me so" (ibid., 53). The father is an ardent disbeliever and the time is ripe for a struggle between dissonant credos. Yet nothing happens. To his credit, the father understands that his daughter has been won over by a biblical narrative whose power he cannot match: "[Evolution] stinks of extinction," he knows, "and nothing // exciting happens for centuries" (ibid., 54). His tacit hope is that his daughter's conversion may be temporary:

> I didn't have a wonderful story for my child
> and she was beaming. All the way home in the car
> she sang songs,

> occasionally standing up for Jesus.
> There was nothing to do
> but drive, ride it out, sing along
> in silence. (ibid., 54–55)

The opposition remains, but we are nudged into thinking it might disappear in time. And we're also asked to recognize that the father's singing in silence despite his reservations signals another handshake, a momentary truce that brings the world a little more genially into our ken.

In "The Sudden Light and the Trees" (*LE*, 42–43), another speaker deals with a more immediate danger, a neighbor living in the same apartment house who is "a biker, a pusher, a dog / and wife beater" (ibid., 42). He also owns a pistol and wishes to use it on a sparrow that's been trapped in their common basement. The poem has a suspenseful edge, and we don't know how things will turn out until the speaker offers to catch the bird and set it free:

> . . . I got it in my hand, and how it burst
>   that hand open
> when I took it outside, a strength
>
> that must have come out of hopelessness
>   and the sudden light
> and the trees. . . . (ibid., 43)

The bad neighbor in this case, even though he still seems dangerous, nevertheless is subverted by a small act of kindness that in no way changes him—he keeps slapping his gun against his open palm—but perhaps bewilders, maybe even surprises him into benign inaction and silence.

The examples I've mentioned are poems that bring antitheses together and chronicle the reverberations that ensue. Sometimes, they make a pact with "everything / strange, inchoate, like living / with someone / like living alone, / settling for the partial" (*ND* "Essay on the Personal," 32). Other times, they hold out for a better world: "May you make men better / than they are" (*FL*, 54), the father in the hospital waiting room wishes for his new daughter, and the world, though it has its dangers, is also congenial and forgiving in many instances. Dunn, of course, has always been richly attentive to our immediate and domestic lives and the quiet but necessary negotiations we maintain to keep them intact. I would argue, however, that as he begins to include in his work larger political and historical considerations, he becomes more attuned to paradoxes that have no reconciliations, no halfway meeting of minds or compromises.

Such a politico-historical dimension makes its first conspicuous appearance in the final section of *Between Angels*, and it's interesting to also note the slight shift in Dunn's compositional strategy because of it; we register how his inclination toward accommodation shrinks a little in light of the terrible but understandable reasons why people do bad things to each other. "To a Terrorist," for instance, written long before the Towers fell on 9/11, acknowledges that what we find hateful might nonetheless have its urgencies:

> For the historical ache, the ache passed down
> which finds its circumstance and becomes
> the present ache, I offer this poem
>
> without hope, knowing there's nothing,
> not even revenge which alleviates
> a life like yours. . . . (*BA*, 79)

Though there's an understanding of terrorist motives, Dunn nonetheless registers his moral indignation of their murderous calibrations: "Still, I must say to you: / I hate your good reasons. / I hate the hatefulness that makes you fall // in love with death, your own included" (ibid., 79). There is, here, both a convergence and a parting of ways, but no synthesis of positions, no adjustments to include what the speaker feels he must turn away from, and the poem exists not to be commodious but to register an act of resistance, to cancel silences. Similarly, in "About the Elk and the Coyotes That Killed Her Calf" (*BA*, 86–87), the elk's fierce struggle against deadly attacks earns our admiration; we feel ourselves attached to her heroic but doomed courage. And yet, though we perhaps side with her for now, how easily, it seems, our affiliations might change: "Ah but tomorrow, / desperate, and night falling fast // and with a different sense of family . . ." (ibid., 87).

Who can say what we are capable of in the right circumstances? How could we not wish to be as "wild" and "brilliant" as the cunning coyotes in times of extremity? And isn't it true, while we indict the torturers and hatemongers of vicious crimes, we "put out the poison" for any rat we wish to rid ourselves of, asking always forgiveness for our small but effective exterminations (*BA*, "Forgiveness," 83)? We indict indecencies; and yet, often, our decent lives are flecked with blood.

This notion of irreconcilability leads us to Dunn's *Riffs and Reciprocities*, prose poems that are paired to play off, and in many ways, resist each other. They are unlikely couplings whose titles may give us only an elliptical sense of their mutual subversions: "Bourgeois/Religion" (*RR*, 26–27); "Sky/Weather" (ibid., 50–51); "Luminescence/Seriousness" (*WG*, 60–61). But there they are, praising on one hand the democratic principle of one person, one vote while arguing for a more judicious electoral public on the other; in league with lovers who are enviably in the full flush of love but conceding the attraction of flirtation, dalliances without obligation; espousing "the cold light of intelligence" (*WG*, 60) as well as the whimsical but seductive bewitchments of intuition; reason and also the heart's reasons. That they are separated from each other both by page and predilection reinforces our sense of their discreteness, but their proximity to each other allows us to bounce back and forth, seeing how the same general subject matter may be approached in at least two different ways, the pairs swinging apart from each other like repelling magnets though nonetheless connected because of their antinomian nature.

One of the poems in his Pulitzer Prize–winning collection *Different Hours*, which elegantly exemplifies for me this idea of contrarieties, is "The Reverse Side." The epigraph, a Japanese proverb, is instructive: *"The reverse side also has a reverse side."* We enter the poem through its directive as if through a hall of mirrors, our mind's eye overwhelmed by innumerable reflections and their opposites. The poem understands how we try to arrive at only one truth in order to excuse ourselves from the terror of considering multiple truths:

> It's why the terrified and the simple
> latch onto one story,
> just one version of the great mystery.
>
> Image & afterimage, oh even
> the open-minded yearn for a fiction
> to rein things in—
> the snapshot, the lie of the frame. (*DH*, 73)

If there is only one version of truth, then its re-version is suppressed or dismissed; and if there is an unreciprocated "verse," then its uncreated "re-verse" is a failure of the imagination: though the poem may be shapely, its inattention to contrary positions destroys the raw, sometimes enlivening quality of disagreement. But here's the wrinkle: we hunger also for the great mystery of something that is not bilateral or binary, something that has yet to be spoken because speaking it would diminish its amplitude, its myriad contiguities:

> How do we not go crazy,
> we who have found ourselves compelled
> to live with the circle, the ellipsis, the word
> not yet written. (ibid., 73)

It is a proposition that finds attraction in the blank page, the unutterable, something which all poets must find compelling for the openness of the territory. Once something is said, its shadowy other appears, floating up out of the murkiness onto the available surfaces of our consciousness. Even as Dunn writes the poem, he half wishes it to disappear, creating, of course, another opposition. It's almost as though he concedes that language begets discrepancies, displacing us from the primary and intrinsic world of our first waking into one that seems linguistically invented. The more we refine language, the more we fall under its constructed thrall. Yet a withdrawal into silence is unconscionable for Dunn. As he said in an early poem, "Those of Us Who Think We Know," "The words we find / are always insufficient, like love, / though they are often lovely / and all we have" (*FL*, 49). Even though our compulsion to speak "out loud" is doomed to become mere words (*BA*, "To a Terrorist", 80), we are compelled to speak them because we can.

If our attraction is to many-sidedness, or in the circle's case to no-sidedness, how then do we strategize to include all that we feel the subject matter compels us to include without the work becoming incoherent or unwieldy? In the poem "Oklahoma City" (*DH*, 113–14), the triggering subject is Timothy McVeigh's bombing of the Alfred P. Murrah Building in Oklahoma City in 1995, an event that killed 168 people, many of them children. A lesser poem might have offered to counteract the horror with instances of generous and compassionate acts that occurred subsequently, but Dunn's poem for the most part skirts accounts of the catastrophe and describes the more trivial event of a same-day cocktail party whose guests are more intent on each other's intersections than anything else:

> Not one of us wouldn't be smiling.
> There'd be drinks, irony, hidden animosities.
> Something large would be missing. (ibid., 113)

Dunn is well aware that to parrot moral platitudes about goodness and evil in dealing with such an upheaval is to diminish its enormity; we acknowledge the wisdom of the poem to resist iterating our complacent beliefs or allowing us to feel in a time of broken connections a comfortable sense of shared communitarian values. Of course we know that the beautiful and the bestial live in the same place, but our hope might be that if we did *x*, then *y* should follow, a logical construction whose integrity, we might feel, gives us influence over the outcome. Dunn, however, will not subordinate one quality to the other, and the poem's surprising, and perhaps liberating, syntactic and philosophic belief is in the ampersand:

> It's the naïve among us who are guilty
> of wondering if we're moral agents or madmen
> or merely, as one scientist said,
> a fortuitous collocation of atoms.
> Some mysteries can be solved by ampersands.
> *Ands* not *ors*; that was my latest answer. (ibid., 113–14)

What Dunn eschews here as a poetic aesthetic is the causal, hypotactic sentence in favor of a paratactic approach: clauses not subordinated, declarations of one form or another, significant ones, held in equal valuation to each other. The physicist Niels Bohr has famously said that the opposite of a great truth is another great truth. The danger of such a proposition is that nothing of value might be declared, no moral positions espoused, and life might revert to a random perpetration of actions without significance. Its dismissal, however, leads to the constriction of a large and open-minded perspective that is the foundation of any consequential thinking. When we are able to hold two mutually exclusive declarations together in our minds, connected only by an *and* without resolution or integration, without even any connection other than the syntactic, then we are on our way to salvation because we are ready for anything. And so is the poem, its capacious doorway able to admit all that it has felicitously discerned in the world beyond:

> At the party two women were talking
> about how strange it is that they still like men.
> They were young and unavailable, and their lovely faces
> evoked a world not wholly incongruent
> with the world I know. I had no illusions, not even hopes,
> that their beauty had anything to do with goodness. (ibid., 114)

Beauty to goodness, goodness to truth: it's a ladder to paradise and ideality whose rungs are not quite as obliging for us as they have been for other centuries. The oppositions are persistent, but they direct us more keenly to what we finally believe in. "How nice that so few of us count on the negatives / these days to preserve what we hold dear" the character, Hope, declares in "At the Nihilist's Funeral" (*WG*, 165), and of course, it is what Hope should say given her allegorical prescriptions, though she can't help but also confess its converse:

> I loved [the nihilist], in fact for years couldn't live
> without him, he who helped crystallize
> what I thought by being so opposed to it. (ibid., 165)

We might not be sure if Hope can continue to live so discretely without his presence, though the poem comes full circle when the nihilist mourners, by turning their backs on Hope in protest, enact "the kind of negation that [the nihilist] . . . / would have thought might lead somewhere, / might even have thought was hopeful" (ibid., 165). The poem has managed to construct a merry-go-round of sorts, the ouroboros of one truth eating another's tail and being eaten by it as well. Even within the circle we might find peculiarities, different dispositions.

It might have taken a wonderful and sustained poem like "Loves" in *Landscape at the End of the Century* for Dunn to openly declare without compromise and with a sense of joy: "Here is where loveliness can live / with failure, and nothing's complete. / I love how we go on" (*LE*, 94). The inclusive gesture admits both qualities into our lives without settling on the partial or avowing "nothing can be done but know / nothing can be done" (*WL*, "Amidst the Faltering," 61); it prefers to celebrate how in spite of the fragmentary and incomplete character of the world, or maybe even because of it, we can choose to accept both sides of ourselves, recognizing our hates for what they are but able to love and be loved. The pivotal word here is "choose," and the choice that we make is underscored by our understanding of just what our choices are. It is important that our acts be substantiated by our knowledge of the world in all its circumstances, from the heroic to the monstrous, what Simone de Beauvoir, writing soon after the end of World War II, describes in *The Ethics of Ambiguity* as essential for our well-being:

> There was Stalingrad and there was Buchenwald, and neither of the two wipes out the other. Since we do not succeed in fleeing it, let us therefore look the truth in the face. Let us try to assume our fundamental ambiguity. It is in the knowledge of the genuine conditions of our life that we must draw our strength to live and our reason for acting. (2000, 9)

If we can't change the world as often as we'd like by our speaking about its contradictions, then let's speak at least about our acts, and act with the knowledge of what our lives are based on, what, among the multitudes of directions, we have chosen existentially to follow. If we have to confront many declarations connected by *ands*, then that is our world, though it does not prevent us from acknowledging preferences. We can want the beautiful or we can want the bestial. The choice is ours if we recognize it is a choice. Isn't that, finally, what most empowers us: the personal act coming from an examined life that might resonate outward to intersect with other lives, other choices? And isn't it the poet's obligation to make us aware of them, even if he has favorites, even if his final urgency is to "praise whatever you can" (*BA*, "Walking the Marshland," 111)?

The world is an ambiguous place, and to say yes to it is to live in a house whose doors and windows are open to all eventualities. It's not an easy house to live in; it's dangerous and unprotected, but it's a house the more courageous of our poets must inhabit if everyone is to be invited in, and it's a house, I think, that Stephen Dunn has lived in most of his life: like the speaker in "Clarities" in *Between Angels*, he has lived under all kinds of weather and without assurances:

> The weatherman said cold air
>   coming in
> from Pennsylvania. He said sleet

then snow then clearing then—
    speaking to me—days of
        uncertainty.
Once again there seemed room for me

in the world. (*BA*, 81)

Works Cited

Beauvoir, Simone de. 2000. "Ambiguity and Freedom." In *The Ethics of Ambiguity*, 7–34. New York: Citadel Press.

Glück, Louise. 1994. "On T. S. Eliot." In *Proofs and Theories: Essays on Poetry*, 19–22. Hopewell, NJ: Ecco.

A Certain Capaciousness and "The Routine Things around the House"

BJ Ward

In his poem, "The Reverse Side," from the 2001 Pulitzer-winning book *Different Hours*, Stephen Dunn cautions against latching onto one story because that's "just one version of the great mystery" (73). He writes in the title poem of his 2011 volume, *Here and Now*, that he learned "to never again // be a supplicant / of any single idea" (42). And his 1999 collection titled *Riffs and Reciprocities* comprises pieces that resist each other on opposing pages. Throughout his body of work, one detects how resistance to an idea is not a nullifying element. In fact, it is necessary, in Dunn's creative process, to enable the next moment.

A casual look at his books' titles indicates what he's been up to: the name of his first volume to achieve widespread recognition (a National Poetry Series selection), *Local Time*, eventually yields to the aforementioned *Different Hours*, which gives way to the recent *Here and Now*. The title of his book *Work and Love*, initially seeming ambitious in scope, feels limited when we get to *Everything Else in the World*. And how can one not smile realizing that *Not Dancing* ceded to *The Insistence of Beauty*? His catalog is full of titles that, when placed next to each other, generate the tension of small quarrels. This indicates a technique that he often uses to drive individual poems forward: the construction of expectations, then the juxtaposition of the unexpected. Throughout his oeuvre, Dunn harbors a ruthlessness toward what has already been established on the page. His poetry is often busy destroying itself. But unlike quotidian destruction, this breach does not rise out of disregard but rather its opposite—a meticulous attention to the inner world as reflected in our shared language. It's in this infraction that he creates a wholeness for the reader, an acknowledgment that the considered life is one in which we live in a perpetual state of constructing and tearing down at once.

There is a Stephen Dunn poem that I have twice witnessed people walk out on during his readings. It is also a poem that divides my college students into two camps: those who love it and those who are made uneasy by it. "The Routine Things around the House" originally appeared in the *Ohio Review* and was first collected in his 1984 volume, *Not Dancing* (later appearing in *New and Selected: Poems 1974–1994*). The poem maneuvers across risky narrative territory: upon the son's request, a mother shows him her breasts. Rather than striking a moralistic (or antimoralistic) stance on a contentious issue, the poem is, in Dunn's words, more interested in "understanding the dynamics of [a] human situation" (*WLN*, "The Good, the Not So Good," 37). Perhaps people left during the readings because they were offended by the poem's subject matter, or the narrator's depiction of the event, or even Dunn's willingness to write such a piece. But here's where the egress-inclined went wrong: this poem resists advice or dogmatism, other than the modeling of earnest inquiry.

Attention to the first three lines of the poem illuminates how Dunn affects an abrupt reaction, then supplants it with an opposing one, then does it again: "When Mother died / I thought: now I'll have a death poem. / That was unforgivable" (*NS*, 142). What sympathy is elicited by the first line, amplified subtly by the choice of "Mother," as opposed to "my mother." This is big-m Mother dying. The poor boy. He must be devastated.

These three words have arranged the room of the reader's mind for the next line. However, eight words later, one suspects that the speaker is an insensitive opportunist. The jerk. He should be devastated.

Then, three words later, we say, Okay. Mother taught him right after all. He was in shock when she died. The sad man. He was devastated.

This control of tension and energy is impressive, but that is only part of the aptitude on display. The music of the first tercet is affecting as well: all the words are terse, monosyllabic except for two: "Mother" and one of the only words that assigns judgment in the whole poem—"unforgivable." The noise of the latter seems, at first, like the music of conclusion: *Hey, reader—we know the world is complicated. I'm giving you a multisyllabic word amid all these simple ones to reflect that—a V-8 roaring louder than the Smart Cars around it.* The poem, though, is a display of deft navigation across shadowed terrain, and that "unforgivable" is not followed by a period (which would seem like the obloquy of a judge's gavel) but rather by the fecund white space between stanzas, the silence in which formed ideas harden and new growth readies to spring out below, then the corrective and perverse word "yet."

Throughout the piece, he turns the poem's front axle towards unexpected destinations: "I stared into the coffin / knowing just how long she'd live" is a gratifying two-line combination by itself, but he goes on: "how many lifetimes there are // in the sweet revisions of memory" (ibid.). The satisfying quality of "how many lifetimes there are" is facilitated by the earlier "now I'll have a death poem" moment.

One can see how he has already taken some risks. The first overt hazard, though, is in these two tercets:

> I had asked my mother (I was trembling)
> if I could see her breasts
> and she took me into her room
>
> without embarrassment or coyness
> and I stared at them,
> afraid to ask for more. (ibid.)

Dunn made many choices here: "Mother" became "my mother," allowing the reader slightly more distance than the proper noun could afford. There is a pleasing restraint on display in his avoidance of the salacious: the choice of "breasts" over other words, for example. Of course, it's easy to know to steer clear of the lewd ones, but Dunn spurns the meek ones as well: "upper body," "torso," even "chest." None would have been right for the poem. Then he merely implies the action: there is no recounting of the mother's words (if there were any) and no slow-motion verbal shot of the disrobing or any other such gimcrack distractions. Rather, there is a detached statement portraying an extraordinarily personal moment that rose out of the tough, sweet business of filial love.

In this risk-laden moment, there are two gestures to humanize the speaker. One is the parenthetical statement of "I was trembling." If one were to read the passage again without the phrase, it's a different, imbruted moment. There's also the line "afraid to ask for more." "Afraid" is humanizing, sure, but the word "more" is the brilliant note, given that this poem is written in the wake of the mother's death. "More" is what he can no longer have. "More" implies recognition on the speaker's part that this was a gift, even if he didn't recognize it at the time—a kind of generosity unheard of and, until now, not talked about. Both the action and the telling of the action are historically taboo.

Later in the poem, the narrator calls himself "a Cancer," and then, three words later, credibly says, "What luck," destroying the destruction that had just been introduced. In a poem that is about much more than a mother who showed her son her breasts, Dunn runs a satisfying risk with the lines "when girls my age were developing / their separate countries," then the echo of "what luck" followed by "she didn't doom me," making the word "Cancer" shine its little knives in one of the poem's dark corners (ibid., 143). And what didn't she doom the speaker with? "Too much or too little," essentially providing instruction for how to write this elegy (ibid.).

Informing the sophistication of the next six lines is the shifting direction of the address:

> Had I asked to touch,
>
> perhaps to suck them,

what would she have done?
Mother, dead woman

who I think permits me
to love women easily . . . (ibid.)

The first three of these lines accomplish two things at once: they insinuate how far this act between mother and son went (or didn't go) while verbalizing a contemplation some readers would have at this moment—one that that may have caused some over the years to close the book or, alternately, reach for the purse, the coat, and/or the flask and make their ways to the exits.

What was the music they walked out on? It was the noise of love for the recently dead—for this moment is both the climax and the valediction of the poem, an apostrophe in which the speaker directly addresses big-m Mother, the woman who permits him "to love women easily," those beings who had developed "their separate countries" earlier in the poem. They are not enemy outlanders, though, but rather, because of this dead woman who acted extraordinarily (in the original sense of "outside the ordinary"), an otherness he loves. He finishes:

this poem

is dedicated to where
we stopped, to the incompleteness
that was sufficient

and to how you buttoned up,
began doing the routine things
around the house. (ibid.)

After the intensification of the previous lines, on first reading "this poem // is dedicated to where / we stopped," it's natural to infer the "where" as the end of the disrobing—a reading that is supported by the final tercet of the poem. However, as Dunn is a poet of great capaciousness, allowing for multiple (even antipodal) considerations in one work, we realize that the penultimate stanza has an intentionally multifarious construction. The poem has grown out of recollection and flourished into a threnody. Therefore, "where / we stopped" can also allude to the end of the mother's and son's physical time together. The poem itself, with its use of the present tense (for example, "permits me / to love women easily" as opposed to "permitted me"), serves as a testimony to how the relationship endures, to how the tenure of their love and trust was an "incompleteness / that was sufficient" (ibid.)

The denouement, as it were, begins with the next line, as "button[ing] up" is the closure of the incident and the "routine things / around the house" seem impelled by the same mother love as the extraordinary episode that had just occurred (ibid.). By depicting such an occurrence as just another of the "routine things around the house" (it was his choice to title the poem thus), each element alters our perception of the other. As mentioned before, resistance enables.

Conjointly, given the occasion of the poem, the "buttoning up" adumbrates the closure of the casket and the phrase "routine things around the house" intimates those beneficial gestures and habits we engage in that were formed or influenced by the great love of a parent (for those of us lucky enough to have had such love), as if we can see a lost parent's good choices in our everyday actions.

Furthermore, there is another stratum here, which has to do with the telling of the story itself. As mentioned before, the mother's action and the telling of the mother's action would have been taboo. Both the narrator and the mother had to "button up," as in "be quiet," about what had transpired. One surmises from the telling that there were no other incidents such as this, making it exceptional (in both senses of that word). Therefore, the poem is both a buttoning up (closure) and an unbuttoning (exposure) at once.

This is also reflected in the opposing music of the words. The three hard syllabic stops of "buttoned up," the sound signifying both closure and the death portended (the opening line, "When Mother died," has a similar hard stop), contrast with the soft, open sibilance of the poem's final syllable—as if that "house" can go on forever, as it may in "the sweet revisions of memory." All this tension between opening and closing, exposure and covering up, telling and silence, and conferring and restraint charges the poem with a truthfulness that feels both hard-earned and consigned at once. Only a certain capaciousness could accommodate all that had been bequeathed by this extraordinary moment. In the end, "The Routine Things around the House" is an elegy that resists lamentation.

The Poetry Foundation's Web site, in its description of Stephen Dunn, states that "Dunn writes poetry that reflects the social, cultural, psychological, and philosophical territory of the American middle class." The Poetry Foundation is a good organization, but this characterization represents an underestimation. Things are not "reflected" in a Stephen Dunn poem as much as they are questioned, refuted, and, at times, affirmed by a sedulous inquiry that rejects as a possibility only its own hebetude. Through this courting of and fidelity to the "reverse side," Dunn has forged an oeuvre for adults, distinguished by a voice that is marked by candor and tenacious deliberation, among the most accessible and complex in contemporary American poetry.

Works Cited

The Poetry Foundation. "Biography of Stephen Dunn." http://www.poetryfoundation.org/bio/stephen-dunn.

The Reverse Side

David Jauss

"Go in fear of abstractions" (Pound 1968, 5); "A poem must not mean / but be" (MacLeish 1985, 107); "No ideas / but in things" (Williams 1991, 55); and the ubiquitous "Show, don't tell"—these are some of the shibboleths that govern both the teaching and practice of poetry in our time. In his essay "Some Reflections on the Abstract and the Wise," Stephen Dunn argues, in his characteristically contrarian way, against the narrow application of these principles and makes a compelling case for poems that "risk being abstract and unabashedly 'wise'" (*WLN*, 54). *Risk* is a key word here, for Dunn is very aware that a poet who writes "wisdom lines" is risking Polonius-like pomposity, didacticism, oversimplification, and banality. Furthermore, he says,

> With wisdom lines, with any abstractions, we're usually in the presence of a conscious truth, one that we can readily get elsewhere or dispense with hearing at all. Its context doesn't enrich or support it. We feel toward it as we feel toward a preacher who doesn't embody his sermon. It lacks the blood and bone of experience. (*WLN*, 55)

But Dunn isn't really interested in conscious truths, whether they are embodied and supported or not. A wisdom line that conveys a conscious truth is, at best, a "conventional wisdom" line, and sometimes, it's a lie disguised as a truth. For Dunn, a bona fide wisdom line "articulates for us some things that we've probably half known and felt. It gives our inchoate knowledge shape and order" (*WLN*, 58). Wisdom, he says, is something "arrived at out of the personal" and "discovered *in process*," so it's often the case that "the first wise lines occur in the middle of the poem" (*WLN*, 64). "What Men

Want" (*WG*, 192–95) is a good example of this tendency in Dunn's poetry; the first wisdom lines of this ninety-seven-line poem appear after thirty-eight lines of personal meditation on his father's and brother's lives.

Since a genuine wisdom line is a discovery, not a premise, it should come as a surprise to the poet. It's no wonder, then, that Dunn has said, "My criterion for myself is that I'm not in my poem until the first moment I surprise myself" (Dacey 2000). Lesser poets might consider that moment of surprise and wisdom the place where the poem ends, not where it most truly begins, but for Dunn, the process of discovery is plural, not singular. He is never content to rest with the first conclusion he reaches.

The process of discovery that Dunn employs in his work is a dialectic one. As he has said,

> I . . . have learned to argue with myself as I go, to assert then doubt a claim, to compose dialectically. . . . In short, I think I've learned how to "find" the poem I'm writing by resisting where it wants to go and/or resisting my initial impulses for it. (ibid.)

Now, he suggests, that method is habitual, involuntary: "When I say or assert something, I almost immediately hear and start to entertain its opposite" (ibid.). In this, he resembles Simone Weil, who argued that "contradiction is the lever of transcendence" (1970, 134)—that is, contradicting a conscious truth is the way to transcend it and discover an as-yet-unknown truth. Importantly, the purpose of investigating ideas dialectically is not to eradicate one or the other idea, for contradiction, Weil argues, is an essential element of both truth and beauty: "in all beauty we find contradiction" (1977, 379), she says, and "all truth contains a contradiction" (1952, 151). Dunn agrees. In his poem "Circular," he says that those who fail to see the truth of contradictory beliefs are "one-eyed amid the beautiful contraries" (*WG*, 95). Ironically, it's the one-eyed who see with the most clarity—albeit the misleading clarity of false certainty; what the "clear-eyed" see, he tells us in "The Observer," is "the blur" of reality (*NS*, 12). Better a blurry truth, he suggests, than a clear falsehood.

Behind the dialectic method Dunn practices is the belief that something can be true on one level, its opposite can be true on another, and when they are synthesized, both of them can be simultaneously true on a higher level. As Jean Cocteau said, "All creation is the spirit of contradiction in its highest form" (1972, 63). And in its highest form, contradiction transcends the either-or mentality of simple negation—"This is true, that isn't"—and achieves the complex affirmation of what Cleanth Brooks called the both-and mode of thought (1956, 81). In his poem "Oklahoma City," Dunn seconds Brooks, saying, "Some mysteries can be solved by ampersands. / *Ands* not *ors*"—but characteristically, he refuses to let that wisdom be his final word on the subject: his very next words are "that was my latest answer" (*DH*, 114). Clearly, the process of transcendence through dialectic contradiction is one that continues, never reaching a permanent conclusion. And how could it be otherwise, since ultimate truth is unattainable?

H. L. Hix has described the unattainability of truth in a wonderfully memorable way. "If truth is an extinct totem animal," he has said, "argument is the map that specifies the place it would be found if it still existed, and aphorism is the description of what the animal would look like if you could get there" (1991, 85). Despite the impossibility of the task, Dunn tracks truth through his poetry's dialectic arguments. The aphoristic wisdom lines that result are laudatory not only for their chutzpah—their Napoleonic desire, despite their small stature, to be emperor of Truth—but for their refusal to pretend they've achieved that desire. Always, they provoke thought rather than shut it down. As Karl Kraus once said, "An aphorism never coincides with the truth: it is either a half-truth or one-and-a-half truths" (1976, 67). A wisdom line, too, is inherently incomplete; either it fails to capture a whole truth or it suggests the existence of a further truth that has not yet been captured. In short, a wisdom line, be it a half-truth or one-and-a-half truths, requires the reader not merely to nod in agreement but to continue the exploration for that impossible-to-track animal: truth.

The dialectic method is the principal way Dunn tracks the untrackable. Implicit in this method, at least as Dunn practices it, is the notion of complementarity, a key concern in contemporary physics that is also at the heart of his poetry. In the words of J. Robert Oppenheimer,

> One of the first things the student of atomic structure must come to understand is the rather deep and subtle principle which has turned out to be a clue to unraveling the whole domain of physical experience. This is the principle of complementarity, which recognizes that various ways of talking about physical experience may each have validity and may each be necessary for adequate description of the physical world, and may yet stand in a mutually contradictory relationship to each other. (qtd. in Schevill 1977, iv)

The theory of complementarity that Oppenheimer describes was introduced in 1927 by the physicist Niels Bohr, who asserted that two mutually exclusive explanations of the nature of light (as a wave and as a particle) were both true and that we can achieve a complete understanding of light only by recognizing their "complementary" relations. "There are the trivial truths and the great truths," he said. "The opposite of a trivial truth is plainly false. The opposite of a great truth is also true" (qtd. in Becker 1957, 52). William Blake makes a similar distinction in his poem "Jerusalem" when he says that "Negations" cannot "mutually Exist" whereas "Contraries" can because they "are equally true" (1988, 162, 196). Bohr's theory of complementarity doesn't apply only to light, or even only to quantum physics; in his opinion, it is an "all-pervasive principle," one that applies to all of nature, both human and physical (Holton 1973, 150). That all of life is paradoxical and complementary is not a new theory, of course. As revolutionary as Bohr's theory was, and remains, its philosophical roots are ancient, a fact that Bohr acknowledged when he chose for his coat of arms the symbol for yin and yang (Holton 1973, 121). Bohr's contribution was in revealing that this ancient concept of unity as the marriage of opposites was not just a mystical notion but a matter of literal physical, subatomic reality. In Dunn's poetry, it is also a matter of literal physical reality—and of psychological and philosophical reality, too.

Dunn's complementary vision of truth pervades his nineteen books of poetry and prose. We see examples of it in "Between Angels," where he says,

> I do not mind living
>
> like this. I cannot bear
> living like this.
> Oh, everything's true
> at different times
>
> in the capacious day . . . (*BA*, 46)

and in "The Past," where he says, "Nothing in nature is a metaphor. / Everything is" (*IB*, 39), and in his prose piece "Personal," where he says, "I know that nobody's problem was ever solved by feeling deeply about it. I've said the opposite of this, and stand by what I said" (*RR*, 73). In all of these cases, and countless others throughout his work, the second statement doesn't correct or cancel the previous one; rather, it *completes* it, for neither truth by itself approaches a whole truth. As this suggests, Dunn's most characteristic poems consist of—to borrow the title of one of his books—riffs and reciprocities; each discovery reached through a riff is followed by its reciprocal.

Sometimes Dunn even conveys the process of considering one truth and then its complement through his lineation, as in these lines from "The Soul's Agents": "Trust us, your secrets differentiate you / from no one" (*WG*, 144–45). Taken as a sentence, this statement is not paradoxical. But Dunn's strategic line break makes the reader pause and momentarily think the thought "our secrets *do* differentiate us," a thought the next line contradicts. Thus the reader must simultaneously hold within his or her mind, if only for an instant, two diametrically opposed thoughts.

As these examples should suggest, complementary contradiction is not only Dunn's compositional method, it's also one of his central themes. "Halves" is one example of a poem that takes as its theme the complementary nature of existence. Its title alludes to the ancient Greek belief that men and women were originally complementary halves of one androgynous being. According to their creation myth, Zeus split these beings in half to prevent them from becoming too powerful and challenging the gods. As Aristophanes says in Plato's *The Symposium*, "The innate desire of human beings for each other started" when they were divided in half, and now desire "draws the two halves of our original nature back together and tries to make one out of two and to heal the wound in human nature" (2003, 24). The name for this "desire and pursuit of wholeness," he says, is "love" (ibid., 26). Much of Dunn's poetry is about this pursuit, this attempt to marry opposites and achieve wholeness, both in human relationships and in his understanding of himself and the world. In "Halves," he suggests that we sense this original wholeness in that moment halfway between sleeping and waking when such seeming contraries as dream and reality and night and day coexist. At this almost mystical moment, the dichotomy between male and female also disappears and we are whole, not halves. After describing this moment between sleep and waking, Dunn writes,

> Soon the equally mysterious world of women
>   and men, of momentary
> common agreement and wild misunderstanding,
>
> will impose itself naturally on the simplest event.
>   Anatomy will send
> its differing messages to syntax and sense, . . .

But now, he continues,

. . . while the secret
intercoms in our dream rooms
are still open and each separate body knows

but does not reach for what it wants,
we all live in the same
country, share the same absurd flag.

We keep our eyes closed as long as we can,
hang on to the vestiges
of night as if we were balancing

two delicate and always vanishing halves.
Then the alarm, and the body rises
to yearn for what is here and gone. (*LT*, 24–25)

In this poem, the contradictory worlds of men and women are one world, not two, and in that world, which shares "the same absurd flag," men and women are also one, their separate bodies and souls fused in the wholeness they desire. Here, as in much of his work, the author of *Work and Love*—those seeming opposites—pursues the wholeness of love, trying to balance the two halves that are both here and not here.

Of all of Dunn's poems, "The Reverse Side" is perhaps the one that most reveals the complementary nature of his vision. It also reveals his instinctual tendency to go beyond the nod of agreement with a wisdom line—in this case, the Japanese proverb that provides the poem's title—to an open-ended consideration of its implications. Here's the poem:

The Reverse Side

The reverse side also has a reverse side.
—a Japanese proverb

It's why when we speak a truth
some of us instantly feel foolish

as if a deck inside us has been shuffled
and there it is—the opposite
of what we said.

And perhaps why as we fall in love
we're already falling out of it.

It's why the terrified and the simple
latch onto one story,
just one version of the great mystery.

Image & afterimage, oh even
the open-minded yearn for a fiction
to rein things in—
the snapshot, the lie of a frame.

How do we not go crazy,
we who have found ourselves compelled
to live with the circle, the ellipsis, the word
not yet written. (*DH*, 73)

Notice that Dunn says that speaking "a truth," not a falsehood, is what makes him feel "foolish." The opposite—the reverse side—of a truth is not a falsehood, it's another truth. The "folly" of asserting the first truth isn't that it's false but that it's incomplete, that it needs its complementary opposite to approach a whole truth. And the process doesn't stop after we've created a complementary truth out of two opposing truths; rather, the next step is to consider that new, complementary truth's reverse side. This process is never-ending; thus the poem concludes with Dunn recognizing the need "to live with the circle"—that is, with what has no beginning or end—and with "the ellipsis, the word / not yet written"—that is, with the need to continue searching for the truth and the words to express it. The poem acknowledges our natural yearning "for a fiction / to rein things in," for a belief that will give us the peace of certainty and closure but admirably refuses to succumb to it.

The ending of this poem is a good example of how a wisdom line—and a poem derived, like this one, from a wisdom line—can and should lead the reader to further contemplation, and to a greater acknowledgment of the ambiguity and mystery of experience. The words "How do we not go crazy" could mean two contradictory things: that those who hold opposite, complementary beliefs can't help but go crazy and, conversely, that they remain sane. The fact that this final sentence ends with a period, not a question mark, further suggests that it is simultaneously a question and an answer. But if those who recognize the paradoxical nature of truth *do* go crazy, it is, Dunn believes, with that wise kind of insanity that Melville called "the sane madness of vital truth" (1972, 225–26). As Dunn says elsewhere, "paradox helps us / not to feel insane" (*LE*, "Loves," 85), and it does so because it "disturbs our conventional sense of things. It's the jolt that gives us permission to think what in fact we've thought" (*RR*, "Paradox," 29). As these passages suggest, it's the "conventional sense of things" that is truly crazy, and therefore it is those who accept that conventional sense of things—those who "latch onto one story, / just one version of the great mystery"—who are insane. Or, to put it another way, while the brave and complex risk "the sane madness of vital truth," the "terrified and the simple" succumb to "the *in*sane madness of *non*vital, conventional truth."

Without question, Dunn is one of those who risk—and achieve—Melville's sane brand of madness, and he does it, as Melville does, and as all of our greatest writers do, through a rigorously honest pursuit of the paradoxical nature of truth. More than perhaps anyone else in our literature, he has explored the idea of complementarity in that pursuit. Whitman may be large and contain multitudes, and he may willingly and cheerfully contradict himself, but he does so less out of a sense that truth is composed of complementary contradictions than out of an exuberant desire to embrace all of humanity in his "en masse" voice. Emily Dickinson certainly argued as dialectically with herself as Dunn has with himself (and she did this not only between poems but within them—witness, for example, poem 501 [1976, 243], which ends by doubting what its opening line states with such certainty), but hers is ultimately a poetry of either/or, not both/and: it vacillates between affirming first one possible truth and then its opposite, and never seems to consider the possibility that both could be true. Dunn's complementary vision of truth makes his contribution to American literature distinctive, new, and important—and makes him worthy to be read alongside these masters.

In one of her late poems, Dickinson offers a short course in becoming a great poet, and though the course is short, the lesson is anything but simple. To learn it requires a lifetime of intensive examination of one's self, others, and the world. She says, simply,

> . . . faithful be
> To Thyself,
> And Mystery—
> All the rest is Perjury—(1976, 714)

If Stephen Dunn's poems were testimony in a court of law, he might be accused of perjury for his contradictory attempts to track that extinct animal, truth. But in the court of poetry, where truth is so complex and elusive that one cannot ever speak "the whole truth, and nothing but the truth," he has been the most honest and honorable of witnesses. He has consistently been faithful both to himself and to mystery. As a result, he has overcome the risks associated with abstraction and written poetry that is genuinely and "unabashedly wise." And for that reason, and many others, he is one of our most indispensable poets.

Works Cited

Becker, Bill. "Pioneers of the Atom." *New York Times Magazine* (October 20, 1957): 52+.

Blake, William. 1988. "Jerusalem." In *The Complete Poetry and Prose of William Blake*, edited by David V. Erdman. New York: Anchor Books.

Brooks, Cleanth. 1956. *The Well-Wrought Urn: Studies in the Structure of Poetry*. New York: Harcourt, Brace.

Cocteau, Jean. 1972. *Cocteau on the Film: Conversations with Jean Cocteau Recorded by André Fraigneau.* New York: Dover.

Dacey, Philip. 2000. "Interview with Stephen Dunn." *Cortland Review* (March). http://www.cortlandreview.com/features/00/03/index.html.

Dickinson, Emily. 1976. *The Complete Poems of Emily Dickinson*, edited by Thomas H. Johnson. Boston: Back Bay Books.

Hix, H. L. 1991. "Warning Signals." *Iowa Review* 21, no. 2: 84–88.

Holton, Gerald. 1973. *Thematic Origins of Scientific Thought: Kepler to Einstein.* Cambridge: Harvard University Press.

Kraus, Karl. 1976. *Half-Truths and One-and-a-Half Truths*, edited and translated by Harry Zohn. Montreal: Engendra Press.

MacLeish, Archibald. 1985. "Ars Poetica." In *The Collected Poems of Archibald MacLeish.* New York: Mariner Books. 107.

Melville, Herman. 1972. "Hawthorne and His Mosses." In *Shorter Works of Hawthorne and Melville*, edited by Hershel Parker. Columbus, OH: Merrill.

Plato. 2003. *The Symposium*, edited and translated by Christopher Gill. New York: Penguin Classics.

Pound, Ezra. 1968. "A Retrospect." In *Literary Essays of Ezra Pound.* New York: New Directions. 3–14.

Schevill, James. 1977. *The Arena of Ants.* Providence: Copper Beech Press.

Weil, Simone. 1952. *Gravity and Grace*, translated by Arthur Wills. New York: G. P. Putnam's Sons.

———. 1970. *First and Last Notebooks*, translated by Richard Rees. London: Oxford University Press.

———. 1977. *The Simone Weil Reader*, edited by George A. Panichas. New York: David McKay.

Williams, William Carlos. 1991. "A Sort of Song." In *The Collected Poems of William Carlos Williams*, edited by Christopher MacGowan. Vol. 2. New York: New Directions. 55.

Part Three

The Despoiled and Radiant Now

David Rigsbee

For Stephen Dunn, seeing double poses no obstacle on the way to clarity. Double seeing is what we do, and he has carved a much-admired career out of exploring what makes us ambivalent and of how ambivalence typifies something in our moment. Joseph Brodsky, a poet so different from Dunn that it is hard to imagine an overlap, asserted that for a poet, ambivalence was a necessity. Of course, he was largely referring to imagination's survival mode when in Orwellian political (and consequently linguistic) circumstances, and for him the strategies and tactics obtaining in these circumstances were always in play. Dunn goes him one better in finding the necessity for ambivalence inherent a fortiori in daily life, without the heroism implicit in the expatriate's utterances, and his poems describe how that necessity plays itself out in the world of human relationships. In its regularity and dynamism, Dunn's fondness for counter-thesis would make Hegel smile. It's an ability to appear synoptic when reflecting upon the mind's tendency to experience a thing and almost immediately to entertain its opposite. This opposite can take the form of a rejected alternative, a road not taken, an unchosen career, a personal secret, or, in its rare, expanded version, a whole secret life.

The secret, that privatized country of imagination, comes into play trailing a long literary pedigree. Like scarcity and prayer, secrets create value. One value they create for sure, whether as the result of a revelation harbored or the Paternoster, is a more robust accommodation of the imagination to, as we would say, interiority. So in one sense we may allow ourselves to think that the ambivalence poets feel and write about has a positive component. It is the counter-alternative in the ambivalence that is at issue in Dunn, the one he seems interested in setting to theme. It's the imagination's equivalent of the road not taken, and it is none the worse for that, as far as Dunn is concerned. In the long poem "Loosetrife" (*L*, 89–96), Dunn writes in section 5, "Still I can't be sure, as you were, / that what's hidden is any more mysterious / than the palpable immensity that isn't" (*L*, 93).

The sense of ambivalent encounter that so often appears in Dunn's poems reminds me of something else the Russian said about ambivalence, namely that it stood to be a saving trait in a poet. In postponing commitment, the poet maintains a freedom that appears when ambivalence shades into equilibrium—a sort of discount freedom, based on a détente toward positions usually already compromised. This is not magical thinking. Indeed, freedom like this shades also into anomie:

> It was the hour of simply nothing,
> not a single desire in my western heart,
> and no ancient system
> of breathing and postures,
> no big idea justifying what I felt. (*DH*, "Zero Hour," 43)

As strategies go, the relinquishment of any "big idea" is itself the ghost, or trace, or elegy, of a big idea. Even lassitude has its poetry, but you won't get it by flying the flag of a traditional theme. As everyone knows, the Russians and French were onto the heaviness of anomie. It's a testimony to American exceptionalism that Whitman's sunny disposition pulled our poetry toward imagism and mysticism. Anomie's lack of grasp allows the hand to dangle down into the lower depths. As Dunn showed so adroitly in early poems, boundaries are enablers, as his more than passing acquaintance with formalism also shows. As example, in an interview with the editors of *Nightsun*, Dunn said, "The Commandments rose out of somebody's understanding of human nature; given who we are, we need a lot of Thou shalt not's" (2000).

When we go in this direction, we discover not only that wish (and that need) to expand our interiority but that the not-chosen is rife with imagination's fruits. It is not a stone's throw from the not-chosen to a fantasy land of counter-facts that tap the brake pedal of conformist behavior. It's not fantasy so much that matters anyway, but the psychological or human predisposition to imagine alternatives and to have lived with both those chosen and those not. This latter can become a kind of shadow life:

> It's why when we speak of truth
> some of us instantly feel foolish
> as if a deck inside us has been shuffled
> and there it is—the opposite
> of what we said. (*DH*, "The Reverse Side," 73)

Dunn is of the school of Chekhov, one of whose characters remarked (or rather thought) that it's the secret life that chiefly bears our significance. He also reminded us that we should be shadowed by a man with a hammer, who would be there to whack us, by way of reminder, every time we thought fit to avoid the pain of others or, by extension, to deny the secret life with its sorrows and impossible desires. And Dunn knows, like Chekhov, why that life is secret:

> But by the middle years this other life
> had become his life. That was Odysseus's secret,
> kept even from himself. When he talked about return,
> he thought he meant what he said. (*DH*, "Odysseus's Secret,"
> 32–33)

In this Chekhovian view, secrets are a locked part of human interiority, and it is such interiority that has a purchase on a significant portion of modern personhood, just as deeds did in bygone epics if the poets are to be believed. And the difference between secrets, specifically, and other sorts of interiority is the difference between a memory and a prayer. I would even venture to say that this Chekhovian view constitutes the tenor and atmospherics of much of Dunn's poetry. Now it may be, and I think this may be Dunn's suspicion, that the carrying of secrets and the need to divulge or confess them enable us to consider ourselves in a new light of consequentiality, dignified by the knowledge of imperfection, inspired by those same imperfections, to move away from faultless dreams and allowing us something denied the gods, what we grandly call a tragic vision. I mean, it is all intramural, is it not? Neither gods nor animals understand our weeping, our inconsistencies, our need for rhetoric, to say that which is not, as well as that which is.

Meanwhile, we don't know people's secret lives until there is a rupture or an unlocking. The subsequent release paints us as even more partial—even more mortal (that is, discontinuous)—creatures than we had feared. This is tragic in the classical sense: things are not meant to work out. Its revelation as a secret also ruins it as a secret; it is under wraps no longer. Meanwhile there is something usable in discontinuity, in what doesn't finish (even in secrets). Dostoyevsky knew it and fastened incompletion to the tragedy's porch. Dunn mentions elsewhere that as a young writer it was Dostoyevsky who turned his head around. After that, he was good to go: the seeming inconsistency in Raskolnikov's opposition to animal cruelty would pose no problem for Dunn:

> So next week why not admit
> that what Raskolnikov did
> has always made you dream?
> The more you expose yourself
> the more you become unrecognizable. (*EE*, "The Soul's Agents," 37)

The secret not only creates the value of interiority, it gets another project going. An awareness of the value of secrecy kindles an awareness of mystery, and from that flows all manner (but not all) of art.

Writing one's life in public is both anathema to that sense of the sacred and unaesthetic, insofar as poems are concerned. But emerging from the high-water mark of confessionalism, Dunn is unafraid of the potential insult that follows from revelation. Take his well-known "The Routine Things around the House" (*NS*, 142–43), where the speaker both elegizes and thanks his mother for revealing to him her breasts, a bounded moment of tender instruction that left him, he argues, a regular guy without hang-ups. Dunn writes:

> this poem
>
> is dedicated to where
> we stopped, to the incompleteness
> that was sufficient
>
> and to how you buttoned up,
> began doing the routine things
> around the house. (ibid., 143)

Now, no one should be under the illusion that the boundaries of behavior reflected in the boundaries of form or any other aesthetic approach do more than offer the "momentary stay against confusion," which the poem proposes as its contribution to human solidarity. I note that the "stay" is just as mortal as the sayer; only the confusion seems to have a purchase on the long run. In an interview, Dunn puts it this way:

> I do think that in our poems and in our stories we can offer those momentary stays against confusion. We can create coherencies out of the raw stuff of life, the chaos of it, the fraughtness of it. Credible fictions that for awhile seduce us and others into acceptance of them. Versions of a life, not a life. Yes, if we do them well enough they may well indeed constitute a life, especially after we're gone. (Dacey 2000)

There is also the presumption that goes with necessary fictions. Consider the ending to Dunn's "At the Smithville Methodist Church" (*WG*, 183–84):

> Evolution is magical but devoid of heroes.
> You can't say to your child

"Evolution loves you." The story stinks
of extinction and nothing

exciting happens for centuries. I didn't have
a wonderful story for my child
and she was beaming. All the way home in the car
she sang the songs,

occasionally standing up for Jesus.
There was nothing to do
but drive, ride it out, sing along
in silence. (ibid., 84)

Human relationships and dealings are of course layered, as are the ambivalences they foster. It is one of Dunn's strengths to find these layers and write the narratives that are appropriate to them. The thing about authenticity (or *in* authenticity) of feelings goes back to poets like James Wright and John Logan. The fact of authenticity began to lose force when lyric poetry began to undergo a destabilization in the 1970s—and for the same reason: things like subjectivity were put under a microscope and revealed their parts. This shift notwithstanding, Dunn acquitted himself well by building a sense of *knowingness* in the poems he made, and he went right on writing poems about men and women. Part of what he knew was that authenticity is not to be confused with the likes of sincerity: the latter was always self-divided. What better way to say this than to first look in the bedroom. To have a partner is to enact an ambivalence; it is inherently unstable, as the title "Sleeping with Others" (*IB*, 84–85), attests, and in the poem "The Answers" (ibid., 81–83), a partner speaks:

I am unreachable.
If I were standing next to you
you'd see for yourself
how far away I was. (ibid., 81)

Dunn is one of the great poets of domestic mystery, and that mystery is in turn founded on yet another division: the satisfaction and the outrage of solitude. Rilke went so far as to declare that love was the mutual protection of solitude, an insight that would have quite sobered the woozy rhapsodists of Plato's *Symposium*. The ambivalence, the combining power of many viewpoints, in married life is nowhere more apparent (nor so well-hidden in plain sight) than in speech.

Dunn is perhaps our preeminent poet at clarifying what's intractable. It is no small feat. Where other poets are content to gesture or skirt the difficulties of description altogether, Dunn jumps right in and sheepdogs wandering meaning through the gate. Keeping discourse between such navigational guidelines would seem to suggest that Dunn is a realist, by which I mean a poet who steers his way between desire and nothing in a dialectic that has profound stylistic implications. His own poems, for example, owe something to the *sprezzatura* of James Tate while also seeking the aesthetic oneness of closure. Not for him the discontinuous, the merely textual, the fodder of irony. Although his demotic ease might be mistaken for the work of a poet who likes to spin language, his work comes from older stock and his persistent explorations of the id's agenda and the power associated with that, in contrast to redemptive or illuminative moments (secular division) mark him as a poet who has not moved far beyond the gravitational field of the verities. He writes,

> You've faked so many feelings
> in your time you wonder
> if it could have been
> the ghost of faked feelings
> offering you an authentic sadness . . . (*L*, "The Song," 49)

Secrets and lies are often paired. The linguistic ramifications are similar: both secrets and lies are exceptions to a general rule. Just as secrets require a presumption that revelation would be bad, a lie requires general truthfulness in language as normative. This is why, among other things, that Satan's mission in *Paradise Lost* was doomed from the get-go and that there is no honor among thieves. For Dunn, the subject of secrets and lies, of ambivalent suspensions of allegiance, suggests an acquiescence to boundaries even as it requires those boundaries to be manifest at all. And therein lies a paradox, the kind that a resourceful poet can hang a hat on. Dunn also knows the incentive power of temptation:

> . . . the soul on its own
> is helpless, asleep in the hollows
> of its rigging, waiting to be stirred. (*WG*, "And So," 190)

The individual, particularized soul—the poet's, say—becomes the general "the soul," as if to demonstrate a principle, rather than render a confession. It is the principle Dunn is after, almost as if he had discovered an elemental force previously unnoticed by literature. At bottom, the truths to be discovered in the relationships of ordinary people are every bit as significant to the individuals as approved motives or larger, tectonic forces like history—a region American poets have had to struggle to claim in lyric poetry. It is the prison of days that is at issue and how to mend that singularity of which Dunn is aware, unsure at times whether to claim the privilege of singularity (authenticity), whether that singularity be subject to relationships, moral development, or a new historical epoch: "Our solitudes are so populated / that sometimes after sex / we know it's best to be quiet" (*IB*, "Sleeping with Others, 84").

At times in Dunn's poems, you sense something like stoicism:

> The truth is,
> I learned to live without hope
> as well as I could, almost happily,
> in the despoiled and radiant now.
> (*DH*, "A Postmortem Guide," 121)

At other times we experience situational conformity, and at still others, desire for what can't be had, as if imagination were a skyhook. And behind all is the ticking.

Works Cited

Dacey, Philip. 2000. "Interview with Stephen Dunn." *Cortland Review* (March): http://www.cortlandreview.com/features/00/03/index.html.

Nightsun. 2000. "Poet of Restraint and Extravagance: A Conversation with Stephen Dunn." *Nightsun* 20 (March 2). Frostburg State University. http://faculty.frostburg.edu/phil/forum/SDunn.htm.

In-Dwelling

Kathleen Graber

Recently I watched the first two episodes of *Deadwood* with a friend who'd never seen this HBO television series. Before we sat down, shoulder to shoulder in front of his twelve-inch laptop screen, I said I wanted to give the viewing an epigraph, and I read two sentences from a Stephen Dunn essay I'd been reading earlier in the day: "To know where you are requires imagination. To move well requires skill" (*WLN*, "Stepping Out," 10). But by the time *Deadwood* saloon owner Al Swearengen offers up his famously persuasive speech discouraging his paying clients from abandoning their revelry to ride out in "darkest night" in search of "the heathens" suspected of scalping a Norwegian family traveling back to Minnesota—he makes a counteroffer of free drink and half-priced women—we'd both forgotten the orienting words we were supposed to have been keeping in mind (2004).

The next morning, my dog was stretched out on the floor beside me chewing his bone while I reread a chunk of Heidegger's *Poetry, Language, Thought*—that bit in which "poetically man dwells" (2001, 211), a passage written (or at least translated) so that with each reading I'm certain I'm following his unfolding thoughts, right up to the point at which I realize I'm actually not.

A lot has already been written about all of these things: dogs, Heidegger, Stephen Dunn. A lot has even been written about David Milch's western drama *Deadwood*, which aired for only three seasons (2004–2006). Milch, in a voice-over commentary available as a bonus track on disc 1 of the series, explains that he was drawn to Deadwood as an historical actuality for the same reason that many of the series characters claim to have been drawn to it: it is a place without law (2008). Located beyond the borders of the United States on land belonging at that time to the Sioux, the real Deadwood must have percolated in something as much like a half state-of-nature, half social-contract stew as we can imagine. Milch was eager to explore how order might establish itself or be established in the absence of both a written code and its authorized enforcement. Thus, the morals enacted in *Deadwood* are often a rich mélange of the universally accepted and the highly provisional, generally relative, and in some ways self-serving. In other words, they are baldly human, fluid rather than static, neither particularly democratic nor heaven-sent. Another *Deadwood* viewer might replace the word *human* here in favor of something like *inhuman* or *monstrous*, but that would be to miss the point.

The longer I think about poetry, the clearer I am in my belief that writing it is a moral act. Our aesthetics emerge from our ethics, or are co-generated with them, whether poets attach themselves to an *ism* or a manifesto or not. Perhaps I'm naïve when I say that I can't imagine a poem, even one at the farthest end of invention and experiment, that doesn't aspire to deliver a truth of some kind. I like what Stephen Dunn—expanding that famous line from Auden's elegy for Yeats—has to say about this in his essay "Bringing the Strange Home": "Poetry may make nothing happen, and I don't think it's desirable for it to be written as if it could make something happen. I'm interested in those poems that manage to cut through passable truths to another level of truth and connection" (*WLN*, 33). Elsewhere he describes the poem's act of replacing an accepted truth with a more precise truth simply as its having gotten the world right. If you know Dunn's poems at all, you know that I do him no disservice in calling this "getting the world right" his essential project. "The issue is not right versus wrong," he contends. "It's right versus off (the imprecise, the superficial, etc.)" (*WLN*, "The Good, the Not So Good," 44). He wants at all times to disabuse himself (and us) of the easily accepted, comfortable, and comforting truths. What he leaves us with is often a view of the heart that is as appealing and stable as a backroom in *Deadwood*'s Gem Saloon or Heidegger's abyss. Or Mr. Wu's pigpen, the sloppy final resting place into which *Deadwood*'s murdered often disappear. If that's disturbing to some (probably the same folks offended by Milch's use of profane diction), it's because we usually recognize ourselves when we see ourselves, even if we don't like what we see. However, if we want to cultivate our capacities for empathy and compassion and something approaching a genuine comprehension of ourselves and our planet-mates, rather than something like condescending tolerance—or worse, condescending intolerance—then the mirror with its greedy, unseemly reflection isn't a bad place for us to focus our careful attention.

My favorite moment in Stephen Dunn's work might be his rendering of the resurrected Mary Shelley's opinion of the welcoming American neighbors among whom Dunn has fancifully placed her: "Thus Mary Shelley found herself accepted / by those who had no monster in them— / the most frightening people alive, she thought" (*LV*, 91–92). I'm drawn to this poem from *Local Visitations* in part for personal reasons; because I'm from southern New Jersey, the poem's reference to the now-vanished Brigantine Castle haunted house amusement, in which some theatrical version of Shelley's monster once roamed the halls "making children scream" (ibid., 91) means more to me than it would to most readers, and thus it charms me to no end. Yet this passage appeals to me primarily because it offers a nearly perfect crystallization of the ethical inversions and subversions so central to Dunn's aesthetics.

This moment also seems to have tucked within it a deeper invitation. *Ask yourself why, exactly*—it seems to want us to wonder—*these people with no monster in them are the most frightening people alive?* Perhaps because I have been instructed by so many other Dunn poems, I find it hard now to believe that there really are such beings, and, hence, I hear in what seems to be a funny quip a genuine warning. We ought to be frightened by those who do not know themselves, those who hide their darkest impulses not only from each other but also from themselves. This contention that there might not be any purely benevolent souls among us is a harsh knock on human nature, and Dunn has been careful to just barely suggest it. In fact, he distances himself from it even further by imaginatively placing it in the mind of Mary Shelley. Thus he delivers his message with a sort of secondhand sleight of hand, for, as he says in another poem, "Cruelties," "It might be best / to invent others to speak certain things / we've thought and kept to ourselves" (*WG*, 128).

After two episodes of *Deadwood*, every viewer knows that Al Swearengen is a monster. What we have yet to learn is that he's not the worst by far, nor is he even as psychologically or philosophically terrifying as the do-good, handsome ex-sheriff from Montana, Seth Bullock, who is also a monster and all the more unpredictable because he doesn't *know* he's one. Ironically, he thinks he's quite the opposite—a moral compass, in fact—and he's got charisma, so you can see already how far wrong something like that might go. The caveat here should be that in *Deadwood* the central characters are nearly all either brutes or victims, violent actors and schemers, or objects to be exploited. Sol Starr, Bullock's savvy but honest business partner, and "The Doc" are the only two obvious exceptions. Especially in the early going, almost no one else occupies any alternative ground.

Stephen Dunn's poems, like his aptly titled prose collection *Walking Light: Memoirs and Essays about Poetry*, are peppered with images of locomotion. To walk *right* is to exhibit appropriate being; it announces that one moves through a landscape with both sufficient knowledge and self-knowledge. It is not an anomaly, in other words, that one premise of the book of poems *Local Visitations* involves the poet's imaginative reanimation of nineteenth-century novelists in specifically selected small New Jersey towns. The landscape of Atlantic City *fits* Twain, for instance; and if you've ever been to Pleasantville, then you know why Dickens had to end up there. I was thrilled to find Dostoyevsky feeling what I'd been feeling all of my life on the boardwalk on a summer day in Wildwood, my own hometown: "He liked the ocean but hated the beach, / loved people more than he did / a single woman or man" (*LV*, "Dostoyevsky in Wildwood," 88).

With this ambulatory metaphor already in my mind, I began to see how many shots of *Deadwood* participate in a similar understanding of the importance of how one walks. Bullock, from the first moment, has a strikingly idiosyncratic stride—so rigidly upright, so tall, that it seems to be something of a hindrance to his forward progress. He clearly thinks a lot of himself: his gait smacks of puffed-up posturing. There is no easy elegance there. When Swearengen, in contrast, moves through the camp, he walks like a man who knows where he is going and what he is going to do. He rarely leaves his own domain, but when he does, self-knowledge and assurance travel with him.

In his essay "Stepping Out," Dunn recounts his coming-of-age experiences with various local thugs in the Forest Hills section of Queens. He proposes that to escape being bullied one needs to master the right sort of walk. He goes on, however, to qualify his opening claim, suggesting that there are not only many other variables in play but also situations in which no subtle strategy will suffice:

> . . . nonchalance is a bad tactic with certain theorists. If the theory is say Jews must be killed, or some equal aberration, evasive action might make some sense. Acting nonchalant is stupid. The more we know about history, the more we know that in such circumstances we must forget about subtlety, forget even about poetry if we are poets, and attack the theory and its proponents. (*WLN*, 9)

Dunn praises George Oppen, who stopped writing poetry in mid-career in order to be a political activist: a good poem needs to enter complexly and with due complicity into any circumstance, an intellectual indulgence not available, advisable, or even morally acceptable in moments of historical extremity. To not know what you are up against, Dunn argues, is one kind of failure to understand where you are, and such failure can lead to the "political error" of misjudging your adversary.

To walk right, then, you need at least two things: knowledge of who you are and knowledge of the situation—which is to say, you need to be able to measure yourself against the landscape, a landscape understood to be occupied by other potent, willful beings. In "Stepping Out," Dunn is talking on the surface about the unlikelihood of two teenage boys being able to walk past a crowd of drunken hoodlums in front of the White Castle after dark and not get jumped, but as Heidegger reminds us, all sensuous poetic images exist for nonsensuous or suprasensuous reasons, pointing beyond themselves to an unseen metaphysical or spiritual realm. "The superior and the true are what is sensuously represented in the symbolic image," is how Heidegger puts it. "The essence of art stands or falls in accordance with the essence and truth of metaphysics" (1996, 18).

For Dunn, there is no higher ethical and aesthetic value (these walk hand in hand for him) than revealing what is "true," but this doesn't mean a poet ought not to lie, if necessary, to reveal it. The truths that most interest him are psychological, philosophical, and artistic rather than factual. He feels almost no allegiance to the facts at all, except in those cases when someone else has been trying to keep them from us. The muddy sty he is reaching into is most often that swirling, amorphous interior arena where what Freud calls "the drives" meet up with that part of the soul meant to restrain them, and what fascinates Dunn is just how good we are at conning ourselves into believing that any uneasy truce made down in the muck precludes further espionage, intricate machinations, and other forms of less secret warfare. To know the world, "to get the world right," one has to start by knowing the self and human nature—and what a thankless, unending job *that* is.

For what it's worth, Seth Bullock arrives in Deadwood understanding the mentality and abilities of simple murderers, thieves, and road agents. He knows he's quick enough with his own gun to defend himself and others against them. He knows the highwayman's common tactics and motives. However, he doesn't know how to take the measure of himself against a more complicated criminal like Swearengen, who has a couple of terrific personal assets that make us admire him—even eventually like him, something his being fictional permits—despite his ruthless behavior. Swearengen knows who he is and he has, metaphorically speaking, panoramic vision, meaning he knows the landscape in which he's staking his claim. He sees not only to the horizon but beyond it.

I should be clear now. When I say landscape, I refer to time as well as space. When I say landscape, I mean the moral, social, political, and even linguistic landscape. We, like Swearengen and Bullock, and like Heidegger, live in a destitute time. The term "destitute time" is actually Holderlin's, although Heidegger appropriates it. The time of "the world's night" is a destitute time that grows ever more destitute. The gods have fled; what we confront is, in fact, the default of the gods. The world "has already grown so destitute," he proclaims, "it can no longer discern the default of God as a default" (2001, 89). And what he writes next matters:

> Because of this default, there fails to appear for the world the ground that grounds it. The word for abyss—*Abgrund*—originally means the soil and ground toward which, because it is undermost, a thing tends downward. But in what follows we shall think of the *Ab-* as the complete absence of ground. The ground is the soil in which to strike root and stand. The age for which the ground fails to come, hangs in the abyss. (2001, 90)

I don't want to push Heidegger too hard here for a lot of reasons. For one thing, he thinks the gods are coming back and that we can pave the way. All I care about for my present purpose is that he thinks, in the absence of any ground, that it is the poet who has the gift of being able to "reach into the abyss." Perhaps we can find consolation in noting that the god Holderlin and Heidegger seem initially most intent on luring back into our lives is Dionysus, the god of wine and pleasure—a deity whose play for power even self-proclaimed atheists like Dunn and Swearengen might be willing to back.

Recently, when I read aloud Dunn's poem "What Goes On" (*WG*, 86) to a summer class of art and mass communication students looking to fulfill their 300-level literature requirement, the girl in the first row, second seat, burst out, "That's the saddest poem I've ever heard!" I was stunned: happy, as always, for an honest, exuberant reaction, but still surprised. The course, on contemporary poetry, is one I teach essentially as a lesson in how to read poems, and we'd already read harsh poems by Paul Celan and Ceszlaw Milosz—as well as Stanley Kunitz's "The Wellfleet Whale," which always moves me to tears. What could this student mean?

"What Goes On" offers the briefest possible narrative of an unnamed woman who has an affair and leaves her marriage. The affair runs its course; she gets cancer but survives. At some point her husband asks her to come back, and she returns. I don't doubt that the other poems we'd read, depicting violent political realities far removed from this student's own experiences, moved her—but they did not force her to confront any discomforting truths. Even Randall Jarrell's "Next Day" must have felt to her like a poem about getting old, a truly distant event that she had already heard would be depressing.

The "abysmal" moment in Dunn's poem occurs in these three stanzas:

> her husband asked her to come back—
> his wife, who after all had only fallen
> in love as anyone might
> who hadn't been in love in a while—
>
> and he held her, so different now,
> so thin, her hair just partially
> grown back. He held her like a new woman
>
> and what she felt
> felt almost as good as love had,
> and each of them called it love
> because precision didn't matter anymore. (ibid., 86)

How many of a young woman's most sacred delusions about "happily ever after" have been exploded here? They called it love because precision didn't matter, but they probably also called it love because we don't have a one-word name for "what goes on." Compromise? Comfort? It's more than convenience, and there is so much real caring present. Precision doesn't matter to the couple, but it matters tremendously to the poet, who has looked piercingly in order to replace the passable truth with a "sad" corrective.

If this corrective is itself heartbreaking for my student, Dunn's tone—not only as tender and accepting as the husband's embrace but also as completely lacking in obviously negative moral judgment—is probably something even worse. The infidelity, falling in love with someone else, is not only forgiven in the particular but forgivable and understandable in general as something that might happen to anyone who hasn't been in love in a while. Dunn's tone suggests that this isn't an isolated case; this is how it is everywhere for nearly everyone at least some of the time. And, what's more, it's actually fine. It might even be a little better than fine, in fact, something worthy of a toast of a certain kind. The language is packed with monosyllables and delicate repetition, and it is as far from ornamental as language gets. The lines are amazingly muscular: each unit possesses a syntactic integrity while the structure of the sentences—one running over nine lines (we've entered in the middle of things) and the other more than five, replete with dashes, conjunctions, and subordination—embodies the complexity, careful qualification and deployment of the idea being expressed. The perfect pairing of the fragile image ("so thin, her hair just partially / grown back") and the ache of an idea makes the poem lift off the page for me at this point.

Heidegger appropriates not only "destitute time" but the term "dwelling" from Holderlin. He devotes many pages to the explication of the phrase "poetically man dwells." Essentially, "to dwell" is to truly exist in some meaningful human way. It has nothing to do with actual housing or physical geography. We dwell, or in-dwell, in our lives only when we are fully awake to them. That which enables such an in-dwelling is poetry. "Poetry is what really lets us dwell. But through what do we attain a dwelling place? Through building. Poetic creation, which lets us dwell, is a kind of building" (2001, 213). I've come, correctly or incorrectly, to think of in-dwelling this way: If philosophy and logic allow us to dwell *upon* an issue or argument or event, poetry permits us to dwell *within* it, to inhabit it imaginatively.

We would exaggerate Heidegger's intention if we concluded that poetic building might provide us with something like a moral ab-ground or ur-ground into which we could put down roots in a destitute time. Though we remain adrift in an ethical sea of our own design, poetry can, it seems, at least give us enough buoyancy, enough of a sense of who and where we are, to allow us to float a bit on the waves. A Dunn poem, however, is glass-bottomed boat.

And it is glass-bottomed boats all the way down. By that I mean he is a master of revealing the abyss below the abyss. He never allows us to forget our plight, to forget that our present agreed-upon, constructed values—the only ones enabling us at any moment to just barely keep our moral heads above water—are unstable, provisional, and subject to change as the situation demands. He won't give us the solace of our own, or his own, familiar protestations. Not only does he implicate himself in nearly every misdeed and dangerous complacency he diagnoses, he also implicates the solidity of the poetic houseboat he's building even as he drives in the nails. He's not shy about letting us know how little we can trust him—which, of course, has the immediate effect of letting us know that we are in good honest hands.

Here is the first half of "Burying the Cat":

Her name was Isadora and, like all cats,
she was a machine made of rubber bands
and muscle, exemplar of crouch
and pounce, genius of leisure. Seventeen years old.
A neighbor dog had broken her back,
and the owner called when he saw my car
pull into the driveway. He'd put her
in a plastic sack. It was ridiculous
how heavy she was, how inflexible.
For years I've known that to confess
is to say what one doesn't feel. I hereby
confess I was not angry with that dog,

> a shepherd, who had seen something foreign
> on his property. I'd like to say I was feeling
> a sadness so numb that I was a machine myself,
> with bad cogs and faulty wiring. But
> I'm telling this three years after the fact. (DH, 111)

Is Dunn confessing that he was angry with the dog or not? If to confess is to say what one doesn't feel, then he didn't feel "not angry," which is not quite the same as feeling angry, is it? (In another poem, "The Mistaken," which begins with his thinking about the birds that occasionally fly into the glass of his window, he says, "Only wild things need no excuse" [*WG*, 191].) His equivocal claims about the emotions of the moment in "Burying the Cat" ring true to me. He would have been angry if he could have been, but to be angry he would have had to have thought the dog capable of malice, and we know he knows malice is an exclusively human trait. Was he feeling a sadness that rendered him more mechanical than human? The event was so long ago that even he can't say for sure, but he'd like to say so. Who wouldn't believe someone so exacting? In the end, he buries the cat before his children and wife get home—seemingly a generous, compassionate act. Yet the poem also resists this obvious, unselfish reading of his motives, concluding, "I remember that after their shock, their grief, / I expected to be praised" (*DH*, 12). Even when we "walk right," we are probably doing so, at least in part, for the wrong reasons. Think about it. How can it be otherwise when our moral codes are so intermingled with our self-regard and our eagerness to garner the warm regard of others? If we were even once to do the right thing simply because it was right, how would we ever know?

Although Dunn at times employs the term "nihilist," he is not a very successful one himself—or I should say, attempting to be as accurate as he attempts to be, his nihilism is a landscape he must repeatedly traverse in order to "dwell" somewhere else. This view of nihilism is, in fact, similar to Heidegger's interpretation of Nietzsche's central idea: after discovering the foundationless nature of our lives, some of us muster the will to dwell poetically within them anyway, inventing the meanings and morals we'd like them to have.

Here resides the difference between Al Swearengen and Wild Bill Hickok, who doesn't make it through season 1 of *Deadwood*: the character, like the real Wild Bill, is gunned down at Tom Nutall's #10 Saloon in the middle of a poker game while he is holding two pairs, aces and eights. Milch explains in his bonus-track, voice-over commentary that from the start Hickok is for him a dead man walking, and the first image we get of Hickok resembles his lying in state: he is flat on his back in the back of a wagon, eyes closed, nursing a hangover. Hickok has lost the capacity to imagine a ground on which to stand. His actions are reckless and self-destructive; he resists the solicitation and advice of his closest companion, Charlie Utter. He seems unable to take joy in anything, and even his gambling has become a means of self-flagellation. Hickok is a lawman who has realized that there are no laws. Seth Bullock, on the other hand, is a lawman who thinks the laws are transcendent and available everywhere, even beyond the literal boundary of the law. It doesn't matter to him whether they are written down or not.

Swearengen has neither the comfort of Bullock's faith nor the emptiness of Hickok's despair. Schooled in brutality, the son of a prostitute who abandoned him to a life in an abusive orphanage, he's presumably passed through both systems of belief. When he stands on the balcony outside his second-story office and surveys the scene, he is fully engaged. Life may be pointless but it's awfully interesting; it may actually be more poignantly fascinating because its meanings and morals are so illusory. This is not far from the attitude of those in Dunn's poem "The Metaphysicians of South Jersey," who "sought the approximate weight of sadness, / its measure and coloration. But they liked / a good ball game too, well pitched, lots of zeroes / on the scoreboard" (*WG*, 88). They go to bed at night "exhausted and enthralled." These small-town thinkers are better stand-ins for Dunn than the nihilist, and when, in "At the The Nihilist's Funeral," we encounter Hope delivering the nihilist's eulogy, I suspect that this is one part of Dunn's character temporarily interring another, "which will rise again / when needed" (ibid., 165).

In truth, if Dunn's speaker resembles anyone in *Deadwood*, it would most likely be Doc Cochran. Cochran is a man who runs on wonder and intellectual curiosity. His grasp of the terrain is nearly as broad as Swearengen's, although—except for his inventive remedying—Doc is largely an observer who only takes a stand when pushed to do so. He is, for instance, clearly prepared to die himself rather than let Dan Dority, Swearengen's right arm, murder a small child who can identify the men who attacked her family, who might in turn implicate Swearengen himself. To his credit, Dority has been hoping to be stopped on this mission, and to Swearengen's credit he tidies up the loose ends by knifing the man who murdered the family rather than disposing of the child. Doc, of course, has foreseen all of this, which is why he is waiting with his rifle in hand when Dority arrives for the child. When he attempts to map it out beforehand to Calamity Jane, who's portrayed as somehow both vulgar and vulnerable, she's incredulous and thinks this reflects the darkness of his mind. In truth, he is simply a realist, though he is still a little deflated when people don't even manage to live up to his exceedingly low expectations.

Just as we trudge between hope and hopelessness and seem at times to have walked through a wasteland to arrive almost gleeful at the first pitch of a double-header, there is nothing predictable or stable or commensurate in Deadwood. In fact, this is the other reason Milch was drawn to such a locale: it is in the perpetual process of coming into being, redefining itself and its terms at every turn. If the sensuous is an analog for what cannot be seen, then this spot at this time seems like a made-to-order metaphor for the soul burdened with the task of imagining how to dwell in a destitute time. As we build the self, we simultaneously build the landscape it inhabits.

Yet, our nihilistic situation aside, in practical terms we don't get to create ourselves from nothing, and we don't live our lives in isolation. If we did, the obligation to speak a more precise truth would hardly matter. Much of this is touched upon in "The Mistaken," the penultimate poem in *What Goes On*, Dunn's second collection of new and selected poems. This poem, as I mentioned earlier, begins with the sparrows and grackles that fly into glass because they don't understand where they are, "that sometimes the world isn't / what it seems" (*WG*, 191). Do the few who survive learn from their mistakes? Dunn doubts it, but at least they aren't guilty of the error of needing "an invisible Bird-of-all-birds to bring / twigs and worms to, that they aren't supplicants / before their own creation" (ibid., 191). Only humans invent gods. The poem veers dramatically near its conclusion to become a meditation on cruelty and the relationship between the powerful and the timid. Dunn admits he's sometimes gone along, nodded politely, with the strong. And if we are cruel, what do we—who should have learned and for whom something like wisdom might be an actual (if self-created) moral obligation—say for ourselves by way of explanation? "We often say / we were blinded. We say we were not ourselves" (ibid., 191). Dunn clearly dismisses these two justifications. And so he would, for in the ethics he has fashioned there can be no excuse for those who are "blind" to the landscape and lack an adequate awareness of who they are within it.

I started by describing my dog chewing his bone and myself rereading texts and rewatching productions I've already experienced. Even the pre-Socratic Heraclitus knew no river is ever the same river twice. And so, perhaps, this sort of obligatory reentering might just be how perpetually coming into being has to work. We can never declare ourselves done with anything, especially the work of being a self who dwells. Thus, Stephen Dunn finds himself returning again and again to daily occasions, washing them free of their encrusted interpretations like one of Deadwood's miners sifting for gold. Categorically speaking, we cannot, of course, not be ourselves; we can merely be different versions of ourselves. Dunn's body of work argues that only by peering into the mire, as Al Swearengen peers down upon the rabble and filth of Deadwood, and by acquainting ourselves with the jostling multitude within, do we come to dwell within our lives. We cannot achieve, nor should we aspire to achieve, a fixed and final sense of who and where we are. Being is the bone we must worry all of our lives. With diligence, however, we can perhaps enter a landscape in which we and the world are surprising in ever-new ways rather than old ones. And language, too, if we listen carefully to it, can teach us a lot about how things are.

Most of our days are mercifully less eventful than Swearengen's, and certainly most among us walk through them more rightly than he manages to walk through his, despite of, or perhaps because of his tremendous cunning and will. Lacking his gifts, we may simply be less tempted. With real luck, our good mornings might more closely resemble those of Stephen Dunn's humble metaphysicians of South Jersey, mornings no less vital than those in Deadwood—no less rich, and no less a manifestation of an authentic poetic in-dwelling:

> Come breakfast, as always, the metaphysicians
> Would begin to list the many small things
> They'd observed and thought, unable to stop talking
> About this place and what a world it was. (*WG*, 88)

Of course, this bucolic scene also isn't simply what it seems. I used the image of the glass-bottomed boat as a correlative for how it feels to drift with full knowledge above a kind of essential and ungrounded nothing. In his essay "Alert Lovers, Hidden Sides, and Ice Travelers" (*WLN*, 144–56), Dunn, as the title suggests, ups the ante. To walk light or to live right, according to Dunn, is, ultimately, to dock the boat completely and to walk out consciously onto the melting surface of a frozen river. It's a metaphor he's taken from a love poem, "Crossing Over" by William Meredith:

> Here, all we have is love, a great undulating
> raft, melting steadily. We go out on it
>
> anyhow. I love you. I love this fool's walk.
> The thing we have to learn is how to walk light. (ibid., 148)

To be a good poet, a good lover, and a conscious being is to be an ice traveler. If the poet is walking on anything more stable than a melting ice flow, the poem, or the life being lived, isn't animated enough to be worth our time. But this risky journey, as Meredith makes clear, isn't a matter of the body's location but the heart's and the mind's. It is to dwell in a flawed and provisional beauty and to find that beauty sublime.

Works Cited

Heidegger, Martin. 1996. *Holderlin's Hymn: "The Ister,"* translated by William McNeill and Julia Davis. Bloomington: Indiana University Press.

———. 2001. " . . . Poetically Man Dwells. . . ." In *Poetry, Language, Thought*, translated by Albert Hofstadter. New York: Harper and Row. 209–27.

Deadwood. 2004–2006. Produced and directed by David Milch. HBO. DVD.

A Citizen of No State; or, the Politics of Ambiguity

Michael Broek

Absolutes are a problem for any contemporary poet, but particularly for the contemporary white, male, heterosexual, middle-class poet—a poet like Stephen Dunn—who is the inheritor of a history of racist, sexist, and homophobic speech, language that is inherently political. The absolutely earnest declaration is now immediately suspect, and while "political correctness" has become a maligned expression, it still reminds us that language can and often has been wielded as a weapon, often by white, heterosexual males. How is a poet such as Dunn supposed to rally language so as to avoid statements of certitude, when such certitude has historically proven destructive?

This raises the question of whether engaging the political is of any interest or value to Dunn at all. The answer is clear: Dunn says in a 2004 interview with the online journal *Guernica*, "Certainly a good many of my poems over the years have alluded to or taken on the political" (Whitney). But how have they done so? He writes in his essay "The Good, the Not So Good," "The good poem may be political, but is more interested in enacting or understanding the dynamics of any human situation than it is in effecting change" (*WLN*, 37), and the "not so good moral poem often works against some abuse or injustice," but it fails on the level of "composition" (ibid, 44).

So what kind of "political poetry" is this?

His essay "Stepping Out," the very first to appear in *Walking Light: Essays and Memoirs*, offers a clue, both in terms of its placement in the collection and its argument. The essay opens with a political allegory about a mythical totalitarian state in which a young boy rebels against his oppressors and "brings the truth back to the people" (*WLN*, 3). Dunn calls the boy (and by analogy himself) the "emblematic poet" (ibid., 4), but if Dunn's poet is a heroic rebel speaking truth to power, this is not obvious in the language or circumstances of his poems, at least not at first, not in the sense of poets such as Philip Levine, Adrienne Rich, or a host of other poets typically defined as "political," where the language and the tone evince some angry certitude.

Instead, this poet's revolt against tyranny is much more about ideas, or as Dunn writes, "The good poem is implicitly philosophical" (ibid., "The Good, the Not So Good," 37).

So what philosophy is this? "We need to find and champion the poems that are true to the ambiguity of experience," Dunn writes in his essay "Bringing the Strange Home" (ibid., 33). And in a lecture at Pine Manor College delivered in 2012, he states, "Good thinking, it seems to me, involves saying no or maybe before saying yes; that is, holding out for the more satisfactory yes. Then maybe doubt that one, too."

In other words, we have a body of poetry, presented in philosophical terms, that is simultaneously interested in politics *and* ambiguity, or what some might construe as "anti-politics." Turning now to the modern English critic Isaiah Berlin, we find a philosopher who has set ambiguity at the heart of his politics, and it is his work that I think best helps elucidate the complicated philosophical/political stance at the center of Dunn's poems.

Known most popularly for his essay "The Hedgehog and the Fox," Berlin, a former president of the British Academy and a longtime professor at Oxford, establishes two main theses in his essays collected in *The Crooked Timber of Humanity*, spanning almost thirty years of his thought. The first thesis concerns the question of idealism in the West, a question that stretches from Plato through Voltaire and the Enlightenment and to Marx, attenuated by the revolution in scientific thought since Newton. The crux of the issue here is a belief in some universal Truth, arrived at through reason. In "The Decline of Utopian Ideas in the West," he argues that this belief holds, first, that "to all genuine questions there can only be one correct answer"; second, that "a method exists for the discovery of correct answers"; and third, "that all the correct answers must, at the very least, be compatible with one another" (1990, 24). In this conception, Truth is objective and exists for the most part a priori, waiting to be discovered and expounded upon by those rigorous enough to stay the rational course. Such Truth binds all humanity together into a common set of problems, leading to a single set of solutions. Obviously, this is a vein of Christian thought as well, particularly Catholic and Evangelical thought, though it could equally be said of all monotheistic traditions. This conception is also closely related to utopianism, or the idea that once Truth is universally recognized and placed at the center of human endeavor, then a certain harmony will result—Plato's Republic, Marx's classless society. Voltaire, like Locke, while skeptical of certain human institutions, nevertheless believes in the essential validity of rational inquiry to discover, eventually, "what to do."

According to Berlin, the benefit of such thought, at least since the French Revolution, has been the "elimina[tion] of a great deal of cruelty, superstition, injustice and obscurantism" (ibid., 34). The problem that we have come to recognize, as Berlin also points out, is that every claim to universalism (remember that all answers must be compatible with one another) is an invitation to horrendous violence: racism, sexism, colonialism, empire—often abetted by nefarious uses of *language*. Those who stand against Truth, who refuse to recognize its authority (or its language), are apt to be mowed down. Berlin writes in "The Pursuit of the Ideal," "The notion of the perfect whole, the ultimate solution, in which all good things coexist, seems to me to be not merely unattainable—that is a truism—but conceptually incoherent" (1990, 13).

To return to Dunn, he resists all expressions of Truth, occupying instead "the bluesy middle ground / of desire and withdrawal" (*BA*, 45). In this line from the poem "Between Angels," the poet identifies his vantage point, between what the will wants and what it cannot have, not because it is weak but because the speaker's will is empathetic, recognizing the same desire in others, a certain democracy of desire. What Dunn's speaker can't abide is certitude, as in "On the

Way to Work": "I hated bumper stickers, hated / the notion of wanting to be known / by one glib or earnest thing" (*BA*, 35). Or again, in another poem, "Here and Now," more than twenty years later: "I learned, in time, to let heaven / go its mythy way, to never again // be a supplicant / of any single idea" (*HN*, 42). Instead, the speaker in the poem "What I Might Say if I Could" resists the attraction of "some crazed utopian with a plan" (*EE*, 25) and wants to be known, in a sense, for not taking sides, for dwelling in ambiguity, which of course is a form of "taking sides" in itself, although in the Berlin/Dunn world it is the only moral choice.

And yet, there are real difficulties associated with this choice. "Here's to an evening of contradictions, / I say, let's never live without them" (*HN*, 79), Dunn writes in "Evenings Like This," although dwelling in contradiction "suddenly makes me think of the night sky / and large, empty spaces" (ibid., 80). One could argue that Dunn's resistance to certitude marks a character flaw. What is his speaker ever committed to, after all? The answer could be simply "saving face" by not dedicating himself to anything definite, thereby avoiding judgment and failure on the one hand and the burdens of responsibility on the other, a certain bourgeois noncommittance. "But of course things are never that simple," Dunn writes in the poem "The Good News": "The good news is I know who I am; that's the bad news, too" (ibid., 29). The consequence of such ambiguities, which arise from holding many truths to be possible at the same time, is a sense of isolation and even captivity, as in the poem "Leaving the Empty Room": "The door had a double lock, / and the joke was on me" (ibid., 25). The speaker in a Dunn poem is often caught between a desire for action and a recognition that "we must choose, and in choosing one thing lose another, irretrievably perhaps" (Berlin 1990, "European Unity and Its Vicissitudes," 201). Dunn does not wish to lose anything, but he does not wish to pervert himself either. His choice to dwell *between* delineates a political position: a citizen of no state.

There are also consequences for Dunn's position in love and in art. In "Here and Now," Dunn considers "You and I." He writes,

> Heaven did exist,
> I discovered, but was reciprocal
> and momentary, like lust
> felt at exactly the same time. (*HN*, 41)

It is difficult to love under these conditions, in light of the recognition that every "Truth" is temporary and contradictory and "nothing can save us" (ibid., 42). Nothing is ever enough in itself, as in "Turning Yourself into a Work of Art": "A work of art // always is in danger of wanting more / than it can give itself permission to have" (*HN*, 49). Dunn and Berlin share the same problem; they are always in the process of reconsidering:

> And somewhere a philosopher is erasing
> "time's empty passing" because he's seen
> a woman in a ravishing dress.
> In a different hour he'll put it back. (*DH*, "Different Hours," 70)

Again Berlin, in "The Pursuit of the Ideal": "To force people into the neat uniforms demanded by dogmatically believed-in schemes is almost always the road to inhumanity" (1990, 19). The philosopher, like the poet, is never sure. "Time's empty passing," is contradicted by the vitality and immediacy of "a woman in a ravishing dress." Both are true. Both love and art, in this context, demand a simultaneous flinging outward and holding back, a sense of being stranded on the rocks by the sea: "Brigantine—I heard prison and freedom / in that name. Walking a beach so called / felt appropriately in between" (*DH*, "Backwaters," 115). Or in more typical Dunnian fashion, in an empty room with a Scotch on the rocks: "Johnnie Walker Black / coming down now from the cabinet to sing / of its twelve lonely years in the dark" (*EE*, "Summer Nocturne," 72). Or in his 2012 lecture: "The poet resides in the world of ambiguity or ambivalence, qualities that makes one hesitate, reconsider."

So what is left to be lauded, to be striven for, if the "single idea" is always insufficient and the consequences of in-between-ness are always psychologically agitating? Perhaps, if not a "single idea," then a single *action* is required, a revolt against what is "reasonable" and an expression of personal *will*, a romantic Whitmanian gesture, much like the "heroic" boy of Dunn's allegory in "Bringing the Strange Home." As Berlin writes in "The Apotheosis of the Romantic Will," "The romantics have dealt a fatal blow to the proposition that, all appearances to the contrary, a definite solution of the jigsaw puzzle is, at least in principle, possible" (1990, 236). And yet, the essential narcissism of the religious or political idealist is also the narcissism of the romantic poet, as well as the poet of "non-sense."

The idealist's lack of empathy, her or his denial of complexity and nuance, is of a piece with the romantic devotion to the primal Self, the fascination with the "I." This is Whitman's primordial "yawp," correct only because it was *his*. That was enough. Unfortunately, for all his passion and verbal imagination, it is a short road from Whitman's "yawp" to barbarism itself, the tyranny of the relativist. This is Berlin's second thesis, and he makes this point strongly, contrasting the fanaticism of the French Terror (a revolution founded upon idealist/universalist principles) with the fanaticism of fascism (founded upon the elevation of the will above reason, that is, founded upon romanticism).

For Berlin, the answer to the clash between idealism and romanticism is what I will call incrementalism. He writes in "The Pursuit of the Ideal": "The best that can be done, as a general rule, is to maintain a precarious equilibrium that will prevent the occurrence of desperate situations, of intolerable choices—that is the first requirement for a decent society" (1990, 18). This is an equilibrium struck between universalistic idealism on the one hand and debilitating relativism on the other. For Dunn, this equilibrium is embodied in "The Stairway."

The prelude poem of *The Insistence of Beauty*, "The Stairway" is an aesthetic manifesto as well as a personal and political one:

> The architect wanted to build a stairway
> and suspend it with silver, almost invisible

guy wires in a high-ceilinged room,
a stairway you couldn't ascend or descend
except in your dreams. . . . (13)

The architect here is the poet and the philosopher, engaged in an act of creation and thought, and yet the artifact that is engendered is not really one of use but of imagined possibilities. Maybe in some utopia, it could be tread upon, but in this world, it's enough that it exists at all. That it is not of real use does not detract from what it represents.

But like the beach that resists the sea or the Scotch that resists the dark, bounds are crucial, and the straight edges of reason contain the stairway, or at least lend it context:

But first . . .
he'd make sure the house that housed it
was practical, built two-by-four by
two-by-four, slat by slat, without ornament. (ibid.)

Ironically perhaps, the stairway exists as a monument to the human while it resists the application of human labels, the "single" idea of either idealism or romanticism:

The house he'd claim as his, but the stairway
would be designed to be ownerless,
tilted against any suggestion of a theology,
disappointing to those looking for politics. (ibid.)

Although, as I have argued, there are politics at work here, a *politics of ambiguity*. This door in the air leads not to action, at least not directly, but to a greater sense of human community, that Dunn's speakers regularly find around the dinner table, at the party, along the parkway rest stop:

Yet every night when he got home
he could imagine, as he walked in the door,
his stairway going nowhere, not for sale,

> and maybe some you to whom nothing
> about it need be explained, waiting,
> the wine decanted, the night about to unfold. (ibid., 14)

For Dunn, it is that moment of unfolding, of desire, that holds the most promise because it constantly refuses to be any one thing. From the poem "Androgyne":

> I will tell you, Androgyne, what I learned today
> about the sublime. It's that moment
> when a compound changes
> from one state to another. (*DH*, 42)

The androgyne in this poem is the speaker himself, never only just one thing, always in flux, "about to unfold." In his essay "Alleged Relativism in Eighteenth-Century European Thought," Berlin's sense of unfolding is found in his argument in favor of pluralism or the idea that "there are many objective ends, ultimate values, some incompatible with others . . . which, of course, entails the permanent possibility of inescapable conflict" (1990, 80).

There is no single system, whether rational/idealist or romantic/relativist, that will suffice. There is nothing traditionally "heroic" in this, Berlin says, no sense of "the artist, raised above other men not only by his genius but by his heroic readiness to live and die for the sacred vision within him" ("Apotheosis" 1990, 231), but both Dunn and Berlin would agree that this is all for the best. "I've come to understand," Dunn writes in "Here and Now": "a steady, low-voltage hum // of affection / must be arrived at" (*HN*, 41–42). Dunn's "heroic boy" has metamorphosed into a mature political poet to be sure, but not one that is easily recognizable as such, given the language of certitude that traditionally defines such poems, a certitude that is unavailable to a poet such as Dunn today. Instead, the poet has championed a philosophy of politics and art that establishes his work as highly moral, as Berlin would define such morality, balancing on a staircase in the air.

Works Cited

Berlin, Isaiah. 1990. "Alleged Relativism in Eighteenth-Century European Thought." In *The Crooked Timber of Humanity: Chapters in the History of Ideas*, edited by Henry Hardy. Princeton, NJ: Princeton University Press. 70–90.

———. 1990. "The Apotheosis of the Romantic Will." In *The Crooked Timber of Humanity: Chapters in the History of Ideas*. 207–37.

———. 1990. "The Decline of Utopian Ideas in the West." In *The Crooked Timber of Humanity: Chapters in the History of Ideas*. 20–48.

———. 1990. "The Pursuit of the Ideal." In *The Crooked Timber of Humanity: Chapters in the History of Ideas*. 1–19.

———. 1990. "European Unity and Its Vicissitudes." In *The Crooked Timber of Humanity: Chapters in the History of Ideas*. 175–206.

Dunn, Stephen. 2012. "The State of the Union: Diversity and Poetic Craft." Keynote reading and lecture at the Solstice MFA in Creative Writing Program of Pine Manor College, Chestnut Hill, MA.

Whitney, Joel. "The Hard-to-Say (Interview with Stephen Dunn)." *Guernica*, October 27, 2004. http://www.guernicamag.com/interviews/stephen_dunn_on_why_he_writes/.

Part Four

Making Moves in *Loosestrife*

Philip Dacey

Stephen Dunn at his most characteristic is Wallace Stevens's modern poet, his "mind in the act of finding / What will suffice" (1990, 239). As Stevens explains, "The poem of the mind . . . has not always had / To find: the scene was set; it repeated what / Was in the script" (ibid.). In his 1966 book on the acknowledged precursor of modernism, Gerard Manley Hopkins, Todd Bender argued that the modern movement is synonymous with "a shift in the artist's attention from the nominal subject of his work to the operation of the mind which perceives that subject" (3). Thus, when Dunn ends "Aging" with the line "There never can be enough," the speaker is not only distinguishing himself from his wine-tasting friend, whose tour of the vintner's has left him "happy, sated," but also announcing a more general condition determined by the mind's consciousness of itself, that hall of mirrors and its endlessly receding vista (*L*, 37). For Dunn is nothing if not conscious of consciousness: "What's underneath is sure / to have something underneath it. / All the way in: that's where crazy is" (ibid., "The Living," 75). Not to go in at all, of course, is to live the diminished life. To read Dunn is to watch him knowingly and stylishly negotiate between the failures represented by those extremes.

The poem shrewdly offered as a prologue to *Loosestrife*, his tenth collection of poetry, "Solving the Puzzle," is short enough and important enough to quote in full:

> I couldn't make all the pieces fit,
> so I threw them away.
>
> No expectation of success now,
> none of that worry.

The remaining pieces seemed
to seek their companions.
A design appeared.

I could see the connection
between the overgrown path
and the dark castle on the hill.

Something in the middle, though,
was missing.

It would have been important once.
I wouldn't have been able to sleep
without it. (ibid., 15)

The unexpected move is to be expected from Dunn, who here neither solves the puzzle by taking a certain action nor leaves the puzzle unsolved by taking no action. Rather, he acts to prevent the puzzle's solution. In doing so, he takes charge of the situation, creating a kind of "controlled / confusion, which each of us understands" (ibid., "Road Stop," 29). The puzzle now of course can never be finished any more than the bottom of consciousness can be reached, although it's precisely upon his giving up the complete picture as a goal that a "design appeared." Accordingly, the ambiguity of stanza 2 allows for the possibility that the speaker worries he will, not won't, succeed, presumably because completing the puzzle constitutes a kind of death.

The modernity of the stance Dunn has taken in his prologue can be appreciated by recalling Valery's admission: "I don't finish poems, I simply abandon them"; and both the prologue and admission triangulate with Stevens: stasis, like the past itself, is a "souvenir," and although there are "sudden rightnesses," they only exist briefly, vis-à-vis "sounds passing through" them (Stevens 1990, 239–40). It is a wonder that Dunn ever finishes a poem, not because he is loquacious or logorrheic—he isn't—but because there's always one more move for consciousness, the reigning power of his poems, to make. In *Walking Light*, his 1993 book of essays and memoirs, Dunn indirectly describes his own approach when he writes that C. K. Williams not only presents and evaluates experience but also examines a consciousness that presents and evaluates experience. Once a semi-professional basketball player, Dunn most likely faked out many opponents with his moves; he knows the value of anticipation, and in his poems, which abound with phrases like "I'm thinking," "I want to say," and "I'll say," he anticipates himself, the poet of the quotidian less for its own sake than as occasion to exercise an ultimate, if elusive, virtue: that of self-knowledge.

Such a concern places Dunn in a tradition that includes the unlikely combination of Hopkins, whose grammatical and rhythmical innovations were designed to serve the limning of the workings of the mind, with its "mountains, cliffs of fall / Frightful" ("No Worst" 2002, 167), and Allen Ginsberg, whose emphasis on spontaneous composition (hardly Hopkins' practice) also means to make his poetry take as primary datum the flow or jumps of mind and, as the author of *Howl* puts it, "conform to the rhythm of thought" (1956, 20). Enjambment, for example, the technical poetic device long the darling of workshops (in the late 1960s, an Iowa workshop mock-awards list included "Best Line-break by a Rookie"), functions over and over again in Dunn's work in a particularly salient way, serving as a kind of handmaiden to his investigation of mental layering: "What a perfect thing an orange is / to think about" (*L*, "Because You Mentioned the Spiritual Life," 85). When Dunn, with conspicuous reflexivity, writes in "Slant," "I'm seeing myself seeing" (ibid., 31), he creates a dizzying situation in which the reader sees a poet seeing a speaker who sees himself seeing. In "Imagining Myself My Father," Dunn grants his father, a traveling salesman, "many different, agile tongues" (ibid., 53), projecting, obviously, his own agility onto his sire, an agility the son also demands from his readers.

Dunn, however, enlarges this tradition by bringing to it a great fondness for a certain strategy the vertiginous mind paradoxically employs to stabilize itself in the world, that of fictiveness—I fabricate, therefore I am, or, Heraclitus notwithstanding, I can step into the same river twice if I say so. "Slant," whose title of course alludes to Emily Dickinsons's commission to "Tell all the Truth but tell it slant," opens with "early morning sunlight" and other natural "blessings, all" before it makes an abrupt turn:

> But then I saw a cow in a room
> looking at the painting of a cow
> in a field—all of which
> was a painting itself—
> and I felt I'd been invited
> into the actual, someplace
> between the real and the real. (ibid., 31)

"Real" derives from "res," a static thing, whereas "actual" derives from "act." This passage crucially echoes Dunn's active denial of the two most real possibilities in "Solving the Puzzle" in favor of an invention that subsumes one. "The Fallen World" describes a society "untamed by story," when "the age / of enchantment had passed" and "Few sought out the fabulous . . ." (ibid., 57). Thus a reader of Dunn who comes upon the lines "Some people actually desire honesty" (ibid., "After Making Love," 21) and "He realizes that for days now / he hasn't been lying" (ibid., "Nocturne," 39), can be confident the poet is subverting conventional values in service of "some lost fundamental news" (ibid., "The Voice," 41). Such an emphasis on recreating the world has been present in Dunn's work consistently from as early as 1974, when he confesses that "my poems are approximately true" (*NS*, "Biography in the First Person," 41), and through 1986, when he distances himself from "the unforgiveable stories / of the sincere" (*LT*, "Parable of the Fictionist," 49).

Dunn's negotiations as a stylist between the prosaic and the poetic parallel his negotiations between Ahabism and complacency (as distinct from a certain facilitating detachment) and between the false and the true (as opposed to the approximately true). In both "Wild," when husband and wife take their "quieter places in the world" (*L*, 24), and "Paradise," where the "houses are calm" (ibid., 25), Dunn seems to be acknowledging something about the surfaces of his poems, which assiduously eschew inflated rhetoric, as in the case of "Diminuendo," which ends as follows:

> A black fly landed in her hair, and he
>   swept it away.
> A sudden breeze uplifted their napkins,
>
> but that was all there was of action.
>   It was time to go;
> one of them, soon, would say so. (ibid., 20)

The poem's title, besides referring to an affair's dying fall, provides us with a clue to the kind of music Dunn funds most poignant in poetry.

He distrusts the grand or would-be grand, what makes too much of itself, and has approvingly observed that "Astaire's restraint was a kind of extravagance," while adding that "restraint / is worthless unless /something's about to spill or burst" ("Ars Poetica," 32–33). Dunn trusts the demotic as much as William Carlos Williams ever did and even exhibits, in regard to poetic form, the old master's rebelliousness: "The well-made poem," Dunn writes in *Walking Light*, "is increasingly in my own work what I try to avoid" (*WLB*, "The Poet as Teacher: Vices and Virtues," 138). Such an agendum, however, may owe as much to temperament as to literary theory: "woo / a stranger so you'll not be mutinous / alone" (*L*, "Paradise," 25). Dunn knows one of the classic tricks of actors: if you want to get the attention of your audience, lower, don't raise, your voice. When Dunn uses rhyme, for example, it's usually delayed and often not full: in "Tiger Face," "gone" and "done" (ibid., 71) end the seventh-last and last lines with a cooperativeness that is more, rather than less, effective for its near imperceptibility; nor does the context call attention to, while it nevertheless embeds, the poet's name. Conspicuous closure is not Dunn's game. A hush attends much of his poetry; in that hush, a small verbal gesture looms large. If poetry were wine, Dunn's would be very dry. To say so is to say that Dunn as an experienced negotiator of various straits illustrates Cocteau's definition of tact, "knowing how far to go too far."

Unlike the Victorians, in opposition to whom the moderns defined themselves and for whom "earnestness" was a much-trumpeted value, Dunn is wary of what he calls in an essay "unredeemed earnestness" (*WLB*, "The Good and Not So Good," 37). Thus the eight-page title poem, which ends the volume, is especially to be prized because it not only faces important political and historical circumstances—a year after Waco and just shortly after Oklahoma City—as does "The Fallen World," but it maintains a "controlled confusion" that is synonymous with "the act of finding / What will suffice" (*L*, 57). Appropriately, weather in its changefulness weaves through the poem's ten sections to join geography, history, and the individual soul; the suite suggests a meditativeness verging on the Wordsworthian, though Dunn stoically refrains from deriving comfort from anything like the "Presences of Nature." "Loosestrife" begins:

> Storms moved across the Rockies
> and through the plains, rode the jet stream
> east. By the time they reached us: rain.
> And there were other things that looked—
> to other eyes—like welcome news.
> The country tilting right.
> A few more punishments for the poor.
> It was the winter winter never came
> to South Jersey; no natural equivalent,
> once again, to our lives. (*L*, 89)

Indeed, the beautiful "landscape's invitation to forget" history suggests to Dunn "a postcard . . . cropped, agreeably, to deceive." In the midst of a kind of abundance—"loosestrife, goldenrod, pixie-moss" and "pitchpine, crowberry, black oak"—the speaker seems close in spirit to the dogs he used to walk, now dead, "who had so little / of their own." The apostrophization of Pascal comes as no surprise in the poem, which seeks answers "to every hard and bitter question": "There were authorities in those days, / there were soul-maps; it's heartening / you knew they couldn't be yours." "Soul-maps" consorts with Stevens's "script." Pascal's sense of displacement is, ironically, "heartening" for the speaker, who recognizes that "Every month, like every mind, / changed the way things looked" and to "wander in times not ours," as the Frenchman phrases it, is to be at home (ibid., 89–96). A strong sense of the personal and immediate permeates "Loosestrife" so that it seems, like *The Prelude*, "An Autobiographical Poem," yet the intimacy engendered here, so disarming and persuasive, provides no lasting refuge. The poem's final words, in identifying the "intolerable" as that "with which we live" (ibid., 96), brilliantly evoke, return the reader to the prologue, where what "was missing . . . would have been important once" (ibid., 15) although now sleep is possible "without it." Living with the intolerable provides closure, but a deliberately off-balance one—the poet, like the reader, is ready for the next move.

Ultimately, Dunn's "examination of consciousness" shades into an examination of conscience. Just as, according to Eliot, the status of Tennyson as a religious poet is revealed by the quality of Tennyson's doubt, not that of his faith, the moral seriousness of Dunn's work is enhanced, not weakened, by his apparently radical disbelief in the reliability of human judgment, which fails at the simplest of tasks:

> You haven't slept, you swear it,
> though you know
> when it comes to that
> most people are mistaken. (ibid., "The Song," 49)

Flawed consciousness creates such a crisis of conscience for Dunn, who looks unblinkingly at his species' capacity for evil, and therefore his own, that his "easily praised" (ibid., "The Refuge," 82) excludes the human in favor of Canada geese and marshland. Matthew Arnold, whose "Dover Beach" helped to define the modern, can probably be made out here, too, with his armies ignorantly—that is, existentially—clashing by night, in those lines where children get "in the way of gangs / or their parents' close-quartered rage" (ibid., "Loosestrife," 95). Dunn, who sees the postmodern taking its place among us—"Strange music beginning, / the dance floor getting crowded now" (ibid., "Poetry," 69)—may represent one of the last, and brightest, flare-ups of the modern sensibility. In "Nocturne," a certain psychoanalyst "tended by temperament / and profession to want to cure, / and so was not useful" (ibid., 38); conversely, Dunn, who does not profess to cure the human condition he explores but wants only to offer as consolation the pleasures of an unobtrusively but finely wrought poetry, is useful, eminently so because, by means of the stories he tells us, he would have us be, as before "The Fallen World," like children "delighted into sleep" (ibid., 58). The poet of consciousness, by fulfilling its promise, by completing its arc, ironically would ease us into letting go of it, into accepting the necessities of our lives.

Works Cited

Bender, Todd K. 1966. *Gerard Manley Hopkins: The Classical Background and Critical Reception of His Work*. Baltimore: Johns Hopkins University Press.

Ginsberg, Allen. 1956. *Howl, and Other Poems*. San Francisco: City Lights Pocket Bookshop.

Hopkins, Gerard Manley. 2002. "No Worst." In *Gerard Manley Hopkins: The Major Works*, edited by Catherine Phillips, 167. Oxford: Oxford University Press.

Stevens, Wallace. 1990. "Of Modern Poetry." In *The Collected Poems*, 239–40. New York: Vintage.

Claustrophobia, Decency, Truth

One Speaker's Civil War

Tony Hoagland

What *is* the secret of Stephen Dunn's poetry? How can his poems be so consistently good without being verbally flashy? How can the work be at once intelligent and non-intellectual? How does it manage sincerity and make arguments for decency without somehow seeming moralistic, or arrogant? How does one manage to be a realistic poet—that is, a pessimist—without sounding morbid or crotchety?

For, most readers would agree, Dunn's work *is* a poetry primarily of even-tempered discourse. His speaker dwells in the zone of middleness: mid-self, mid-American, mid-life. Yes, the poetry has its lyric and narrative moments, its hot spots and griefs, but principally, more than anything, it *discusses*, it *thinks*, endlessly, fluently, clearly. Dunn's is a poetry of personal and political conscience written from an American middle-class white male perspective—I thought that was all over in the eighties!—and yet, it succeeds, again and again, in casting the spell of companionability, of reflective and intimate conversation, between more-or-less equals. Dunn is "civil" in the old-fashioned sense—civilized and civic—a poet of the middle way, a Horatian advocate of sanity and moderation.

One secret is that Dunn's poetics, with their plain honest face and good manners, are trickier, more turbulent and antisocial than they first appear. Despite his reasonable tone, and his persistent meditations on decency, Dunn is a citizen of modernity, well aware of the unreliability of signs, the elusiveness of self, the transience of truth; and his poems practice a surprising amount of elusiveness, self-consciousness, and reflexivity.

It is a tricky business, and, like any serious conversation, is never resolved. Yet, interwoven at the heart of any poem by Dunn are three recurring and often competing concerns or motives:

1. Trying to say it right; clarity about the way the world is.
2. The effort to be decent; not to hurt the feelings of others or be unfair.
3. Trying to protect the speaker's own right to selfhood; or, as they say, to keep his own space.

This list, in fact, is backwards in priority for, in the Dunn universe, 1 and 2 are dependent upon 3. In Dunn's poems, as it turns out, the ability to be responsible in speech depends upon the essential freedom of the self. The protection of that personal freedom from incursion has precedence over every other obligation, and, looked at in this light, one will notice that many Dunn poems are narratives of soul preservation.

Despite the soothing sound of reason and moderation in his poetic voice, despite a vocabulary that stays within the range of standard American conversation, Dunn is one of the most meditatively acrobatic poets of his generation. And much of his tricky, mobile discussion is performed through what I would call dialectical motion. The term "dialectical" seems to imply dialogue between *two* positions, a back-and-forth sort of arguing between two voices. We humanist readers, with our habitual emphasis on the psychological, like to use the dignified phrase "internal argument," as if the self was a capsule. But more accurately, dialectical process in a poem is embodied by many active presences—scenery, memory, metaphor, irony, and so forth—and the ability to suggest their conflicting claims. As the Polish poet Czesław Miłosz says, "The purpose of poetry is to remind us / how difficult it is to remain just one person" (2001, 241). It is a credo that perfectly characterizes the entirety of Dunn's work.

The poem "Aren't They Beautiful?" (*WG*, 168–69), like so many of Dunn's poems, displays a whole sequence of these dialectical voicings—shifts to the side, confrontations, regroupings, and counter-positions—as the speaker rebuffs and discards one assumption, one stance after another. It isn't so much that the narrator has in mind a final stance, or overview, but that he refuses to be co-opted or incorporated by any singular point of view that might adopt him. Truth is a tall order; a more realistic concern might be to move away from the temptations to bad faith. Or, to put it another way, it is easier to *stay* out of jail than to *get* out of jail.

The poem's dramatic situation could not be more simple; a man and woman are looking at flowers:

> Aren't they beautiful,
> she said, with an edge
> because I hadn't commented
> on these slender,
> some would say splendid,
> purple things
> we'd come upon. The foxglove,
> she repeated, aren't they beautiful? (*WG*, 168)

Just the first few lines of the poem, and already the speaker is embattled and encroached, jammed between alternatives of being either untrue or unkind. More importantly, the occasion of the poem has immediately been displaced by a subtext. Inside our narrator a summit conference is hurriedly taking place, a judicial hearing on diction as a litmus test of Character. Because, it turns out, there are Types of People: those who call flowers *beautiful* and others who say, *"purple things";* flowers which some would call *splendid*, and flowers a more precise person would call *foxglove*. The inexactness of the speaker's diction—"purple things"—signifies the status (not high) he accords these flowers in the realm of named things, or it signifies the amount of attention he is capable of paying to pretty, natural things (again, not much).

"Aren't They Beautiful?" could easily become, at this point, a comic poem about gender difference—the thick-skinned color-blindness of men, the insistent, somewhat irritating sensitivity of women.

The poem doesn't move in that direction, however; for the poem's speaker, the drama here is not gender nor even a matter of aesthetics, a concern for what *is* beautiful. Rather all of Dunn's obsessive subjects are in play: how can the world be correctly described; the tension between honesty and politeness—the social contract; and, of course, perhaps most maximally, the self's freedom from coercion.

When the poem's narrator cannot mirror the rapture of his interlocutor, the internal racket multiplies. Even more interesting, perhaps, is how quickly this interpersonal moment amplifies conceptually. Now the field of battle enlarges to include both memory and social critique. The speaker's thoughts dexterously go towards the whole history of aesthetic coercion, from childhood on—"the fascists of prettiness," the bullies of beauty, the dictators of appropriate response:

> Foxglove, what a nice name,
> I thought, I liked that name,
> and told her so, but I was thinking
> of conversation, the way *beautiful*
> often puts an end to it.
> And remembered as a child
> those long drives in the country—
> Look! a clearing. Look!
> a swatch of wildflowers.
>
> All the tedium of ahs and yeses,
> all that piety before the perfect. (*WG*, 168)

Having defended and justified his own recalcitrance with what is essentially a counterattack, again the speaker, and poem, might rest. That doesn't happen. "The way *beautiful* / often puts an end to conversation" (ibid., 168) is a laugh line, comic because true. But in the development of the next few lines, the stakes are quietly raised from the realm of the personal to the realm of the ethical: "tedium" and "piety" before the "perfect" carry dark connotations about the soul price of easy consensus. To participate in the misdemeanor of "easy beauty," the tone implies, leads to the country of hypocrisy and corruption.

Now, one might think, the poem has arrived home and is in its stall, munching oats. Instead, what happens next in this dialectical poem is a self-rebuttal and a counter-position. Withdrawing from his own self-righteous presumption, our narrator offers an acknowledgment of the existence of other, legitimate temperaments than his own:

> Beauty, for her, was a beginning,
> an honest way in. I knew that,
>
> yet I still wanted to say, Give me
> what a troubled soul might see,
> give me that kind of beautiful,
> but heard the sanctimony in it. (ibid., 168)

So defense is followed by concession, which then becomes accusation, followed by concession, followed by internal dialogue (what one *might* have said, after all, has a place in any authentically recalled conversation). The thinker has become so ensnarled by his open-mindedness that he is exhausted:

> Deprivation is the mother of beauty,
> a wittier man might have declared,
> pointing theatrically
> to all this blinding abundance. (ibid., 169)

And now, the flowers themselves seem to have their say:

> The foxglove were looking smug,
> Uncontestable. And there I was,
> impatient, angling for an argument. (ibid., 169)

Here is the secret of energized engagement in Dunn's poetry—it constantly offers, attacks, and retreats from points of view. The poem “Aren’t They Beautiful?” is not about the topic of beauty nor about the relationship of any particular man and woman. It is about space, about there needing to be enough space for everybody—especially enough space for the narrator’s freedom of mind, his right to be himself. Though the tone is sometimes comic, nothing less than self-preservation is at stake. If, for Wallace Stevens, “death is the mother of beauty” (1990a, 68), then for Dunn, we might say that claustrophobia is the mother of conversation—maybe even of poetry.

The narrator of “Aren’t They Beautiful?” is wise and patient, but repeatedly rebuffs possible compromise and a variety of conclusions. It’s that restless antisocial dimension that often mobilizes Dunn’s poetics and contributes to the richness of their sensibility. And in his narrator’s endless chafing, we see a strong family resemblance to our own tumultuous inner worlds. In Dunn’s poetry, self-preservation hones the edge of decency until it cuts.

As can be seen in “Aren’t They Beautiful?” one of Dunn’s recurrent rhetorical practices is *refusal.* He is a chess player who wins by repeatedly blocking any intended advance of his opponent, a tennis player who wins by simply returning one more shot than the player on the other side of the court. The goal in a good war (even a “civil” war) is to not be cornered or captured. Dunn is a sociable antisocialist who preserves his freedom only by staving off any position or point of view that would presume to adopt him.

“Aren’t They Beautiful?” begins from the subject of beauty. A much earlier poem, “Something Like Happiness,” is about refusing other people’s versions of another great absolute, happiness. The occasion for the poem is simple: the speaker spends an evening at home alone. Yet though the speaker is “alone” in a technical sense, the room is crowded with presences: the dog Buster, “his head in his privates” (*NS*, 19; like a poet, one might say); Buster’s fleas; the principles of Buddhism; the music on the stereo (Joan Sutherland, soprano); the human condition; nature lovers and psychotherapeutic correctness; pragmatism; French literary theory; and a friend who calls. Here is the opening two-thirds of the poem:

Last night Joan Sutherland was nuancing
the stratosphere on my fine-tuned tape deck,
and there was my dog Buster with a flea rash,
his head in his privates. Even for Buster
this was something like happiness. Elsewhere
I knew what people were doing to other people,
the terrible hurts, the pleasures of hurting.
I repudiated Zen because it doesn't provide
for forgiveness, repudiated my friend X
who had gotten "in touch with his feelings,"
which were spiteful and aggressive. *Repudiate*
felt good in my mouth, like someone else's tongue
during the sweet combat of love.
I said, out loud, *I repudiate,* adding words
like *sincerity, correctness, common sense.*
I remembered how tired I'd grown of mountaintops
and their thin, unheavenly air,
had grown tired, really, of how I spoke of them,
the exaggerated glamor, the false equation between
ascent and importance. I looked at the vase
and its one red flower, then the table
which Zennists would say existed
in its *thisness*, and realized how wrong it was,
to reject appearances. How much more difficult
to accept them! I repudiated myself, citing my name.
The phone rang. It was my overly serious friend
from Syracuse saying *Foucault, Foucault,*
like some lost prayer of the tenured . . .
I repudiated him and Foucault . . . (*NS*, 19–20)

What a busy evening! What a crowded room! One of the things revealed by this very affable poem is not how civil but how very *combative* Dunn's poems are, fighting off one enemy, one point of view, one way of speaking after another, including former incarnations of the speaker's own self. He repudiates sincerity, correctness, common sense, Zen, himself, Foucault. Who's left? we might ask.

Who's left is a speaker who has carved out a space for himself large enough to think in or to *be* in or to be unknown and unseen in. The burlesque of repudiating everything has pushed everything away and has made an assumption-free zone. Here again we can refer to Dunn's three central topics and may observe that principles 1, seeing the world as it is, and 3, protecting the space of the self, have required a momentary forsaking of 2, civility to other people, and that's just too bad. The title "Something Like Happiness" suggests that this famous state of mind may in fact be (like much of the world) inexactly named, only a temporary and provisional condition. In the meantime, however, it is, like "the sweet combat of love" (ibid., 19), achieved by the tongue.

Dunn has written many, many other poems that undertake to "unsimplify" abstractions and pieties, as any of his tables of contents will show: "Knowledge" (*LV*, 31–32), "The Perfect Life" (*WG*, 167), "Salvation" (*WG*, 143), "Kindness" (*NS*, 215–16), "Desire" (*NS*, 155–56), "Mercy" (*WG*, 180–81), and "Excitement" (*WG*, 188–89) are just a few of the titles. Such themes, attacked obliquely but sincerely, demonstrate his natural attraction to the traditional preoccupations of philosophy and anti-philosophy. The question "How should a man live?" may sound worn out, but it recurs in Dunn's poems in endless guises. In "Something Like Happiness," the self's renewal of integrity requires the demolition of the social lie, thus, the repudiation of polite agreement with others. Being accurate about the world is the reward for being tough about boundaries. And as to more expansive realisms, in the deep background of "Something Like Happiness," we may note, humans are hurting other humans as they always will. All of these pleasures are expensive.

· · ·

Poets have citizenships in distinct countries, and those readers who love Dunn's work most are those who think that he belongs principally to the country of the psychological. It is easy to see why. They respond to his considerable values of warmth, confession, anecdote, and sympathy. As an analyst of human motive and behavior, Dunn is a keen, insightful, and ruefully accurate technician.

However, Dunn himself has been persistent about refusing the equation of his poem's narrator with himself. Likewise, he has persistently refused to equate the role of poetry with a mission of "truth-telling" or "comfort food." In fact, in his interviews Dunn insists not on the truth but on the *artifice* of all poems, including his; he denies sincerity as a criteria for evaluating poetry. A poem works, he has often said, not because it is true or emotional but because it manages to capture or embody a convincing rhythm or figure of thought, a shape.

Here we come to the terrain of Dunn the aesthetician, and here is where I wish to assert an unlikely kinship between the poetics of Stephen Dunn and those of Wallace Stevens.

At first glance, the two poets seem very different indeed. If Dunn's speaker is plain-spoken and psychological, Wallace Stevens's poetic speaker is deliberately theatrical, linguistically baroque, and robustly romantic. In Stevens's cosmology, the self of the poet is infinite in its freedom and its emptiness at the same time. Though some critics have read Stevens psychologically, he is primarily a metaphysician/aesthetician. Stevens's pleasures exist mostly outside of time and the constrictions of self, which is what grants the typical Stevens poem the irrational freedom of the firecat, the sailor catching tigers in red weather, and the singer who sings beyond the genius of the sea. Dunn's poems are full of second thoughts; Stevens seems immune to regret or self-recrimination.

On the other hand, consider some of the commonalities between Dunn and Stevens: both are poets of the middle-class suburbs, of midnight, and of the interior soliloquy. Like Stevens's work, Dunn's poems frequently sing the pleasures of loneliness and hiddenness, finding metaphysical comfort and reprieve in the powers of fantasy. To be unknown is a great freedom, and, to take one step further, it is the great truth. Unknowness and unknowing are a kind of ecstasy.

There are plenty of poems that exemplify Dunn as a metaphysician as much as a worldling. In the poem "Before the Sky Darkens" (DH, 19–20), we can hear the stylistic echo of Stevens in both preoccupation and resolution.

> Sunsets, incipient storms, the tableaus
> of melancholy—maybe these are
> the Saturday night-events
> to take your best girl to. At least then
> there might be moments of vanishing beauty
> before the sky darkens,
> and the expectation of happiness
> would hardly exist
> and therefore might be possible.
>
> More and more you learn to live
> with the unacceptable.
> You sense the ever-hidden God
> retreating ever farther,
> terrified or embarrassed.
> You might as well be a clown,
> big silly clothes, no evidence of desire. (*DH*, 19)

This is an enigmatic and refined lyric for our so-called regular-guy poet, a poem in which the speaker reaches past the normal towards a self outside selfhood, towards intimations of something empty and encompassing.

Behind the presentation of self in Dunn's poetry is a quiet but recurrent, hinted-at absence that suggests less the down-home, just-plain folks tone of many poems and more of the mystery-self of Stevens. Dunn's poems consistently resist the idea of a solid, knowable "I," in particular the "I" with which the speaker has been entrusted. These metaphysical intimations are especially visible in those Dunn poems that aren't born of friction with society but that *begin* in solitude, enter into it, and discover that there may be nothing at its center. "The Arm" (*LV*, 43–44), for example, is a poem about the rich relationship between reality and imagination, and it displays an illuminating resemblance to Stevens—not in prosody but in poetics.

The Arm

A doll's pink, broken-off arm
was floating in a pond
a man had come to with his dog.
The arm had no sad child nearby
to say it was hers, no parent to rescue it
with a stick or branch,

and this pleased the man to whom
absence always felt like opportunity.
He imagined a girl furious
at her younger sister, taking it out on her
one limb at a time.

Yet the sun was glancing off
the arm's little pink fingers,
and the pond's heart-shaped lily pads
seemed to accentuate an oddness,
which he thought beautiful.

When he and the dog looked for
the doll's body but couldn't find it,
a different image came to him,
of a father who hated the fact
that his son liked dolls.
What was floating there

was a punishment that didn't work,
for the boy had come to love
his one-armed doll even more.
Once again the man was struck
by how much misery
the human spirit can absorb.

> His dog wanted to move on,
> enough of this already.
> but the man was creating little waves
> with his hands, and the arm, this thing
> his wife was sure to question,
> was slowly bobbing toward him. (*LV*, 43–44)

A plain-style narrative, "The Arm" bears little obvious resemblance to Stevens. Without a doubt, "The Arm" can be read psychologically, as a poem about storytelling, about the capacity and the compulsion of the imagination to fill an emptiness, to creatively invent wholeness from only a found fragment. Likewise, the amputated doll arm easily (almost laughably so) can stand as a psychological symbol of being disconnected. We also can be amused by the way that the doll's arm promises to provide the speaker with the perverse future pleasure of being misunderstood by his wife, a kind of sustenance for this character who feels most comfortable, most justified in his distance, when being misunderstood.

Yet "The Arm" is also a poem about the pleasures of merely circulating, about the glories of unresolved fantasy itself, of indefinitely suspended disbelief. There is no true friction at the heart of this poem, and that is part of the subject. The poem may be "attached" to the social realm, but in deeper and parallel ways, "The Arm" is about the experience of mystery, a poem about the way in which the evidence is metaphysically incomplete, unresolved, and unknowable. To this character, "absence always [feels] like opportunity." The self in the poem is not a self striving to be wise, kind, troubled, unique, personable, or even to be there. Rather, the mood is reverie, which is also a state of erasure. To bring out the metaphysical underpinning in "The Arm," one needs only examine the poem "Disillusionment of Ten O'Clock" by Stevens for comparison. In this poem, "the houses are haunted / By white night-gowns," (1990b, 66), and the poem illustrates the hypnotic mode of hypothesis and retraction; hypothesis and erasure is a typical, and perpetual, rhetoric and philosophical rhythm in the work of Stevens. In "The Arm," Dunn, like Stevens, seems happiest when he is engaged in such orbital rotations. Nothing exists, he implies, not even the self, and it doesn't matter. These fabrications of poetry are weightless, and all is permutation. "The Arm," however psychological it seems on the surface, is cut from the cloth of pure speculation.

"Of what was it I was thinking?" ("Metaphors of a Magnifico" 1990d, 19), asks Stevens. "It has slipped away while I was paying attention to something else." In this same way, there is a stratum in many of Dunn's poems that implies that beneath all this turbulence of self and world, beneath all this worry and striving, these entertainments and costumes, this self pitted against the selves of others, there is something like a soul, or a non-soul, an essence that isn't within reach of names. Its unreachability protects it from us and it, in turn, protects us. The world is a world of endless appearances displacing each other—poetry too is that because being is itself a fluidity, and unknowable.

Much more could be said about Dunn as a philosophical poet, one consciously and intricately involved with the legacy of Stevens. The godlike freedom of the poet depends upon remove, and poetry finally has no obligations other than to speculation. The major drama in Dunn's poems is nearly always thinking; that the poems seem intimate and down-to-earth is their great card trick, for in fact they are written at a peculiar distance. "I was in danger of being terribly understood" (*HN*, 89), Dunn says drolly in the poem "Connubial." A few pages later, in one of his many poems about friendship (something Stevens doesn't seem to know about), he describes the limitations of intimacy:

> And they in turn would allow me my distance
> because, after all, we were friends, each of us
> quite sure, after many mistakes and infringements,
> a person's pleasure must be his own serious business. (*HN*, 95)

Maybe this parallel I am claiming between the poet from New Jersey and the poet from Connecticut can only be taken so far.

Stevens's appetite for transcendence seems inexhaustible. Dunn's thirst for remove, for philosophical rapture is something he resists and often repudiates in his serious and lengthy conversation with Stevens. One of many instances can be found in Dunn's poem "The House Was Quiet" (*IB*, 29), which echoes the title of a Stevens poem of imperial calm, "The House Was Quiet and the World Was Calm" (1990c, 358). Stevens often aligns himself with clouds and the sun, the elementally eternal hubs. But a man is not a cloud, Dunn would remind us, and his own poem revises the sentence of his predecessor: "The house was quiet and the world was vicious" (ibid., 29).

Stephen Dunn is one of the most philosophical of contemporary poets—or, let me say, one of the most *effectively* philosophical. The proof of intelligence in a poet, after all, is not that he seems smarter than the reader but that he makes you smart in concert with him. Meditation, in the hands of such a poet, even on such intangible topics as the soul, beauty, and responsibility, seems relevant to the quality of an individual life.

If Dunn constantly reminds us of the imperfections of the self, of its embattledness, he also stands up finally for its mysterious beauty and enigma, its elusive unknowability, and in that way, its transcendental dimension. If the poems strip one of illusions, they also grant the reader the dignity of a place to stand. And then there is the threshold of mystery, at which Dunn's poems often arrive. From my thirty years of reading the poems of Stephen Dunn, I firmly believe that this poetic house has a back door as well as a front. The whole body of work is a mystery of openness. As Dunn probably would say, understatedly, *Human nature should not be oversimplified.*

Works Cited

Miłosz, Czesław. 2001. *New and Collected Poems 1931–2001*. New York: Ecco. 240–41.

Stevens, Wallace. 1990a. "Sunday Morning." In *The Collected Poems*. New York: Vintage. 66–70.

———1990b. “Disillusionment of Ten O’Clock.” In *The Collected Poems*. New York: Vintage. 66.

———1990c. “The House Was Quiet and the World Was Calm.” In *The Collected Poems*. New York: Vintage. 358–59.

———1990d. “Metaphors of a Magnifico.” In *The Collected Poems*. New York: Vintage. 19.

Part Five

A Manifesto of the Spiritual and the Sacred

Ilyse Kusnetz

Stephen Dunn is not a poet that one would immediately associate with the spiritual or the sacred. His poems often take as their subject matter the concrete, everyday world—dogs, divorces, the job he once held writing in-house brochures for the sales force of a corporation. But much of his work, through its contemplation of these and other subjects, becomes deeply spiritual, deeply sacred. The spiritual and the sacred are two related but unquestionably distinct concepts, and Dunn's essay "Poets, Poetry, and the Spiritual" (*WLB*, 159–74) clarifies how Dunn regards both.

Within the essay, Dunn's use of the word "spiritual" describes a number of aspects of poetic content and process; however, toward the end of the essay he writes, "Language successfully arranged to evoke the mysteries of the world is sacred" (ibid., 172). One might infer, then, that successful poetry—poetry arranged to evoke the mysteries of the world—is sacred. This notion of poetry as a sacred text with access to the mysteries of the world is highly romantic, a position that seems at odds with Dunn's reputation as a skeptic, someone firmly "willing to leave God out of the matter" (ibid., 159) of spirituality entirely, but the two positions are not as polarized as they might appear.

A closer examination of how Dunn views the spiritual allows for these positions to enhance rather than to contradict one another and explains how the spiritual, for Dunn, relates closely to the sacred. When he cites a former student's observation that "at the highest levels of thought a distinction may not exist between the spiritual and the aesthetic" (ibid., 172), Dunn hints that successful poetic language (the aesthetic) is, for all intents and purposes, indistinguishable from the spiritual. We can extrapolate that in the realm of aesthetics, at least, insofar as the "spiritual" concerns itself with "the mysteries of the world," it is, by Dunn's criteria, also "sacred."

Still, "mysteries of the world" seems a nebulous phrase. And indeed, Dunn uses the phrase to refer to variety of things. It has partly to do with the fact that "celestial hopelessness" (ibid., 159–60)—looking to the heavens for more, and knowing you'll be frustrated in that longing—"is earthly opportunity, a challenge to our capacity to endure and give meaning to our lives" (ibid., 160). Celestial hopelessness leads to an opportunity to seek out earthly mystery and earthly solace; such solace can embody the spiritual, and the conveyance of that solace—in this instance, through language—is a spiritual act. Dunn writes, "Poems . . . that address what's most difficult and elusive about our experience, correlatives to the nether regions of our feelings and apprehensions" are perhaps "the greatest solace, evidence that we're not alone, and no doubt where some of what we mean by 'spiritual' resides" (ibid., 160). For the poet, one component of the spiritual is this gift of comfort, an affirmation afforded to the reader that he or she belongs to a greater community, a balm to the reader's feelings of alienation or separateness, or an anvil of meaning upon which, like a forger's hammer, the self can beat experience into shape.

This is not to say that spirituality is all lightness of tone and positive feeling. "Can there be spirituality in negation? Need solace always arise out of good news?" Dunn wonders (ibid., 171). He concludes that while "faith is tested by realizing that there might be nothing to inspire it" (ibid.), communing with others who have experienced this same crisis (and here Dunn cites Yeats, Frost, Roethke, Eliot, and Ginsberg) produces "the solaces of recognition, my half-thoughts and feelings finding companions and words" (ibid.). A contemplation of despair paradoxically may lead one to experience solace, that manifestation of spirituality, in the knowledge that one shares the existential void with others of sympathetic mind.

In another sense, mystery also has to do with the dual propositions that its contemplation can imbue the everyday with a sense of the sacred and that, conversely, observing the world deeply and attentively can lead us toward mystery and a sense of the sacred. Dunn writes, "Here is a possible definition of spirituality in poetry: what exists in the intimations we (as readers) feel as the poet finds language and music for what he leans toward but doesn't know" (ibid., 165). The poet's pursuit of mystery, the clothing of that mystery in language and music, gives rise to a sacred text, the world rendered sacred through language. The spiritual is "ineffable" (ibid.)—"just beneath or beyond our grasp" (ibid., 168) and "the pursuit of the ineffable may lead us into a radiant dailiness" (ibid.). In other words, the poem that is drawn to mystery transforms and transfigures the everyday; in striving to make the unseen seen, it reaches toward a sense of spirituality, a sense of the sacred, that infuses the world it describes. Dunn recognizes, however, that the reverse may also be true: "Similarly, the naming of what's around us may lead us toward consideration of the ineffable" (ibid.). In focusing upon worldly objects and propositions with the appropriate kind of attention and attentiveness, we may also evoke the sacred. It is important to note, however, that for Dunn the spiritual response is predicated by the physical: "Spirituality in poetry, most neutrally put, arises from our breath-driven, form-seeking pursuits of what is" (ibid., 173). "Breath-driven" and "form-seeking" poets, hungry for "what is"—some tangible manifestation of existence—give rise to the spiritual. Within such a paradigm, the spiritual poem cannot, by definition, be separated from the physical world of breath, of form, of existence.

There is one more sense of the mysterious that Dunn alludes to in his essay, and it is an important one though perhaps the most difficult to quantify. He quotes Paul Eluard: "There is another world and it is in this one" (ibid., 160). Dunn's "credo as a poet," he says, has been to "enact and deliver both worlds, which involves giving voice to interiorities and evanescences and to the surfaces that conceal and evoke them" (ibid.). It would be impossible to define such a world, precisely because it refers to that which is not visible, that which can only be guessed at, coexisting with the visible world. We see this in the way Dunn writes of how "spiritual experiences resist the language that might describe them. [. . . W]e therefore need to be conscious of silence, perhaps try to approximate it . . . to limn and deliver the unsayable, sometimes even to let the white space around our words do some invisible work for us" (ibid., 162). If we access the spiritual, the mysterious, through language, he suggests, it must be done with language that paradoxically aspires to the condition of silence. But it is also important to note Dunn's view here that "the truest poems of spirit" (ibid., 167) are usually *not* about religion or religious issues, per se (ibid.). Regardless of the broad nature of spiritual poetry in this instance, the question remains: How does one write silence; how does one write those "truest poems of spirit" beyond an exemplary display of craft?

For Dunn, the way beyond this conundrum seems to involve a process that echoes the Catholic act of communion. Crucial to the poem, he writes, is "our measured breath *(spiritus)*, a component of voice: Pitched just right, voice reveals the spirit behind it, which is part of what we receive when we take in a poem's content" (ibid., 160) Poem as communion wafer, poet as Christ? Perhaps it is this dynamic Dunn pokes fun at in "Testimony" (*New Yorker*, 32), where the narrator dreams of Jesus offering him a plate of cookies: "And Jesus took it off the tray and put it / in my mouth, as if He were giving me / *communication*, or whatever they call it" (ibid.). In the dream world, that subterranean counterpart of Heaven, Dunn's narrator receives not communion but "communication." It is not divine presence the eater ingests, then, but a sharing of mind and emotion, the negation of loneliness, that "solace" that is, at its core, an expression of the spiritual. The poem veers from an emphasis on communion to a parable about not being greedy, but even in satire we see Dunn's philosophy of the sacred, or at least part of it, at play.

Another aspect of Dunn's philosophy is that the spiritual, or the sacred, exists in poetry as a result of conversations poets have with themselves. Of conversations with a muse, or likewise with a god or gods, Dunn asks, "What else can these be except heightened conversations with oneself?" After all, he speculates, "Poets are not far removed from, say, prophets and shamans who believe into existence what they intuit" (*WLB*, 162). Here Dunn might be seen to wander into the territory of English romanticism, in keeping with Blake, Wordsworth, Shelley, Coleridge, and Keats, in whose poetic philosophy a sense of "heightened" conversation and intuition would not seem out of place, as well as the idea of the poet as prophet or hieratic figure. The similarity does not end there. Dunn writes, "The spirit that's in voice, that comes from the entire wherewithal of a person, is one aspect of the spiritual. The spirit that seems to come from outside of the person is another. . . . I don't want to say that a spirit-world exterior to oneself doesn't exist. My two experiences with ghosts persuade me that it does" (ibid., 163). The poetic voice as a spiritual distillation of the poet and the existence of the supernatural (though this appears rarely in his poetry), are also both hallmarks of a kind of high romanticism. While Dunn may be expounding upon a well-known poetic tradition (poet as prophet), this tradition is very much present in how he describes his own views on spirituality and the sacred. We might also compare Dunn's observation "The world, properly seen, is vital, various, contradictory" (ibid., 165) with William Blake's famous line from "The Marriage of Heaven and Hell": "Without contraries is no progression" (74). Properly seen, in other words, seen with the kind of attention that allows us access to mystery, the world becomes both itself and the contradiction of itself—other, oppositional, illuminated—yet still, ultimately, once again mysterious. That this sense of contradiction underpins Dunn's sense of the sacred is clear when he writes, "Spirituality in poetry. Here's another attempt at a definition: A journey through travail toward an understanding that leads back to mystery" (*WLB*, 170). By the end of a spiritual poem, understanding and mystery, seeming opposites, must find a way to coexist.

One can, in poem after poem of Dunn's, witness a philosophy of the spiritual and the sacred. In a poem titled "The Sacred" (*BA*, 55),

Dunn's narrator is a teacher who asks the students in the class if they have "a sacred place":

> . . . the car kept coming up,
>   the car in motion,
> music filling it, and sometimes one other person
>
> who understood the bright altar of the dashboard
> and how far away
> a car could take him from the need
>
> to speak, or to answer, the key
>   in having a key
> and putting it in, and going.

Music fills the car just as musical language fills the sacred poem, and the dashboard is a "bright altar"—a manifestation of the sacred within the physical. The car becomes a vehicle of transport not just physically but spiritually, taking the student away from both the need to speak and the need to respond; both student and poem allude to the condition of silence necessary for the spiritual to manifest. By the poem's conclusion, we are left with both understanding (the key) and mystery, the final destination left unknown, open.

In the prose piece "Religion" (*RR*, 27), Dunn writes, "The sacred cannot be found unless you give up some old version of it." The result is "an emptiness it'll take a lifetime to fill" (ibid., 27). This fresh version of the sacred paradoxically creates an emptiness, a challenge that demands a response. "Religion" concludes, "Indulge, become capacious, give up nothing, Jack my corner grocer said. He was pushing the portobellos, but I was listening with that other, my neediest ear" (ibid.). Open to the sacred rather than religion, the narrator listens with his "other" ear—the ear capable of hearing that other world within this world, which affirms the narrator with the promise of indulgence, largesse of self, and hope.

The notion of a world within the world appears in the poem "Afterlife" (*DH*, 106–7) as well. After imagining his pared-down, decomposed body in the ground, the narrator admits while, "out among the wayward dazzle / of the countryside, / which is its own afterlife, wild, repeatable" (ibid., 106), that he wants his body "to keep making its sloppy // requests" (ibid.). The natural world, with its sense of newness and continuity, creates, if not the reality of "sense // and importance" (ibid., 107), then its very convincing "phantasms" (ibid.). The rain the narrator smells "before it rains" evokes "the odor of another world." Even though it "means nothing," it comes "sweetly" and manages to penetrate "the small openings" of the world (ibid.), and of the narrator's perceptions. The physical world, with its palpable sweetness, creates a sense of the sacred that, although it "means nothing" (ibid.) is in itself enough; it opens the narrator, whose pessimism seems to evaporate in the last stanza, to the invisible world, to mystery. This other world manifests with a pleasant odor, in contrast to the poem's beginning, which evokes the smell of decay that accompanies "the dissolution of the body" (ibid., 106). The narrator comes to understand that while the afterlife is an illusion, there exists something *beyond* life that can neither be denied nor fully explained, only experienced.

The tongue-in-cheek poem "At the Nihilist's Funeral" (*WG*, 165), is probably as close to an unmitigated expression of hopefulness as can be found in Dunn's work. The eulogy is delivered by Hope, admittedly a biased narrator, but the optimism expressed by the poem is undeniable. One suspects that the eponymous nihilist might be a reference to the poet himself, having some fun; the nihilist, we are told, "was always so interestingly wrong" (ibid.). Instead of a belief in nothing, he should have believed in something. But Hope needed the nihilist, it turns out, to "crystallize / what [Hope] thought by being so opposed to it" (ibid.). The nature of the world, when properly seen, is contradictory; this contradiction, as noted earlier, is a necessary precondition for the return to mystery. We might think of contradiction as one diction—or choice of words—in opposition to another; Hope's thoughts are formulated more clearly in opposition to nihilism.

But hope and nihilism are two sides of the same coin, as can be seen at the poem's conclusion when the funeral-goers turn their backs on Hope to honor the nihilist: "It's the kind of negation that he, I suspect, / would have thought might lead somewhere, / might even have thought was hopeful" (ibid.). Here is the idea of finding solace, an aspect of the spiritual, even in the negative. Contraries run through the poem: "Some of the invisible roads / that run parallel to the great boulevards / can be seen now; the era of darkness- / as-illumination has passed" (ibid.). The world within the world is visible, a sign that the sacred is present, and darkness will no longer paradoxically be illuminating. But these hopeful forays are only a temporary reprieve: "May the odors of lilac and laurel waft / across the river, and float over his grave. / The great nihilist is dead. He'll rise again / when needed. He always has" (ibid.). The sweet odors of flowers (in "Afterlife," it was the scent of rain), evidence of the spiritual in the physical, are triumphant for the moment, but the great nihilist, like Christ himself, will "rise again / when needed." The irony that forces a comparison between the nihilist, a man who believes in nothing, and Christ, a figure whose belief is allegedly unshakeable, is another deliberate contradiction. This contradiction highlights the idea of belief itself, whether in something or nothing; both, as we see by the end of the poem, can lead to solace and thus to the spiritual.

The poet can, of course, refuse the spiritual. In "Aren't They Beautiful?" (*WG*, 168–69), even the natural world with its physical beauty cannot transport the narrator beyond his own bitterness. His female companion enjoins him to celebrate the beauty of the foxglove in front of him. The narrator instead finds himself thinking how the word "beautiful" often ends a conversation and, reflecting on childhood drives in the country, writes, "Look! A clearing. Look! / a swatch of wildflowers. // All the tedium of ahs and yeses, / all that piety before the perfect" (*WG*, 168). What is beautiful and perfect feels false to him, as if it were the piety of a tedious and predictable "perfect" religion. "Give me / what a troubled soul might see,

/ give me *that* kind of beautiful," he wants to say in response, but hears "the sanctimony in it" (ibid.). In this instance, the narrator recognizes that even the contrary point of view to a falsity is another falsity, in this case one that reeks of an almost religious hypocrisy—a particularly scathing self-criticism for a Dunn narrator.

Instead he admits that, until his female companion asked him, he had seen "nothing, almost nothing" (ibid., 169). It is a moment that calls to mind Adam and Eve in the Garden of Eden after the Fall, as if Eve is checking to see how Adam's perceptions have been enhanced by eating fruit from the Tree of Knowledge. What do you see now that you have knowledge? But all Dunn's narrator can think about as the poem concludes are, *"the lies of daylight, the failures of language, / God the vicious, hiding behind another veil"* (ibid., 169), suggesting there is no solace, only light that does not illuminate and a failure of language to give access to the world within the world. And there is anger at a "vicious" deity who allows suffering and cruelty to exist in the world, and anger at the toxicity of religion, concealed behind a treacherous veil of beauty, just as the foxglove, *Digitalis purpurea*, is beautiful and even potentially medicinal for the heart, yet highly poisonous. The italics of Dunn's closing couplet suggest that the narrator has not spoken his thoughts aloud. Here is a poem that ends in silence: it is not the silence of the sacred but a silence poisoned by a god that masquerades as sacred. While the poem conveys a deep anger and bitterness at God, the fact that extracts from the foxglove—if administered in the right quantity—can aid the heart holds the suggestion that the "right dose" of religion, or "extracts" from religion rather than religion in its entirety, might offset its negative aspects. And although the poem focuses on the negative, according to Dunn's philosophy, readers of this poem who felt a similar negativity, anger, or bitterness still had the possibility of finding solace, of affirmation, of spirituality.

At the conclusion of "Poets, Poetry, and the Spiritual," Dunn writes, "Obviously faith and devotion can lead one to profound attentiveness. I clearly prefer to be attentive to what the world looks and feels like when some of the illusions that help us live in it are stripped [a]way" (*WLB*, 173). He immediately qualifies this, however, referring to a Charles Wright poem he admires, "Disjecta Membra," which, he maintains, fuses "an acute attention to experience *and* a longing for something more" (ibid., 174). One could intimate that Dunn is loath to entirely relinquish a poetic space that longs, unashamedly, for something more, something that is illusory yet no less desirable for being an illusion. Perhaps that is simply one more "contrary" to contemplate in the work of a poet who celebrates contention.

Works Cited

Blake, William. 1998. "The Marriage of Heaven and Hell." In *Selected Poems*, edited by Michael Mason. Oxford: Oxford University Press, 74.

Dunn, Stephen. 2012. "Testimony." *New Yorker*, March 5, 32.

The Poet as Theogonist

James Hollis

It might be argued that the last time the Western world made sense, that is, had a *Weltbild* to which those of all stations might subscribe, was around 1320, the time of the publication of Dante's *La Comedia*. For that brief while, king and commoner alike could look in one direction and see the medieval castle with its claim of spiritual and civil authority, and in the other direction see the medieval cathedral with its similar claim. Together they provided the psycho-spiritual benchmarks, the points of reference, the longitudes and latitudes that allowed one to know where one stands in some larger, cosmic picture. Moreover, Dante's vision crystallized an implicate hierarchy of values: directing one toward certain choices, measuring their worth, and construing their enduring consequences.

But by 1348–49, almost half of Europe had perished in the Black Death, the veins of royal claim began their long slow hemorrhage, and the mercantile, bourgeois, secular city emerged as an alternative future. With the erosion of those old hierarchies and fixed values, where then does one now stand, and how are our choices to be made? The first true "moderns" may be seen by 1600 in the spiritual desolation of Macbeth and the neurotic anguish of Hamlet, for, as Ulysses in *Troilus and Cressida* has it, "Untune that string, and hark what discord follows."

Put most succinctly, the intellectual and emotional duty of literary, philosophical, and artistic modernism is to critique the received structures and dismantle their explicit hierarchy of values. And the project of postmodernism, from Beckett to Stephen Dunn, is to figure out how one is to live amid enormous spiritual ambiguity thereafter: how does one make choices, in service to what, and framed by what larger perspective, if any at all?

As the epigraph to one of his early poems, Stephen Dunn cites the bon mot of Oscar Levant that an atheist is "someone with no invisible means of support." While there are so many themes one may profitably explore in Dunn's considerable oeuvre—the anfractuosities of intimate relationship, the ghosts of family past, the vanities and banalities of daily life—tracking the wisps, the fading traces of the departed gods makes him postmodern, and causes me most to hold him in regard. His work over the decades lies at the heart of this postmodern dilemma where one is obliged to reside, as the title of one of his books describes, *Between Angels*, in this hour Heidegger described as lying between the gods who have fled and the gods who have not yet come. Since we are all denizens of this dismal day, what Dunn explores is worthy of our respectful consideration, for the persistent question remains: what happens to the soul now, whither its journey, and by what lights does it navigate the tenebrous currents of our time?

Other modern and postmodern poets embodied this spiritual dislocation through the fracturing of their metaphors. Accordingly, we no longer find natural analogs such as the beloved described as "a red, red rose" (Burns) but rather discordant, dislocated images: a "patient etherized on a table" (Eliot) or ourselves as "the eyelids of defeated caves" (Tate). Quite consciously, Dunn takes up the project proclaimed by C. Day Lewis to "move then with new desires," because Dunn understands what it means to be unable to live "between two fires" (1940, "The Conflict," 45).

From his first book to his most recent, a replicative Dunn assignment is the ambiguous task of living in a god-haunted, god-abandoned world. With every flight from this task, its implicate importance reasserts itself. As Kenneth Burke suggested of Yeats's line, "that dolphin-torn, that gong-tormented sea," something presciently echoes in our unconscious as "that devil-torn, that god-tormented sea." In his first book, *Looking for Holes in the Ceiling*, Dunn describes how his poem's protagonist drills a hole in the ceiling, answers silly questions about it, and turns it into a joke until

> Gradually, I forget about it
> only a spider now and then
> reminds me
> of what foresight I had
> though there have been no messages
> not even a pole,
> nor a fireman. (1974, "A Poem for Atheists," 40)

In this near-comic trope, a hole in a ceiling, one nonetheless witnesses the dismantled hierarchy, the severed link between metaphysical layers once provided by sacred scriptures, tribal myth and ritual, and ecclesiastic authority to the transcendent Other—"thems what lives *upstairs*," as it were. This theme is echoed not only in Beckett's two tramps waiting by the roadside in perpetuity, but in Pinter's *The Dumbwaiter* where two inept thugs await their instructions from "on high." Comically garbled, absurd demands descend upon them via sinister, scribbled scraps of paper, ending in murderous denouement. Or one thinks of Yeats again, who announces that since his "ladder" is gone, he is left only with the resources of "the foul rag and bone shop of the heart."

The Dantesque hierarchy, Jacob's ladder, Yggdrasil's spinning world-tree, the sacred mountain, the totem pole, the central axis of tent or tabernacle, the smaragdine tablets of Hermes Trismegistus—all vanished! When the vertical is gone, only the horizontal plane remains, though echoes linger: "My voice still reflects the time / I believed in prayer as a way of getting / what I wanted" (*NS*, "Biography in the First Person, 41"). And, in search of some fine simulacrum spirit,

> dig up the brandy
> you buried the year before.
> Taste it. It will taste like
> the musk of a religion
> you gave up
> for the sweeter taste of women. (*NS*, "Chipping Away at Death,"
> 42)

In these last lines, one sees two perennial but pallid surrogates for the gods: booze, sex, and many other seductions of soul.

An elemental psychospiritual fact, or better, psychodynamic, is that when "the gods" are not experienced as felt presences, we will project our need for them onto objects of desire. The generalized answer to the spiritual aridity of modernism has been either the infantilizing regression of fundamentalism or the distractions of popular culture. Neither is new. In the seventeenth century, mystic and mathematician Blaise Pascal noted that his contemporary popular culture was a vast *divertissement,* or diversion, lest anyone stumble into the magnitude of their emptied souls. As Jung put it in a letter, the "modern" fell off the roof of the medieval cathedral into the abyss of the unconscious. When the gods are lost, the concomitant vacuum experienced generates disorders of desire; materialism and narcotics of various stripe serve as our chief treatment plans for this existential dilemma. If either anodyne worked, we would know by now. The dirty little secret of our time is that we all *do* know and pretend that we do not. I once had a client who incessantly bought automobiles, several a year. A child of poverty and a harsh domestic life, he projected the numinous onto those shiny pieces of metal that cruised by his emotionally sterile home. To him they were freedom, mobility, and, most of all, emotional connection. While he laughed at his automobile obsession, a failed fetish to an unknown god, he could not shake their hold on his psyche, a measure of how deep the need for connection with the transcendent Other runs in us. All addictions, all disorders of desire are, in Rimbaud's memorable phrase, *une saison d'enfer*, a season in Hell, mostly because it is a hell we cannot help but keep choosing.

So what, then, is the alternative? How does one accept one's estrangement, live in this world, and manage to make any sense of it? So much of Dunn's work has been to address this dilemma, and yet is clear that his answers are his alone and not meant as recommendations to the rest of us. He despises prophets, pedagogues, demagogues, preachers, and politicians. As for his own alienation, he readily confesses that he carries metaphors dangerous to complacency concealed in the heel of his shoe (*NS*, "On Hearing the Airlines Will Use a Psychological Profile to Catch Potential Skyjackers," 46–47) yet when "they wanted me to tell the truth, / . . . I said I'd lived among them / for years, a spy, / but all that I wanted was love" (*LE*, "What They Wanted," 21). Dunn finds his personal path in the precincts of love—the love of friends, of a good drink, of a fall-away jumper that swishes the net, in the absurdity of the pompous, in irony, perversity, surprises and reversals—and, most of all, this most spiritual of men confesses,

> . . . I love the corporeal body itself,
> designed to fail,
> and the mind, the helpless mind,
> so often impelled to think about it. (*LE*, "Not the Occult," 55)

Yeats writes, "Man is in love, and loves what vanishes. / What more is there to say?" Could we find a more succinct definition of our common condition? Granted the dual gift of life and the consciousness of its precious transience, we owe two things, a life fully lived and a life relinquished finally. In the meantime, there is the living to do, with only the shabby tools, the inadequate instruments provided us. We remain "designed to fail" but impelled to ruminate on its perplexities. Again, Yeats reminds us that out of the quarrel with others rhetoric rises, and out of the quarrel with ourselves the possibility of poetry, or perhaps an honest psychology. Designed to fail and yet impelled to ruminate—what better definition of the split we carry, the neurosis we serve? From such ruin, only creativity rises to soften and ennoble our suffering and thereby move us from the merely pathetic to the occasionally tragic.

R. M. Rilke suggested that that the vocation of the poet was, at heart, to praise—to praise what is, to praise the wonder and terror of it all. In *Between Angels,* Dunn depicts a metaphoric guardian angel who might also be seen as both the persona and ministry of the poet himself:

. . . in for the long haul, trying to live

beyond despair, he believes, he needs
    to believe
everything he does takes root, hums

beneath the surfaces of the world. ("The Guardian Angel," 16)

This hope is not hubris; it is the genuine contribution of the creative soul to our fragmented world, a world in which poetry, as Edna St. Vincent Millay noted, does not build the bridge nor mend the broken bone but may still feed the soul, the deprivation of which causes us all to sicken and to die long before we are dead. Rilke spoke of the poet as "a bee of the Invisible," Pound of the poet as "the antennae of the human race," and for Dunn this hum he hears and tracks is the sound of *Dasein* ("thrown there," *da*, + "being-itself," *sein*), thrust into this world, humming within our veins, the same resonant energies that move the stars and once constellated the myths of our ancestors.

Dunn's "myth" for a myth-impoverished time is that we are between angels now, and their ancient task falls, absurdly, to us.

Between angels, on this earth
absurdly between angels, I
try to navigate
in the bluesy middle ground (*BA*, "Between Angels," 45)

Whatever the old forms the gods incarnated, when one of them appears to Dunn in "Dancing with God," he is attired rather shabbily, still mysterious, still perplexing, and still always leaving:

He left then, no thanks,
no sign
that he'd felt anything
more than an earthly moment. (*BA*, 57)

But the speaker remains, confused, puzzled, fully aware of being, as Yeats put it, "sick with desire and fastened to a dying animal."

Dunn accepts the absurdity of this moment in which we are vested. When Camus observed that life was meaningful precisely because it is absurd, I take it that he argues that any "meaning" presented to us is someone else's package and not necessarily ours. Ours is to be pieced together through our existential revolt, in our hopeless, extinction-bound but luminous pause between the great mysteries. Both Camus and Dunn turned to Sisyphus as the prototype of this paradox. When he *chooses* to roll the fated boulder up the fated hill to fall back in its fated way, he wrests from the gods their terrible autonomy and with it a measure of spiritual freedom. At such a moment, Dunn imagines,

> The gods sank back
> in their airy chairs, Sisyphus sensed
> he had taken something from them,
> more on his own than ever now. (*LV*, "Sisyphus's Acceptance," 21)

As an artist in this Sisyphean mélange we call our lives, Dunn proffers a final wish for us:

> I've tried
> to clear a late-century place for us
> in among the shards. Lie down,
> tell me what you need.
> Here is where loveliness can live
> with failure, and nothing's complete,
> I love how we go on. (*LE*, "Loves," 94)

So, we are here, for now, and then we are *not* here . . . and in the meantime, we go on. In *Walking Light: Essays and Memoirs*, Stephen Dunn approvingly quotes fellow poet Stanley Kunitz: "I dream of an art so transparent that you can look through and see the world." This is Dunn's achievement: a lens through which we see ourselves, in which the absurdities and opacities of our moment are briefly illumined, and in which—through the connective tendrils of art—we resonate with what hums beneath the surface.

Works Cited

Lewis, C. Day. 1940. "The Conflict." In *Selected Poems*. London: Hogarth Press. 44–45.

Facing Masks and Masking Faces

Timothy Leyrson

In western society, certain masks are well known, such as the classic Greek comedy/tragedy masks. Others are imagined within limited contexts, involving masks used for rituals by African tribes, masks for Asian theater performances, or masks worn by children on Halloween. While there are many differences between the cultures that use masks, as well as differences in the purposes of varying masks such as religious, theatrical, and so forth, one commonality that exists between masks worldwide is that they all hold some type of power.

Throughout his work, Dunn repeatedly uses masks, as well as other images, that link to an idea of a person—or perhaps a truer sense of what it means to be a person—being hidden under the surface of how we present ourselves to one another. A prime example is found in his prose piece "Faces," originally from *Riffs and Reciprocities*, which begins with the speaker reflecting on high school reunions, and in the opening Dunn emphasizes the importance of physical appearance in youth and how the perception of appearance changes over time. He writes, "So interesting to see how character can overcome bone structure. Pretty, handsome, cute—how those attributes, those intimidations, once seemed permanent" (*RR*, 64). The power of appearance is mighty; as stated here by Dunn, appearance can lead to intimidation. One's surface appearance has the ability to influence those around them through fear.

Fear, however, is not the only emotion that masks can evoke, and toward the end of "Faces," Dunn describes the changes that have taken place in some of his former classmates: "We never knew how intelligence could insinuate its way into eyes and mouth, could become a kind of glamour. We never knew one could grow a face" (ibid., 56).

The concept of "growing a face" is especially interesting in the author's choice of the word "grow." Growth is usually thought of as a physical change, but in Western society we also often refer to "inner growth," "spiritual growth," and so on as synonyms for an inner change manifesting itself through an outward projection. Dunn leads the reader toward a rethinking of how the person we view ourselves as creates an outward power to be observed by others.

For Dunn the idea of perception, and the differences between inward and outward perception, is worth exploring. In his poem "Capriccio Italien" (*DH*, 28–29), Dunn writes,

> You buy the most expensive tie you've ever bought,
> silk and wide, blue with subtle, well-spaced dots.
> You try on a flamboyant scarf. In the mirror
> someone foolish stares back at you. (ibid., 28)

Here we see the challenge of the speaker of the poem changing the view he holds of himself. While masks and other pieces of clothing can create a new perception for others, Dunn highlights the importance of the internal view we hold of ourselves. But where does that inner view arise from? To answer this we can again turn to Dunn, specifically his essay "Artifice and Sincerity" (*WLB*, 107–15). Dunn states that "artificial simply means 'manmade.' It's the opposite of 'natural'" (ibid., 107). This perception of artifice, compared to the natural, further explains the use of masks in Dunn's poetry. The masks that are artifice are pointed out to be so; however, those that have "grown a face" have caused their masks to occur naturally and are therefore treated with respect.

A primary example of respect for a masked, or hidden, face can be found in Dunn's poem "A Spiritual Woman" (*DH*, 83–84), where Dunn writes, "Her neck is visible, but not her face— / a placid mountain tarn, I imagine— / unreachable except by snowshoes and guts" (ibid., 83). Here Dunn indicates the danger of attempting to reveal what another has hidden. While uncovering the persona of someone else is possible, to do so should never be taken lightly, if at all.

Another example of this trepidation is found in "Backwaters" (*DH*, 115–16):

> I looked seaward, forced myself back
> out into the bracing wind.
> There at the end of a crude jetty made of rocks
> a hooded man was staring into the monotony.
> You don't speak to a man like that.
> You give him all the room he needs. (ibid., 116)

The speaker is attempting to focus on his or her personal journey, but again, we see the power that the mask, or hidden, possesses. Not only does the "hooded man" create a shift in where the speaker is placing his attention, but this leads to an implied physical change, the giving of a wide berth to the man who, either because or in spite of their disguise, is able to perceive the monotony of life from an outside perspective.

This viewpoint is merely hinted at in Dunn's work, but something the poet himself possesses, as indicated by Dave Smith in his essay "Can We Talk? The Welcome Poetries of Dunn and Dobyns." Smith credits Dunn with the ability to focus "on the pulse reality, however small, and tasks himself to make that the link between the always floundering inner and outer lives, a link with the complicit acts of a loving self who will be responsible for what he is but not culture-ridden" (Smith 1995, 163).

Dunn's ability to shift between "inner and outer lives," linking them together into a cohesive unit, is something Dunn admits to working to achieve. In his essay, "Artifice and Sincerity" (*WLB*, 107–14), he writes,

> The use of pure artifice, devoid of moral issue, is apparent in the work of the half brother of the poet, the magician. We judge a magician entirely by the success of his artifice. . . . We trust a magician by how well he fools us, and by how well he conceals the devices he uses. . . . On one level, poets have to be at least as good as magicians. . . . Yet most poets are different from magicians in

> that their actions and gestures wish to point to realities outside of the poem. Serious poets *must* be magicians, but they must in some way engage the larger world we live in. Artifice serves this end; it is not an end itself. (ibid., 111)

From this standpoint, we can see the artificial being "made" as previously described, but additionally how the construction of the writing needs to direct the reader toward an issue regarding the natural—or sincere—in the same way that a beautiful painting is a made thing that stirs something greater inside of us.

This sincerity, the respect for the natural, is stressed by Dunn in poems such as "Tiger Face" (*WG*, 29–30), wherein he describes the change of a tiger raised by goats:

> And because once you know who you are
>   you need not rush,
> and good parents are a blessing
>
> whoever they are, he went back to them,
>   rubbing up against
> their bony shins, keeping his secret to himself.
>
> But after a while the tiger who'd found
>   his true face
> felt the disturbing hungers, those desires
>
> to get low in the reeds, swish his tail,
>   charge. (ibid., 29)

This poem shows the importance of the overlap of the natural compared to the constrained, the sincere versus artifice. The tiger does not create, nor force, the change within him, but rather *finds* "his true face," in much the same way we speak of "finding ourselves" during college or a trip overseas. While the change itself is natural, as are the hungers and desires of our truer selves, they would not come about if not for the actions we take.

These aspects of perception, reality, masked selves versus true selves (if there is indeed a difference) are perhaps given the greatest credence in Dunn's poem "Achilles in Love" (*WG*, 135–36), where Dunn lays the cause of Achilles' death at the feet of an unnamed lover.

> . . . You could sense it
> in the rigidity of his carriage, as if under
> his fine-fitting suits were layers of armor. . . .
>
> Then she came along, who seemed to be all
> women fused into one, cheekbones and breasts . . .
>
> And so Achilles began to live differently.
> Both friends and enemies were astounded
> by his willingness to listen, and hesitate
> before responding. Even in victory he'd
> walk away without angering a single god.
> He wore sandals now because she liked him in sandals.
> He never felt so exposed, or so open to the world.
> You could see in his face something resembling terror,
> but in fact it was love, for which he would die. (ibid., 135–36)

Dunn's imagery reflects the power of Achilles as a warrior as well as the power he possessed as a gentleman after meeting "her." This shift in personality is reflected through the change of his dress, but Dunn still returns to the face and what one sees in it. While he could have referred to Achilles' helm, his sword, his shield, or any other weapon, what Dunn chooses to focus on are Achilles' sandals (foreshadowing his impending death), and the mood others perceived through his facial expression.

The role of the mask or the perception of one's face, clothes, or hood varies from poem to poem. However, the message is consistent: the power of the mask lies in what is unseen. Masks represent the changes that we cannot articulate, the shifts in ourselves, and the realm of communication beyond the purely physical. This impact on the inner world is far more important than the outer world. Stephen

Dunn reminds us that the mask is an object and the person is a physical being, but the combination of the two accrue to something greater.

Works Cited

Smith, Dave. 1995. "Can We Talk? The Welcome Poetries of Dunn and Dobyns." *New England Review* 17, no. 2: 147–65.

Part Six

The Poet's Women and the Ordinary Mysteries

Alicia Ostriker

What's in a name? With a different name, would he have been a different poet? When he writes of women, which is to say when he writes of loving women—for a moment or for decades—Stephen Dunn sometimes seems like an uncanny twentieth-century version of John Donne. I mean the smooth, clever, charming, and rakish Donne who comes on as a man of the world, bragging "I can love her and her, and you and you" ("The Indifferent" 1896d, 9), but also the earnest Donne who takes desire both wittily and seriously in poems like "The Good-Morrow" (1896c, 3) or "The Canonization" (1896a, 12), and can write in "A Lecture Upon the Shadow," "Love is a growing, or full constant light, / And his first minute, after noon, is night" (1896e, 78).

I doubt that any label can define the range of relationships with women in Stephen Dunn's poetry. In poem after poem, he defines himself as one who is pleased by pleasure, who likes "a kiss . . . when it's especially undeserved" (*LE*, "What They Wanted," 21), who is ruefully aware that "as we fall in love / we are already falling out of it" (*DH*, "The Reverse Side," 73), but who also announces, celebrating a sixtieth birthday, "I've had it with all stingy-hearted sons of bitches. / A heart is to be spent" (*DH*, "Sixty," 21). Dunn is a man of many confessions, among which is the archetypically male confession that "what I choose to reveal / is my way of withholding" (*WG*, "What Men Want," 194). He is a guide to flirtation, sensuality, romance of the destructive and self-destructive sort and of the trivial and cheerfully lingering sort. He gives us quintessential renditions of married love, with its comforts and discomforts—oh, how I recognize these. He lets us see, sidelong, the marital betrayer, and he even lets us see a man who finds a late-in-life soulmate.

Part of what I appreciate in his work is the fact that Dunn is aware of what it is about men that baffles and infuriates women. That withholding bit, for example. Or the way he casually remarks, "I called my wife to tell her everything, / or, as husbands do, some of everything" (*EE*, "Poker Night in Tornado Alley," 83). This candor gets points in my book. When he speaks of the "ordinary mysteries" of women and men as "the broken bridge / between us" (*LE*, "Not the Occult," 53), I feel mournfully that he may be right, and that he regrets this state of things just as I do. Well, perhaps not *just* as I do, for I find myself commonly in denial, trying to reengineer the damn bridge. Mostly, what I appreciate is that women in Dunn's poetry may be sex objects, or love objects, or objects of pity or awe, but they are always also people. Real people, understood by the poet to be as real as himself. Isn't it odd how rare this is? Ask yourself, gentle reader: how many poets can you think of, in any century, any language, who write love poems in which the other person comes across as a real person, a person who is both like oneself and different?

The key may lie in one of Dunn's most famous early poems, "The Routine Things around the House" (*ND*, 39–40), an elegy that moves subtly through three time frames. The poem begins with a memory of how, when his mother died, he thought, "Now I'll have a death poem," which was

> unforgiveable
> yet I've since forgiven myself
> as sons are able to do
> who've been loved by their mothers.

This coolly problematic confession segues into remembering a time in the distant past "before the world / unbuttoned its blouse" and "when girls my age were developing / their separate countries." Trembling, the twelve-year-old Stephen asked his mother if he could see her breasts. Without a question, she took him to her room and he "stared at them, / afraid to ask for more." Back in the present, the poet recognizes his luck that he had a mother who frankly showed him her breasts and let it go at that: giving not too little, not too much. The close of the poem turns from speaking of the poet's mother in the third person to addressing her directly:

> Mother, dead woman
>
> who I think permits me
> to love women easily,
> this poem
>
> is dedicated to where
> we stopped, to the incompleteness
> that was sufficient
>
> and to how you buttoned up,
> began doing the routine things
> around the house.

Many nuances, many gestures of verbal respect unfold here. The address is at once intimate ("Mother") and distant ("dead woman"). The "I think" expresses a courteous uncertainty, as if making too grand a claim would be hubristic. The "permits" in the present tense reveals that in some sense his mother continues to be a real presence to her son—who is grateful of course for her ongoing permissiveness. The "easily" seems to me both the voice of a rogue and a nod to the fact that many men can't love women at all. Finally, the lovely dedication of the last two stanzas makes mother and son a cooperative "we," pragmatically accepts that incompleteness can be sufficient, and accepts as well the closure of intimacy and the return to the ordinary. It is a poem about limits. If its language has slightly inclined to formality, the colloquial "you buttoned up" corrects for that. All these qualities will frame Dunn's depictions of himself in relation to women throughout his poems. There is always a sense about them of a "we" equally engaged and responsible (or irresponsible) yet irrevocably separate. There is typically an acceptance that incompleteness is what you get in life. You get it in his poems, too, since Dunn always stops short of telling all, just as he doesn't tell us what his mother's breasts looked like or how he actually felt when he looked at them. His is the art of partial telling, partial evading. Perhaps that is a factor in the reader's engagement: he appeals to our imagination rather than our literalism. A mouth can be buttoned up too, saying not too little, not too much.

Some of Dunn's women are merely observed, or hypothesized. In a sly variation on the sex wars using the metaphor of a card game, the "woman with five hearts" in the poem of that title makes a fool of the man with not enough clubs, "a man with nothing puffing himself up" (*NS*, 17). I must say how I enjoy the assonances of that line—*nothing, puffing, up*—along with the put-down of the dumb guy. In "Decorum," the shy girl in the creative writing class who bravely insists that her poem should say "making love" not "fucking," even when her fellow students disagree, is altogether believable; while Dunn as teacher plays the insensitive cad who isn't quite sure what the mot juste should be, Dunn as poet ensures that we empathize with the girl (*NS*, 24–25). Condescension toward a blond "midwestern Fatima" shifts to admiration in "The Belly Dancer at the Hotel Jerome," with one of Dunn's wittiest remarks when the girl starts dancing: "no Protestant has moved like this / since the flames stopped licking their ankles" (*CN*, 27). Dunn admits without shame that he likes beautiful women; in the poem of that title he is as interested in what life is like for them—their mistrustfulness, their loneliness, their sadness—as in how to seduce them (*NS*, 26–27). And in "Dancing with God," he takes a woman's point of view to imagine what a woman might feel about being briefly chosen by a cold and sexy partner possibly somewhat like himself (*BA*, 56–57).

If in poems like these Dunn carefully preserves his insouciant political incorrectness, what I'm thinking of as his "rakehell Jack Donne" persona, it is in his marriage poems that the poet really spits on his hands and gets down to business. Avoiding the Scylla and Charybdis of romanticism and cynicism, he navigates the waters of incompleteness.

A wife is "the woman I love with all / the normal difficulties" (*WL*, "Amidst the Faltering," 61). When "Sisyphus in the Suburbs" spends an evening at home without his traveling wife, "he missed her / and he did not" (*LV*, 38). The devastating account of a domestic fight in "He/She" never tells us what they are fighting about, for that is inessential; the essential thing is that she has screamed indictments in words that have skewered him into silence, that he isn't sure he can recover from them, and that he wants her to retract, failing (the poet observes) to understand that women use words differently from men—that "her wrong words / meant so much hurt and love" (*LT*, 27). The poem following this one in *Local Time*, a volume dominated by marriage poems, depicts the way grim silence follows a fight because "whoever spoke first would lose," according to the "stupid / unspoken rule" ("After the Argument," 28). Finally one speaks because neither can "stand hating / each other for more than a day," and sex takes over (ibid., 28). In "All That We Have," the poet marks "that little invisible cloud / in the living room" that a man and woman must use the best of their resources to transcend (*LT*, 45). In "Long Term," he observes how forgiveness in a marriage both works and fails to work:

> It was easy to forgive, so much harder
> to be forgiven. The forgiven had to agree
> to eat dust in the house of the noble
>
> and both knew this couldn't go on for long.
> The forgiven would need to rise;
> the forgiver need to remember the cruelty
>
> in being correct.
> Which is why, except in crises,
> they spoke about the garden,
>
> what happened at work,
> the little ailments and aches
> their familiar bodies separately felt. (ibid., 31)

Perhaps we have all experienced the way unsatisfying domestic compromise leaves residues of minor trouble in the body, but Dunn makes exquisite art of this theme, not only with the fine metaphor of eating dust, of petitioner and noble, but with the brusque curtailing of the "correct" line that makes it enact what it says and the quiet sonic effects: the alliteration of *forgive*, *forgiven*, and *forgiver* morphing to *familiar* and *felt*, the alliterative balance between *rise* and *remember*, and between *cruelty* and *correct*, the several little *l*'s at the close reminding us that there's no great tragedy here. Glancing back up at this poem's title, I realize that "long term" may refer to a relationship but also to a prison sentence. Yet nothing in the poem itself points this out; it's up to the reader to notice or not. The "marital arts" (*LT*, "All That We Have," 44), Dunn's pretty variant on martial arts, include tones of speech and tones of silence, which is just what his poetry itself is so deft at.

A break comes in the 2004 volume *The Insistence of Beauty*. In an interview with Philip Dacey in a *Cortland Review* of March 2000, Dunn describes himself this way:

> It's amazing isn't it, the complexities we can live with? I have loved and been loved, I've been a gambler and an athlete, I have wonderful children and a wife I love to whom I've been married for 35 years. It would be a lie to say I must choose between happiness and art. I can live with many things. Just to admit that I've been married for 35 years means that I've experienced joy and diminution and quiet evenings and tumultuous evenings and betrayal and dishonesty and tenderness and withholdings and forgiveness and cowardice and boredom and friendship—the list could go on.

But if his readers have become accustomed to the Stephen Dunn of that more-or-less contented suburban married man, *The Insistence of Beauty* changes the game with poems of divorce and remarriage. Two of the strongest poems in this book are "Juarez" and "The Answers." Neither is a typical Dunn poem; both, in quite different ways, are veil-lifters. Together, they bookend the tale of the old and now defunct pairing. In the first, the poet opens by announcing "What sad freedom I have, / now that we're unwed," and goes on to usurp a story the wife wouldn't let him tell when they were married, a story about herself as a young adventuresome girl who didn't know that her gesture of independence "was toward me. I was waiting / in the future for such a woman" (34–37). The tenderness of this poem is matched by the brutality of "The Answers," a bitter dialogue in which the wife keeps asking, in italics, "*Why did you leave me?*" and the husband responds with one reason after another, including "We had grown tired together. Don't you remember? / We'd grown tired together, were going through the motions," and "She is . . . I don't wish to be / any more cruel than I have been." Cruel enough, but the poem's close seems to me still crueler:

> *Will you not explain it to me?*
>
> No, I will not explain it to you. I'll say anything
> Rather than explain it to you. Even things that sound true. (42–45)

Offsetting the old, poems of the new love appear to locate a new source of pleasure. The typo "She pressed her lips to mind" is the epigraph of "The Kiss" and leads to the quiet exclamation "How many years I must have yearned / for someone's lips against mind" (*EE*, 71). This poem's close seems to me half facetious and smutty, half quite serious, like John Donne in "The Ecstacy" declaring, "Love's mysteries in souls do grow, / But yet the body is his book" (1896b, 56):

> I was thinking this is intelligence,
> this is the wisest tongue
> since the Oracle got into a Greek's ear.
> speaking sense. It's the Good,
>
> defining itself. I was out of my mind.
> She was in. We married as soon as we could. (*EE*, 71)

There's a confession quite different from earlier ones in "Achilles in Love," which describes first the thoroughly armored hero, then the woman whose beauty was "evidence that evolution doesn't care / about fairness, and a mind so good, well / it was like his" (*IB*, 66). What does this woman do? She softens him. She gets him to wear sandals.

More recent poems, too, recount what it's like to be with a woman who is mind as well as body, wisdom as well as wiles. In "Connubial," the trite marital experience of being "terribly misunderstood" is turned on its verbal head. Dunn finds that as the new wife identifies his little tricks, he is "in danger / of being terribly understood" (*HN*, 89). In "Bad," when she shows her impatience at his interrupting her writing time, and he tries to turn on the adorableness like a dog apologizing for peeing on the rug, she'll have none of it (*HN*, 87–88). Here is a Dunn apparently quite transformed from the player of old, a Dunn who has evidently met his match:

> Forget it, she says, this stuff
> is old, it won't work anymore,
> and I hear Good boy, Good boy,
> and can't stop licking her hand. (ibid., 88)

A blurb by Billy Collins on the cover of *The Insistence of Beauty* remarks that Dunn's poems "would not be so strikingly naked were they not so carefully dressed." Clearly this speaks to the poet's craft and craftiness. There is also the fact of literal nakedness in the poems, the theme of sex like an undertone everywhere, in the poems as in our lives. Writing about what I'm inclined to call "pure" sexuality, Dunn has always leaned toward making love rather than fucking, which means that the one he's making it with is understood to be a person, not a score. Surely this is one of the characteristics that endears him to the female reader. "Tenderness," to take a relatively early example, describes a youthful affair with an older woman whose husband was in jail and who had "never [been] touched / gently" (*BA*, 42). Mutual loneliness and kidding around in the office brings them together, the poet's body "existing with hers / like rain that's found its way underground / to water it naturally joins" (ibid., 41–42). I remember being touched, back in 1989 when this poem appeared in *Between Angels*, by the way the language equates the two people. I am still pleased by the way the metaphor uses water and descent, both so often feminine-gendered images (remember Adrienne Rich's "Diving into the Wreck"?), to evoke the way we can, when sex goes well, temporarily shed the distinct selves that usually imprison us. Does this make Dunn a feminist? Well, not exactly, but it does make him appealing. So does the much later, more exuberant, happily enjambed "Best," which I here quote in its entirety because it is so much fun:

> Best to have a partner whose desire matches yours
> so you each feel there's no time
> to pull back the covers, your respective clothes
> Pollocking the floor, perhaps the beautiful accident
> of her bra commingling with your sock on a bedpost,
> and just a stain or two to prove nothing like this
> could ever be immaculate, Jesus Christ having come
> involuntarily from your lips, Oh Jesus Christ,
> all four of the hospital corners intact
> in what has been without doubt an emergency room,
> both of you having died and gone to heaven
> and now, amazingly, breathing evenly once again. (*LV*, 53)

I admire the way "Pollocking" evokes a whole world of abstract expressionist rule breaking, the casual play of the non-immaculate Jesus Christ coming, as it were, smack in the middle of the poem, blending the sacred and the profane, and the giggle of the "hospital corners" of bedsheets undisturbed in the haste of the emergence/emergency of desire. Dare I say that I could live without the last line of this poem? Yes, but Dunn has so often remarked in interviews that a habit of his mind is to reverse anything he finds himself thinking—to think the opposite—that I must bow to his choice. Wedded as he is to the normal, his fling with the ecstatic is necessarily temporary;

he needs to remind us of that. We, his willing and intelligent readers, need to be reminded. Still, the ordinary mystery remains. When he writes, as he has throughout his career, of his father, or sports, or hanging out in bars, or friendship, or New Jersey weather, or the absurdities of politics or religion, or other writers, or language itself, Dunn teaches both disappointment and wonder. Wonder and disappointment. "Restraint" and "Extravagance," as he observes in "Ars Poetica," can "unshackle the other" (*L*, 32). Not one or the other but both. He writes, as has often been noticed, like an adult. And so he teaches that men and women can sometimes be partners, can sometimes attain what Blake calls gratified desire together, and can sometimes recognize that breathing evenly together, afterward, is also amazing.

Works Cited

Donne, John. 1896a. "The Canonization." *The Poems of John Donne*, edited by E. K. Chambers. Vol 1. London: Lawrence and Bullen. Google eBook. 12.

———. 1896b. "The Ecstacy." *The Poems of John Donne*, edited by E. K. Chambers. Vol 1. London: Lawrence and Bullen. Google eBook. 53–56.

———. 1896c. "The Good-Morrow." *The Poems of John Donne*, edited by E. K. Chambers. Vol 1. London: Lawrence and Bullen. Google eBook. 3.

———. 1896d. "The Indifferent." *The Poems of John Donne*, edited by E. K. Chambers. Vol 1. London: Lawrence and Bullen. Google eBook. 9–10.

———. 1896e. "A Lecture Upon the Shadow." *The Poems of John Donne*, edited by E. K. Chambers. Vol 1. London: Lawrence and Bullen. Google eBook. 78.

Dunn, Stephen. March 2000. "Interview with Philip Dacey." *Cortland Review*. http://www.cortlandreview.com/features/00/03/index.html.

The Penumbra

Jason Schneiderman

It can be easy to think of Stephen Dunn as a sort of miniaturist in the Raymond Chandler mode, presenting, as one reviewer put it, a "regular guy cursed with an understanding of human nature more subtle than he'd prefer" (Brouwer 2009). Dunn's self-consciously plainspoken style often allows him to play with the gap between what is being said and what is being communicated. There's a wonderful moment in the poem "Mercy" that illustrates this technique: "My wife whispered to me / *This music is better than it sounds*" (*WG*, 180). In context, the wife is apologizing for the bad performance of a good score, but the gap is clear. This is funny because we recognize the speech act as the intended apology, but also a clear denial of reality. Dunn frequently creates ambiguity and dissonance in language that could not seem clearer or more natural, and I call this space "the penumbra." The penumbra is that excess meaning surrounding the dense flame of the straightforward and literal that drives his poems. Hovering in the margins of Dunn's poems, especially the poems that deal with the men and women, are wonderful contradictions and undermining implications. Dunn's poems are not simply the recordings of a sharp observer but observations that sharp observers will call into question. It often seems like Dunn's speaker has said all there is to say, but there is a huge amount of work remaining for the careful reader.

The poem "What Goes On" is the title poem of Dunn's second volume of collected poems. At first it seems to tell an unpleasant story of an unpleasant marriage. The wife cheats, leaves her husband, and ends up alone. She gets cancer, the treatments become debilitating, and her husband asks her to return. They live what seems to be a *marriage blanc*. The husband gets back the wife he never stopped wanting; the wife is cared for in her weakness.

The poem has a plural narrator, a "we" that speaks about the marriage as it is observed from the outside. What is interesting here, what goes on in what I am calling the penumbra, is that the community is not distressed by divorce but by caretaking without passion. A divorce makes perfect sense to the community, and it is narrated as a more or less familiar situation. Similarly, to care for a lover who is ill or dying would be familiar territory. But the combination of the two—the end of passion followed by the tenderness of caretaking—is distressing and tender and poignant at the same time. Two-thirds of the way into the poem, we are told that "each of them called it love," but the narrator both undermines this assertion and highlights the pathos: "because precision didn't matter anymore" (ibid., 86).

This is clearly a poem about love, and yet this form of love is a deep threat to the community that watches this couple, a community that has no words for what they want to name this relationship. In the penumbra, we see the community closing ranks, insisting that this dis-eased and de-sexed couple's love is not the love they themselves possess. In having no other word, they have to acquiesce to the couple, and yet this cause of distress pushes against the poem, owned by no one member of the communal voice telling the story.

The focus is on the sick wife. Her feelings are frequently revealed and considered. The narrator tells us that "we watched her life quiet" in the third line, and we are told that she was "happy for the narcosis // of the television" (ibid.) after her lover has been sidelined. In fact, the "each" in of "each of them called it love" is a bit shocking if one has been tracking the almost entire absence of the first-abandoned, now-returning husband. In fact, this "each" comes shortly after we are told that "what she felt / felt almost as good as love had" (ibid.). In other words, we are told that she felt that their reunion approached the joy she had felt in love, while we know nothing of his affective experience. Was caretaking as good for him as being taken care was for her? Still, we are told that if "precision" were to matter to this couple, neither would use the word love.

Considering how closely the poem tracks the experience and emotions of the wife, it seems odd that the narrator tells us that, in fact, the "we" has been involved equally with both parties: "often rejoicing with one / and consoling the other" (ibid.). This suggests the awfulness of the relationship. The cause of joy in one is the cause of pain for the other. More acutely: joy for the wife involves a departure from the husband and pain for the wife involves a return to the husband. Inversely, the husband seems only to want his wife, and for this reason we may not need the husband's experience as it is clearer from the contours of the story. He is also less is need of empathy as the wronged party in relationship. The wife certainly seems the wronging party in the dissolution of the marriage—though it turns out that the marriage never actually dissolved.

This is clearly a poem about love. The narrator tells us that the word "love" is merely acting as a placeholder and that precision would demand a different word—but the joy of language is in its imprecisions, as is the danger, and we see that danger approaching the community. Certainly, this is love, but this is a terrifying version. The husband remains loyal, waiting; the wife is happiest alone and yet called back into his arms by illness and incapacitation. Only the looming specter of death can return her to his arms, and yet, in the shadow of death, those arms are welcome. The wedding vow "in sickness and in health" suggests the necessity of good and bad times, but this couple finds that only sickness can hold them together.

The communal wisdom that this is not love is clearly wrong. Still, this love is indeed distressing. This love is not reciprocal, not passionate, not romantic, not sexual. This love is lopsided and emasculating, and for those reasons frightening. The husband possesses a decreasingly vital version of the woman he married. The poem ends with the diminution of the wife's vitality as she regresses from "truly alive" to "merely alive" (ibid., 87), and the community is helpless in the face of this monstrous affection that requires them to "revise / our phone book, our hearts" (ibid.). That singular "phone book" may suggest that the narrative "we" is simply one husband and wife, but a community of two is still a community.

The glancing reference to "precision" is the key to its necessity. We haven't words for what these people feel, even though I would insist that it is a species of love. "What Goes On" seems like a straightforward narrative, and yet in the penumbra we see the ways in which the wrong kind of love can threaten those outside of it while still having no way to name itself. The word for "emotions we don't have words for yet" may be "poem."

Dunn's poem "What Men Want" also explores desire in the penumbra. The poem initially seems to be about the way that men live inside a giant circuit of anger and praise: "My brother . . . brought the yelling home / the way others bring bread" (*WG*, 192). Parts of "What Men Want" initially feel a little dated, as though Dunn is reaching back into the archive of Tim Allen's 1990s stand-up routine, or even further into Bukowski territory. The speaker's brother only wants to "retreat to his garage, / desiring some honest praise / for fixing something broken" or "an evening out / with the boys" to enjoy "shouting at an umpire" (ibid., 193). But then there are pieces that markedly violate the gender norms he's playing with in ways that are almost unnoticeable. As Dunn moves from family to generality, he arrives at "What a man wants is the power / to name the terms of his rescue" (ibid., 194), which is the opposite of manly independence and rugged individualism. "Rescue" has long been the province of femininity, with men playing the manly role of rescuer.

However, manhood turns out to be a tenuous state. After a stroke, the speaker's father's "anger left; / he never yelled again" (ibid.). He became an "insistent hand-holder, / at sixty-one he discovered / tenderness" (ibid.). Dunn's position within this space of masculine community is retreat. As a writer, he says, "I feel like an escapee, / one big step ahead of my past" (ibid., 192). What it ultimately seems that men want is the ability to depart from masculine strictures. Dunn continually pushes back against a straightforward or normative masculinity, letting the cracks in the façade show. His father's post-stroke desire for tenderness is mirrored by his pre-stroke façade of friendliness, when "his smile would look/ like a stuck, decide-on thing" (ibid., 195). The implication is that Dunn is mostly ducking the world of men, while his brother and father are deeply invested in it—but suffer deeply from their acceptance of manhood and its roles.

Almost at the end, this stanza disrupts the stories being told: "*Just be yourself*, he once counseled. / Who would want to know me then, / I thought, who would forgive me?" (ibid.).

At that point, the crux of Dunn's masculinity is clear. Outside of the ballgames, privacy, money, and respect is the question of forgiveness. As the others bluster about, Dunn recognizes that underneath the public displays of fiscal and worldly responsibility, is a deeper question of guilt and responsibility. The speaker's self is precisely what is not on display, what makes the highest demand. While the brother and father traffic in blame, anger, jocularity, and camaraderie, Dunn is at a remove, insisting that his privacy is different from theirs. The poem creates the illusion of a private space, but truly, any revelation with an ISBN is as public (if not more so than) as a ballgame.

Dunn's poet persona ends the poem as the central man of the poem. Describing his writing life, the poem concludes, "A man wants the power to erase" (ibid.). In that moment, Dunn becomes the man of the title, the stand-in for all the men of the world. Far from his initial position of retreat and retiring, the poem ultimately makes the speaker the paragon of manhood. The writer takes central position. Dunn achieves his goal. The father and brother pursue drives that can never be satiated, and yet the writer, who initially withdraws, can set the terms he wants. He creates the public space he inhabits. In his play with masculine tropes, Dunn demurs only to triumph. Of the many definitions of masculinity put forth by the scholars of masculinity studies, my favorite remains this one: being perceived as masculine by other men (Kilmartin and Lynch 1999). In the penumbra, Dunn gets what all men want: to control the perception of himself.

The pleasure in Dunn's work is the space that opens up after the first reading. The first reading feels almost obvious, but in later readings, the penumbra comes into sight—if I can be forgiven the metaphor—as my eyes adjust to Dunn's specific light. All poets play in the space between what language is supposed to do and what language actually does; poetry is almost always a way to discover the states and feelings that we have yet to find words for. Dunn's genius is for creating poems that feel entirely natural and straightforward, as he narrates stories and offer meditations that feel familiar and need neither explanation nor interpretation. There is something comforting about the immediacy and familiarity of his voice, but the challenge is in the space that his voices open onto.

Works Cited

Brouwer, Joel. 2009. "Poetry Chronicle." Rev. of *What Goes On: Selected and New Poems 1995–2009*, by Stephen Dunn. *New York Times*. 24 April 2009. http://www.nytimes.com/2009/04/26/books/review/Brouwer-t.html.

Kilmartin, Christopher, and John Lynch. 1999. *The Pain behind the Mask: Overcoming Masculine Depression*. New York: Haworth Press.

Leaving Everything Behind in "The Affair"

R. Dwayne Betts

I began framing this essay around an idea of beauty in "The Affair" (*LV*, 46), of Stephen Dunn being willing to invest this poem with an uncomfortable truth about what drives a man into another's arms. I called it the awful beauty, then realized I'd misread it all. In "The Affair," the love song becomes less about plaintive longing and more about what bridles beneath all the mundane ways we have resigned ourselves to talk about marriage, love, and the way these things fail.

Dunn's poem was first published in *Poetry* (2003, 254) under the title "Sisyphus's Affair." Removing Sisyphus from the title, in many ways, guarantees that a certain kind of sentimentality isn't consciously introduced into the poem. Because "The Affair" was published in *Local Visitations*, a collection that found Dunn deploying the figure of Sisyphus often, the decision to remove Sisyphus from a poem title is telling. This poem, as the others in the Sisyphus series, deals with sin and the price that is or isn't paid; yet here, where the subject is illicit love, the danger of cliché overwhelms. Instead, what Dunn relies on is a language that matches the mundaneness of the situation: "A door would open in a faraway city; / inside, everything felt like its own good reason" (*LV*, 46). Dunn embraces a certain kind of failure to find explanation by admission "everything felt like its own good reason." The dramatic tension is built through the logic that the poem develops—how is it that you want it all, even when wanting it all will ruin you, is the question the poem explores. The poem is a journey through the specific ways in which Dunn is able to move the reader through the thought process of his speaker. In the end, if there is anything that endears the speaker to the reader, it is not brashness, nor even a particular kind of insightfulness, but rather the speaker's willingness to abandon the illusion that the affair is more than what it is.

> His wife was his better half by more than half.
> His lover was the everything
> he allowed himself partially to have.
> When their sex turned into love
> adultery suddenly felt wrong—the word,
> he wanted another word for what they did.
> And there were the bones of his marriage
> in plain sight, meat on them still. (ibid.)

If there is a beauty here, it is an awful one, the beauty of an admission that is not enough. Dunn's language is unadorned; his syntax does not invite questions about the movement of thought, questions about a mind reluctant to admit the truth. No, the power here is built into the way the poem drives itself forward, always seeming to look for something more—something that is never realized.

"The Affair" doesn't bore. Dunn writes without etiquette, without honoring the social decorum that demands we write poetry with characters who wrestle with the difficulties that we all confront, but who are somehow able to float above the ruckus that pulls so many of us down, which is all a way to say his speaker is in the muck of it and both unable to dig himself out and unwilling to make excuses. His lines are both failed explanation and failed exorcism.

This telling by pointing to what may not be true is how Dunn makes do without metaphor—his silences suggest what goes unexplained, unannounced. Where one might expect metaphor, there is the unraveling of the situation. This approach puts emphasis on the importance of the human drama and moves the poem away from the need for the distraction ornamentation often causes. The tension is on the narrative moment. The tension is the narrative moment. "Just when it seemed his marriage had settled" (ibid.) begins this poem, and given the poem's title, there is already a sense of foreboding placed on the word "settled." It is in fact not a word but a world,

Dunn is implying, that some find themselves lost in, a world filled with the "sleepy comforts and an occasional boost / from a blue pill" (ibid.). The first six lines form one sentence but hold three caesauras. These pauses, combined with the pauses that mark the line endings, create a space, a moment of contemplation, in which the words challenge themselves by so boldly stating the controversial. This, then, is Dunn's dark space, the space where the ideas that Dunn uses to drive this poem resonate most—ideas of fidelity and choice.

It is also true that Dunn's poem would fail if it only made sweeping generalizations to be argued over. Here, even the generalizations are explanations of a sort, a way to answer the question that persists, unsaid, throughout the poem. Each line offers a variant answer to the question of "why?" But the lines do more. "A door would open in a faraway city" (ibid.), writes Dunn in the seventh line, and it is such a startling change of pace from what preceded it that it is an answer in itself.

And yet, this poem could still fail. This narrative is not a new narrative, and if it needs to be redeemed, the need is more because the hill that it must climb to hold attention is steeper. Dunn relies on an exquisite juxtaposition to hold the reader's attention for the latter half of the poem.

> His wife was his better half by more than half.
> His lover was the everything
> he allowed himself to partly have.
> When their sex turned to love
> adultery suddenly felt wrong—the word,
> he wanted another word for what they did. (ibid.)

Here there is no escaping what is at stake. Dunn leaves the reader dramatically with what runs through the subject's head, and contrary to what might be expected, the wife is not diminished in the sense of "he" no longer wanting her. What is troubling is how the "love" of the "lover" causes the need for a word less dirty than "affair" but not a movement away from the affair. When Dunn writes "It came to a choice, and he chose everything" (ibid., 47), the proclamation isn't really the declaration of a womanizer. Nor is it a hubris that should be embodied by Sisyphus—it is just the way it happened and finally the "why" of it all: that desire to have everything, and have it all while knowing how close disaster is.

Ultimately this is what Dunn achieves in a poem that, in many respects, is as self-centered as one imagines the speaker to be. Although Dunn leaves much unexplained within the poem—the details of the intimacy, the aftermath of the revelation—there is still all that lets us recognize that something has shattered. Isn't this what affairs are sometimes about? The shattering that makes sense and then doesn't? But then, too, aren't they about the tenderness and insatiable cravings that lead us to "choose everything" (ibid.)? If the presumption is that to confess love in verse is the worst kind of confessional, then maybe we are all at risk. Definitely we all need moments of nakedness, where we risk it all and almost leave "everything behind" (ibid.).

Works Cited

Dunn, Stephen. 2003. "Sysyphus's Affair." *Poetry* (February): 254.

Part Seven

Angels and Terrorists

Sociopolitical Identity in the Lyric Figure

Wendy Cannella

At best and worst, Dunn's sociopolitical figures have revealed sides of ourselves in their capacity for compassion and for brutality, just as—read as outsiders—they stand as manifestations of middle-class American fantasies and anxieties. They explore the limits of what we can do—as people, and as poets, just as their abilities and limitations inform Dunn's poetic structure—eliciting lilting tri-stepped music, ancient forms, great tests of metaphor, and on occasion the obsessive lingering of a villanelle. More and more little "pinpricks / of decency" (*HN*, "Evenings Like This," 80) occur in Dunn, as the poet explores a politics concerned increasingly with problems of social injustice and American complacency.

The earliest angels and terrorists in Dunn's work often evoke a shift in consciousness, an enlightenment the poem itself facilitates. In "Teacher Answering Young Radicals," the speaker appears to resist the deeply political and its insistence for violence: "Given the choice of blowing up the Empire / State Building or a department store, he said balloons / took his breath away, too" (*LH*, 12). The teacher's deflection, his use of philosophy or nonsense, purports to offer a way out of destruction's path, but it is the poem itself that yields a truth, as the professor's fist, the fist which he had raised "into a hammer and slammed it to the table, / to show what weakness was," eventually yields a "dull pain" (ibid., 12).

The problem with politics, Dunn believes, is that you already know what you think about a subject. A poem would shrivel under such predetermination, would become, Dunn fears, "a tract instead of a poem" (Amen, interview). Requiring the freedom to abide by its own conditions, the subtle leaps in "Teacher" enact a heuristic process, leading us through a philosophical rendering of weakness and power, ultimately producing an unanticipated difficulty: a show of force hurts back. The teacher learns from the poem's process, too—speaking of misused power, he resists misusing his own: "He had them, / and could have lifted them with his voice" (LH, 12). Rather than perpetuate that violence and its "honest rage that suffocates in the throat" (ibid., 12), he narrates instead the larger discovery, that of narration itself. It is poetic, over political, language that holds the capacity to alter knowledge, to impact the way we conceive our world: "He told them instead about his fist / the dull pain up his arm, turning warm" (ibid., 12).

While Dunn's "Teacher" finds that political terror takes root in the body, where violence impacts both the powerful and the weak, his angels suffer from their incorporeal forms. In Dunn's "The Guardian Angel," the angel himself recognizes the deficits of his powers of protection:

> When the poor are evicted, he stands
> between them
> and the bank, but the bank sees nothing
>
> in it's way. When the meek are overpowered
> he's there, the thin air
> through which they fall. Without effect
>
> he keeps getting in the way of insults.
> He keeps wrapping
> his wings around those in the cold. (*BA*, 15–16)

Dunn creates a portrait of futility so musical it presents an inherent defense of the angel's failed efforts—clusters of sounds develop like constellations: the airy *r*'s of "are overpowered / he's there, the thin air" are chastened by the chilled *t*'s in the slant rhymed "effect" and "insults." It is a lilting, poetic demise, the guardian angel sliding down the tri-stepped lines, slipping, trying, failing as an agent of change. The word "keep" itself shifts from a sense of protection—my soul to keep, say—to a sense of continuing on with Sisyphean tasks: "keeps getting in the way of insults" and "keeps wrapping / his wings around those in the cold." The poem saves the angel from his fallen state; he moves from failed divinity to the good work of earthly endeavor. If he can't "keep safe" at least he will "keep on," believing ultimately—as the poet must, as each of us must—that "everything he does takes root, hums // beneath the surfaces of the world" (ibid., 16). With its formal music and kernels of renewed meaning, the poem is an antidote to futility.

Poetic form might make solid what is ghostly in the angel's ideals, but his "invisible presence" remains a metaphor for the American poet, a fact that Dunn discovered after twenty years. "The poet does his job," Dunn at last laments, "and hardly anybody listens or cares" (2009, 10). Like Dunn's guardian angel, the poet is required to bear the knowledge of his own ineffectuality, to face "the reality that there's little evidence that he makes anything happen" (ibid.). Of course the savvy modern reader has always felt that the angel and the poet are interchangeable, accustomed to looking for the self-referential in lyric poetry—especially in Dunn who above others has crafted a plausible voice, a seeming surrogate for the man. But if Dunn finds that the guardian angel wears his own face, what do we do with the angel's politics of social welfare? It remains a subject in need of excavation.

That is not to say that Dunn would sanction a political reading of the poem. After all, he believes the successful poem must enact a "transformation of outrage" not "outrage pure" (*WLB*, "Complaint, Complicity, Outrage, and Composition," 86). The fact remains that the figure of Dunn's guardian angel is clearly forged from a guiding "principle of selection" that is concerned specifically with social injustices (2009, 6)—a fact that exposes, I think, Dunn's latent concern for issues of class and power, a concern that has grown more overt in his latest work. This angel seeks to protect humans neither struck by the death of a loved one nor displaced by a tsunami—no god can be blamed in this poem. These are political problems—"when the poor are evicted," "when the meek are overpowered," "insults," and "those in the cold"—problems of man-made imbalance, hierarchy, cruelty, impoverishment. This angel is bowed by an unsympathetic system. Unable to impact the cultural issues of his day, the immaterial angel fails time and again to protect the impoverished and disenfranchised. In the type of coy paradox Dunn is known for, "the guardian angel" fails to do his intrinsic job; he is, to disappoint Wallace Stevens, "unnecessary." If the definitive do-gooder fails as an agent of change in the face of social inequality, what chance has the poet, or the average American citizen with best intentions? Perhaps little to none, the poet worries. "Inexcusable, the slaughter in this world. Insufficient, the merely decent man," Dunn will come to declare (*DH*, "At the Restaurant," 25).

To recognize the political figure in early Dunn is to act as the poem's "revisionist reader" (2009, 5). As the guardian angel attempts to protect the poor from eviction, standing "between them // and the bank" in futile effort, we can't help but understand acutely the social significance of the angel's efforts, steeped as this country currently finds itself in home foreclosures and corporate bailouts. So many in need of Dunn's guardian angel; the disappointment of his ineptitude felt even more keenly today. That is a problem of political poetry, as David Orr points out: "it exists at the mercy of time, history, and other people" (2008).

When *Between Angels* appeared in 1989, American culture was soon to become haunted by the feathered bandits—a phenomenon that crossed media, from film to fashion to literature, bedecking the cultural mind-set. We gave guardian angel pins to our grandmothers. We saw, or avoided, movies titled *Dark Angel*, *Bright Angel*, and *Night Angel*, all three released in 1990. We watched Michael Stipe sport a convincing set of feathered wings in R.E.M.'s "Losing My Religion" music video. We were filled with the spirit back then.

Or so thought Roger Gilbert, the critic who counted the twenty-seven volumes of American poetry with "angel" in their titles published that decade, a quantity that doesn't account for all the uncollected angel poems that must still ghost the journals of that age.

Gilbert's essay, "Awash with Angels: The Religious Turn in Nineties Poetry," appeared in 2001 just a few months before 9/11. The essay's uncanny timing allows it to encapsulate the decade's fad just before it would morph into the skulls and crossbones of the new millennium. Lest you fear I exaggerate this unsubtle shift in cultural emblem, I would like to point out that around this time, a $210 skull-print silk scarf became a top seller on the men's designer floor at Barneys New York (Colman 2006), skulls began to adorn baby onesies (Skrypek 2007), and one designer produced a life-size platinum skull encrusted with 8,000 diamonds (Colman 2006). Consider in this light the tenor shift from Dunn's lyric poems in the 1990s to those of the new millennium. His determinedly optimistic *Landscape at the End of the Century* closes with "Loves" heartening final line: "I love how we go on" (94). By 2000, however, the poet was talking, presciently, about skulls and crossbones, his angels grown dark. "If only she could see," the tattooed speaker muses, "my new skull / & bones" (*DH*, "Another Man," 100).

It is interesting that Gilbert (2001, 239) understood the angelic opulence of the 1990s as a symptom of religiosity, that he could believe these ubiquitous angels were "instruments of divine revelation," that could grant "poets access to visionary possibilities." It was already widely accepted that post-1960s American poetry marked a departure from belief, the poet no longer elevated to a prophetic stature (Altieri 1984, 191–224); still, Gilbert desired to locate within the nineties angels a sincere form of spiritual quest, one that pivoted away from the so-called ironic eighties. The problem is that the angels of the nineties are themselves highly ironic, intrepidly incongruous in their fast cars. They are more us than they are divine.

It is not surprising that Dunn would be allured by the postmodern figure of the hopeless angel—his Hegelian love of paradox found plenty of fodder in 1990s New Jersey. Dunn realized the man who is "button-downed and wing-tipped, / reading *Sonnets to Orpheus* in paperback // at the mall's Orange Julius stand" (*LE*, "Smiles," 27) complicates the world for us—whispers of angels and the underworld appear within the mundane, distinctions of highbrow and lowbrow colliding. Dunn's poem "The Sacred" makes evident enough the irony of angelic appearances in twentieth-century New Jersey when, in response to their teacher's request to name a sacred space, student after student responds: "the car in motion, / music filling it" (*BA*, 55). It is not a spiritual quest they are after, then, but a coming to terms with the disappointment of the spiritual that gives the poems of the nineties their relative optimism and tenderness. These poems make of their modern circumstance a sacred place on "the bright altar of the dashboard" (ibid., 55).

In the reconfiguration of their quest, Dunn's angels have more to do with politics than divinity. Their irony rests in their earthliness and their ineptitude—in other words, the ways in which they are like us. Other angels have come and gone in Dunn, ones who "have urged us / to change our lives" (*BA*, "The Retarded Angel," 108). Their missions have fallen short on a complacent populace: "we drift," the poet asserts, "stumbling / toward even the smallest // improvement" (ibid., 108). There have been angels who could not win out against "those little Calvinists, the ants," who make "it all the more difficult / for a person in America / to close his office, skip to the beach" (*LE*, "Landscape at the End of the Century," 76). An increasing ineffectiveness shows in their very form: the ghostliness of the guardian angel, the retarded angel "off balance" with "one wing // apparently useless" (*BA*, 108), and the "tattered / mute angels no one has called upon in years" (*LE*, 77). Like the notion of the soul that Wallace Stevens (1951) claimed obsolete earlier in the century, Dunn's noble angels find no use on earth.

As the angels and their good missions deteriorate, the figure of the terrorist ascends. Our poet of oppositions, Dunn's anti-angel arrives to counterbalance the universe. Another problematic political figure, Dunn addresses him directly in the now famously prescient "To a Terrorist":

> For the historical ache, the ache passed down
> which finds its circumstance and becomes
> the present ache, I offer this poem

without hope, knowing there's nothing,
not even revenge, which alleviates
a life like yours. I offer it as one

might offer his father's ashes
to the wind, a gesture
when there's nothing else to do. (*BA*, 79)

Like "The Guardian Angel," the poem is hopeless, "doomed to become mere words" (ibid., 80), nothing more than an apostrophe to the terrorist who, like god or thunder, is unreachable. The poem's form further insinuates the doomed repetition of human politics: its alliterative verse is ancient, Germanic, echoing Beowulf's battle against a terrorizing force. With four strong beats per line and a chiastic sound structure—the "historical ache" and "ache passed down"—the accentual lines formally render that ache as Dunn drums out the ancient echoes of humanity's ageless fears, hatreds, and ignorance.

Against these fears, Dunn sets our artistic impulses and renderings, stays against the old impulses toward mutual destruction. Like Wallace Stevens's "Well Dressed Man with a Beard," the shrewd figure who knows "It can never be satisfied, the mind, never" (1942, 224), Dunn's speaker pendulates discontentedly through the world's conflicting politics—discovering, as he does, a connection to the terrorist ("Like you, the rest of us obey the sting, / the surge"), and to our collective historical penchant for mythologizing the threat of the unknown ("the first poet" who "spoke to thunder"; *BA*, 79–80). Those discoveries allow the poem's ending to arrive unbidden in a moment of clarity—the poet coming to understand his own modern capacity for empathy, no longer "the first poet" who naïvely believes these immoveable threats have "an ear and a choice" (*BA*, 80).

Dunn's shifts in sound attend the mind's restless pursuits. The sibilant alliteration of "historical" and "passed," then "finds," "circumstance," and "becomes," whispering against the open-mouthed *a*'s of the first stanza's three "aches." From moan to hiss, the mouth moves from grief to anger, accommodating the disparate sounds, and then keeps moving, "just speaking out loud / to cancel my silence" (*BA*, 80). Dunn's free verse has been called "homely," and he is widely known as "plain-spoken," (Baker 2000, 224) but here again his organization of sound is highly musical. The poem provides a sophisticated example of what Jonathan Holden says of late twentieth-century free verse: that, in its best moments, it provides "a flexible medley of older prosodies . . . rich in echoes" (1991, 48).

The political complexities that engendered "To a Terrorist" predate 9/11 by more than a decade, and the Oklahoma City bombing by half a decade, and yet "To a Terrorist" is not the first prescience of disaster in Dunn's oeuvre. In "On Hearing the Airlines Will Use a Psychological Profile to Catch Potential Skyjackers," which appeared in Dunn's first collection of poems, the cheeky speaker tells us:

> "There is no one cause for any human act,"
> I'll tell them, thinking *finally*,
> a chance to let the public in
> on the themes of great literature.
>
> And on and on, celebrating myself, offering
> no resistance, assuming what they assume,
> knowing, in a sense, there is no such thing
> as the wrong man. (*LH*, 50)

It is difficult to imagine that this poem—with its sense of playful complicity, its modernized Whitmanian sense of selfhood—could be written in a post-9/11 America. With its focus on literature, humor, and self-involvement, the last line nonetheless rings with the weight of something beyond the poem's drollness.

The playfully dangerous political mind grows increasingly pernicious in Dunn. Our capacity for destruction: when does it move from theory to threat, from language to violence? The speaker of "Bringing It Down" tests that line when "against decency" and "for reasons // he didn't want to know," he embarks on a negative fantasy "to bring / that jet down" (*LE*, 37). As with the early "On Hearing the Airlines . . . ," "Bringing It Down" could not be written today in light of the lingering insinuations of 9/11—even with the understanding that the speaker's fantasy lives in the secret life of the mind—in his "imagination of disaster," as Henry James once put it (Trilling 1950, 60), where the violent daydream is tempered slightly by the speaker's illusive heroism: "a fire in the fuselage, / then the few lives / he'd help save" (*LE*, 37). Dunn has always allowed the reader to see the worst and best of his speaker's humanity, his capacity for violence as well as for generosity, latent or explicit.

The threat of terrorism from within and without, the insufficient help of angels or poets or activists; we can locate in Dunn's turn-of-the-millennium poems the desperation of a nation grasping for morality in a postindustrial age spiraling towards Y2K. In the futile efforts of Dunn's political figures and the implicative prosody that takes shape around their profound ideals, we recognize humanity's grand—and often ridiculous—quest to locate meaning and purpose in our world. "One man's holiness another's absurdity" (*BA*, 79)—the world and the poem both tremble with problems of signification, complicated by the way our desires and histories impact interpretation. "Aside from the question of whether a poem is political," David Orr has noted, "there is also the question of *when* a poem is political" (2008).

At the turn of the millennium, the quest for meaning became increasingly pressurized. The secretary general of the United Nations warned that while the year 2000 could bring new hope, it could yield "new dangers—or old ones in a new and alarming form" (Annan 2000). Dunn, in his own reserved take on the occasion, declared, "The millennium, / my dear, is sure to disappoint us" (*DH*, "Sixty," 22). By then, the figure of the terrorist had lodged itself in the body of Dunn's speaker, becoming the very language of his mortality: "my heart itself a city with a terrorist / holed up in the mayor's office" (ibid., 21).

The terrorist attacks of September 11, 2001, intensified the political for the Queens-born poet, and this from an intellect that had always been cautious to avoid treading near "deaths we won't experience":

> Advocates of revolution, I agreed with him, poor,
> screwed for years, angry—who can begrudge them
> weapons and victory? But people like us,
> Joan Sutherland on our tapes and enough fine time
> to enjoy her, I said, let's be careful
> how we link thought and action,
> careful about deaths we won't experience. (*NS*, "Something Like Happiness," 19)

Dunn understands the delicacy a poet of middle-class suburbia must extend toward a political subject, "careful / how we link thought and action."

Such subtle treatment of the world has become a crucial condition of the Dunn poem, so I was surprised when the poet confessed he longed for "the kind of historical circumstance that would make the personal—my personal—political" (Wald 2004, interview). It is a wish that burrows into the poems of *The Insistence of Beauty*, where Dunn's speaker is caught between the personal loss of his divorce and the communal loss of 9/11. "I don't, of course, wish for tragedy in my life, or a spate of 9/11s, but I confess to being a little envious of [those] for whom historical circumstance heightened and deepened their immediate concerns" (ibid.).

Dunn's desire for such circumstance explains the unlikely tangling of the divorcé and terrorist in *The Insistence of Beauty*, where the personal and political figures inform each other, if not interfuse. "The House Was Quiet" creates a post-9/11 portrait of "The Room and the World," a new incarnation of Dunn's early room that could not lock out the world: "how pointless it was," Dunn had written then, "to change the lock" (*ND*, 34). Here, the world and its intrusions have invaded fully, the quietude of Stevens's original poem turning ominous in the twenty-first century. Dunn's speaker, knowing what he knows, can no longer pretend Stevens's silence suggests calm. The meditatively iambic opening of Stevens's original, "the house was quiet and the world was calm" (1947, 311) becomes Dunn's "The house was quiet and the world vicious" (*IB*, 29)—the shift towards viciousness reinforced by the replacement of the soft, iambic "was calm" with the hissing surprise stress of the trochaic "vicious."

Throughout *Insistence*, Dunn returns to themes he has explored all along, themes now enlarged, "heightened and deepened," by historical circumstance. The speaker knows that beauty, like politics, implies perception, knows that our terrorists are another's heroes: "And at impact, no doubt, certain beholders / and believers from another part of the world / must have seen what appeared gorgeous" (*IB*, "The Insistence of Beauty," 86). The poem "Grudges" provides Dunn's greatest exercise of complicity to date; to what degree can the speaker who boldly stated "there is no such thing as the wrong man" identify with the terrorists who murdered thousands? The villanelle form obsesses over the problem, and it's not long before the form's repetitions yield a relationship:

> It just takes a little training to blur
> a motive, lie low while planning the terrible,
> get good at acting one way, feeling another.
>
> Yet who among us doesn't harbor
> a grudge or secret? (*IB*, 40)

But surely the deceptions of a man going through a divorce—the man who has gotten "good at acting one way, feeling another," who elsewhere recognizes "what sad freedom" (*IB*, "Juarez," 34) his divorce has earned him—cannot equal those of the terrorist mole? In "Grudges," Dunn challenges the language to solve the discrepancy. The effect is jarring in the envoy:

> Before you know it something's over.
> Suddenly someone's missing at the table.

> It's easy (I know it) for anything to occur
> when men feel one way, act another. (*IB*, 41)

Dunn's parenthetical "I know it" rings of Bishop's "*Write* it!" in "One Art," and Dunn borrows that great poem's fluency of loss in which Bishop builds a schema to sort loss by size, from the smallest object—keys, a watch—to the largest—cities, a continent. But the classification falls out of order as the body of the "you" appears in the final stanza—relatively small, emotionally vast—the loss of the beloved breaks the poem's system, which in turn exposes the underlying deceit: "Even losing you (the joking voice, a gesture / I love) I shan't have lied" (Bishop 1999, 178). Bishop's loss too, like the missing person of "Grudges," carries the intimation of both breakup and death, a duplexity borne out by Bishop's biography. In the broadest strokes of metaphor, Dunn's poem has followed the double entendre of divorce and terrorism through to the end, right up to the vanishing of the beloved's body: "someone's missing at the table."

But can such losses be conflated? Many poems of the volume illuminate that question as Dunn tests the metaphor for its breaking point. Consider in this light the language of "Dismantling the House" as the poem describes the breakup of a family home:

> It's over. It's time for loss to build
> its tower in the yard where you
> are merely a spectator now.
>
> Admit you'd like to find something
> discarded or damaged, even gone,
> and lift it back into the world. (*IB*, 31)

The image of the speaker's loss, which will "build / its tower in the yard," superimposes with the collapse of the World Trade Center; in the mind's eye, those towers fall as the poem's symbolic tower is erected. Against that double spectral image, it is the desire to save something or someone—the guardian angel's impulse to protect—that remains intact, whether personal or political. "To find something / discarded or damaged, even gone, / and lift it back into the world," has become the thorny task of the poet in the twenty-first century, as much as it is the task of the departing husband and of the ground-zero rescue worker—all working for different stakes. The equivocation of the personal and political tests the limits of these poems, and when the language fails to differentiate degrees of value, Dunn assigns that task to our moral conscious—our job now, too, to lift something back into the world.

Dunn's sociopolitical figures mark a continuum between "the room" and "the world"—political crises deepen the poem; the successful poem expands to accommodate the political symbol. In Dunn's early work, the world's pressures illuminated the inner life—the angel in the poet, the terrorist in the imagination—it is the poems of 9/11 that risk what Dunn understands as art's greatest gamble, "to make a 'beautiful' construct out of material that is heinous" (*WLB*, 86). Dunn has long demurred the purity of his political impulses and now further contends "I did this for myself, / not for community or beauty's sake, / yet soon it had a rhythm and a frame" (*IB*, 87). A craftsman first and foremost, Dunn honors the "empathetic imagination whose impulses are as literary as they are moral" (*WLB*, 86). The political, the personal, the mundane, and the grand all yield to the demands of the poem, which is run by its own exacting government. "To take on the political in poetry is not much different than responding to the weather," Dunn (Amen, interview) has contended, his political figures inevitable elements of the poem's world.

The seeds of political inclination planted in "The Guardian Angel" and "To a Terrorist," culminating in *The Insistence of Beauty*, have germinated in Dunn's recent years. If there has been doubt that Stephen Dunn—the poet who has long believed a poet should not approach a poem "as if it could make something happen" (*WLB*, "Bringing the Strange Home," 31)—would touch the U.S. mortgage crisis, there can be none now. "Picture a certain banker's house," Dunn writes in "The Revolt," "then imagine a circumstance in which he has to crawl" (*HN*, 70). Dunn's rebel is one who has yielded "to revenge's sweet surge," reveling in insurrections that are, what else but symbolic: "the waste in his pipe, his very own waste, well / you might say I've liberated it, let it out. / My plan is to be sitting in his chair when he returns" (*IB*, 86). We are incited, even graciously invited, to engage in a communal retaliation: "If you want to be part of this, perhaps bring a friend" (*HN*, 70). Gone is the "Teacher Answering Young Radicals" whose language provided a philosophical response to violence. Here we are told explanations are useless, mere nonsense, a ruse of the banker himself: "He wrote a letter explaining this, the fallout / from the windfall, the gobble and the gobbledegook" (*HN*, 70).

But "The Revolt" ends with a shadowy speculation about the danger of power and greed, an old story of revenge and replacement: "Who knows what we'll do when his room is ours." Will we, after all, prove better than the corrupt man before us? The ominous note overpowers any strain of hopefulness: *who knows what we'll do when his room is ours*. Its insinuation wavers between our potential goodness and the terrible of which we are capable. Ah, the poem is not so far from "Teacher Answering Radicals" after all. In the end, a warning surfaces from Dunn's new meditation on power: tread carefully, the poet might say, we are each at risk of greed's corruptions. After all, "you are only a few decimal points from being me" (*HN*, 70).

As Dunn moves deeper into the twenty-first century, his angels and terrorists are supplanted by new hapless figures likewise caught in the net of history. The figures of the impostor and alien have invaded Dunn's latest work, manifestations of the poet's growing political consciousness. The speaker of "Impostor" who regrets "playing husband, / playing father," comes to understand such a performance as a social exercise in self-control. Consider, Dunn says, the alternative:

> what used to sound good—someone
> earnestly trying to be himself,
> as if being oneself couldn't be hideous,
> you and people you've known:

> pigs in the slop, men in the throes
> of discovering the joy in their malice. (*HN*, 27–28)

The figure of the impostor challenges the fetishism for "being ourselves" that we express as a culture; Dunn knows the extent of what that implies. Still, there is a balance the impostor hasn't found. He may not be hideous, but he is someone else's version of sane.

Distancing himself from his malicious, lower self, the impostor risks a loss of identity, as Dunn's "The Melancholy of the Extraterrestrials" explores. Problems of hierarchy expand interplanetarily in this poem where the guardian angel and his generous, doomed efforts have been replaced by the figure of a space alien less certain of his mission on earth. "Blend in, the elders told us, / be effective," the alien reveals, but "To what end? / That was only hinted at" (*HN*, 75). To work without a sense of import is to lose yourself, and this figure's melancholic stupor stems from his lack of purpose: "Why were we doing what we were doing?" (*HN*, 76). The question rings out from the poem's purported science fiction, confronting the abyss of middle-class "workdays and country clubs," bureaucratic wastes of time, and suburban distractions—a way of life the alien has achieved and, like many a human, found tedious—"seats / on school boards" and "those future sinecures / of leverage in local government." His is the melancholy of a borrowed life without meaning. The tenor of such a voice sounds like any dissatisfied American: "After a while, I'd bring home a weariness, / and when I'd look in the mirror I'd see a creature / made of smoke and pretense" (*HN*, 75).

If Dunn's extraterrestrial replaces the guardian angel in taking on Sisyphean tasks, the tasks themselves have grown meaningless. Further, the figure now carries within him the threat of the terrorist as well: "I've begun to fear," he worries, "that soon I might be asked to break into that stash // of electro-atomic weaponry we were given, / and do something otherworldly to these people." It is a conceit that opens up a new awareness in Dunn's power figure: "They are guilty," the alien comes to understand of the people of Earth, "only of being born / on the wrong planet at a time of our ascendancy" (*HN*, 76).

Dunn's newest sociopolitical persona disorients us as the alien's mask transforms into our own face, to the face of the other, shifting from impulses of generosity to destruction, angel and terrorist both.

For we are Dunn's sociopolitical figures too—we who, like any sad space alien, have consciousness enough to ask *why are we doing what we are doing?* These figures have grown empowered, evolving from those caught in the web of history to those conscious of creating it, in whatever flawed or inexplicable manner. It is a complex identity we find in Dunn's extraterrestrial and impostor, one that demands multiplicity from our sense of self. The old masks no longer deceive, the poet warns us: "We often say / we were blinded. We say we were not ourselves" (*WG*, "The Mistaken," 191). The language insinuates our complicity and reveals our lies, personal and political both. Dunn is a poet who affirms the lyric mode's capacity to illuminate humanity's—and at times inhumanity's—every side; his sociopolitical figures divulge what we hide from and what we wish to hide.

Works Cited

Altieri, Charles. 1984. *Self and Sensibility in Contemporary American Poetry*. Cambridge: Cambridge University Press.

Amen, John. Undated. "Interview with Stephen Dunn." *Pedestal Magazine*. http://www.thepedestalmagazine.com/gallery.php?item=3756.

Annan, Kofi. 2000. "The Secretary-General's Message for the New Millennium." http://www.un.org/millennium/3112sge.htm.

Baker, David. 2000. *Heresy and the Ideal: On Contemporary Poetry*. Fayetteville: University of Arkansas Press.

Bishop, Elizabeth. 1999. "One Art." In *The Complete Poems: 1927–1979*. New York: Farrar. 178.

Colman, David. 2006. "The Heyday of the Dead." *New York Times*. July 27 2006. G2, 1.

Dunn, Stephen. 2009. "The Poem, Its Buried Subject, and the Revisionist Reader: Behind 'The Guardian Angel.'" *Midwest Studies in Philosophy: Special Issue in Philosophy and Poetry* 33, no. 1: 5–10. http://onlinelibrary.wiley.com/doi/10.1111/j.1475-4975.2009.00181.x/abstract.

Gilbert, Roger. 2001. "Awash with Angels: The Religious Turn in 1990s Poetry." *Contemporary Literature*, special edition, "American Poetry of the 1990s," 42, no. 2 (Summer 2001): 238–69.

Holden, Jonathan. 1991. *The Fate of American Poetry*. Athens: University of Georgia Press.

Orr, David. 2008. "The Politics of Poetry." *Poetry* (July/August) http://www.poetryfoundation.org/poetrymagazine/article/181746.

Skrypek, Erin. 2007. "Anatomy of a Trend: Inspired by the Human Body, Designers Flesh Out New Looks." *Boston Globe*. 21 June, E2.

Stevens, Wallace. 1942 (1997). "The Well Dressed Man with a Beard." In *Collected Poetry and Prose*. New York: Library of America. 224.

———. 1947 (1997). "The House Was Quiet and the World Was Calm." In *Collected Poetry and Prose*. New York: Library of America. 311–12.

———. 1951. "The Noble Rider and the Sound of Words." In *The Necessary Angel*. New York: Vintage.

Trilling, Lionel. 1950 (2008). *The Liberal Imagination: Essays on Literature and Society*. New York: New York Review of Books.

Wald, Elissa. 2004. "An Interview with Poet Stephen Dunn." *Poets and Writers*. http://www.pw.org/content/interview_poet_stephen_dunn?cmnt_all=1.

The Poet, the Ice Traveler, and the Other

Andrea Hollander

Throughout his many years of publishing poems, Stephen Dunn has managed to keep a steady eye on the "I" of himself and, in so doing, on the "I" of all of us. It's as though Dunn's words were simply the black and white of our own often secret thoughts. But he does not write confessional poems. He seems to have what he refers to in his essay "Complaint, Complicity, Outrage, and Composition" as an "empathetic imagination": the ability to imagine himself as someone else and to thereby empathize with that other person, to sometimes speak as him or her. The poet's task, Dunn claims, is to "find ways to measure and evaluate experience that uniquely draw more attention to the subject than to [the poet's]" (*WLN*, 100).

How does he accomplish this? What makes a Stephen Dunn poem a Stephen Dunn poem?

While writing guides emphasize the importance of sensory language, Dunn demonstrates his ability to use other kinds, including ontological. Dunn is a kind of philosopher poet whose poems—like the philosophical statements by bona fide philosophers—are sometimes composed of mostly abstract language and relatively few images. And yet the speaker of a Stephen Dunn poem does not behave professorially. Instead, it's as though his speaker sits beside the reader at a bar or in a restaurant and relates an anecdote that leads to some uncannily wise and/or mysteriously—even paradoxically—accurate truism. Or he makes some at-first-outlandish-sounding philosophical claim about life and concludes with a quick parallel to something soundly anchored in the actual world. How does he do what he does, and do it so smoothly, making his mark so indelibly?

One key component of Dunn's ability is the way he orchestrates his poems' points of view to the best possible advantage. Sometimes a poem is cast in first person or the kind of third person that has the *feel* of first person because Dunn uses third-person omniscient, as in "The Unsaid": "To him, consolation was a network / of agreements" (*LV*, 45).

Nor is it unusual for Dunn to use second person as a stand-in for first. For example, in "And So," the *you* is not a specific other person; it is an *I* that suggests the reader as *I*: "And so / you take a walk into the neighborhood" (*WG*, 190). Dunn's second-person point of view in such poems is an offering: Reader, along with or instead of me, imagine yourself in this poem's situation.

Casting a poem in first-person plural allows the speaker to include and implicate the reader. Here is the entirety of "The Reverse Side," which opens with an epigraph:

> *The reverse side also has a reverse side.*
> —a Japanese proverb

> It's why when we speak a truth
> some of us instantly feel foolish
> as if a deck inside us has been shuffled
> and there it is—the opposite
> of what we said.
>
> And perhaps why as we fall in love
> we're already falling out of it.
>
> It's why the terrified and the simple
> latch onto one story,
> just one version of the great mystery.
>
> Image & afterimage, oh even
> the open-minded yearn for a fiction

to rein things in—
the snapshot, the lie of a frame.

How do we not go crazy,
we who have found ourselves compelled
to live with the circle, the ellipsis, the word
not yet written. (*DH*, 73)

Such use of first-person plural is not unusual for Dunn and assures readers that the speaker is speaking *for* us, as well as *to* us. *Hey, isn't life like this?* he asks, our comrade at the bar, the good guy who has bought us all a round of drinks.

The journey of this poem progresses as a series of responses to the Japanese proverb, which the speaker acknowledges as true. He seems to say, Therefore *this* and perhaps *this* and then *this*. By stanza 4, there is less supposition—no "it's why. . . ." The speaker, who may or may not be Dunn himself, has earned authority and speaks without hesitation. By the final stanza, he is sure that his compositional "argument" is so well constructed that whatever he says at the poem's close will be as if spoken not only for himself but also for all who are like him—in other words, his readers.

Also important is the fact that "The Reverse Side" is comprised almost entirely of abstract language. The only real image used is in the analogy in the first stanza where Dunn compares "[feeling] foolish" after having spoken some awkward "truth" with the feeling of "a deck inside us [being] shuffled." And perhaps it is the inclusive point of view (first-person plural) that allows Dunn to compose a poem of so much abstraction. In his essay "Some Reflections on the Abstract and the Wise," he argues for poems that risk being both. Praising and explicating specific poems by Wendell Berry, William Carlos Williams, and William Stafford, Dunn demonstrates that "if a poem has created an emotional climate it can more easily get away with wisdom lines" (*WLN*, 65), or if the poem phrases "a statement as a question" (ibid., 66), or if it incorporates a "useful epigraph" (ibid., 70) as Dunn himself has done in "The Reverse Side," to which the entire poem responds and upon which its existence depends. The important component, Dunn claims, is that a "wisdom line" satisfies only when "it arises inevitably and naturally out of what preceded it" (ibid., 72).

"The Reverse Side" is composed almost entirely of wisdom lines, but never does the speaker claim to be any kind of guru; instead he assures us of his one-of-us status; he's no professor; he's still the fellow at the bar whose apparent wisdom and the confidence with which he speaks are earned by his using the inclusive first-person plural voice, thereby allowing us to feel as though we've participated in the process of discovery.

In this same essay on abstraction in poems, Dunn focuses at length on William Meredith's "Crossing Over," a love poem that wins Dunn's highest admiration as an example of a poem that succeeds at abstraction for all the reasons mentioned above. He also praises Meredith's poem in another essay, "Alert Lovers, Hidden Sides, and Ice Travelers: Notes on Poetic Form and Energy," in which he differentiates among three kinds of poets: (1) ice skaters, who either "avoid or don't arrive at their real [discovered] subjects" or who are "confident that the ice will keep [them] safe while [they do] a few dazzling figure-eights" (*WLN*, 148); (2) sedentary ice fishers, who "formalize the act of fishing" and whose caught fish are nothing we haven't already encountered (ibid., 151); and (3) ice travelers, who are "always willing and able to go a little farther, perhaps even deeper" (ibid., 148), whose "fish are recognizably fish, but [that] have no names" (ibid., 151). Ice travelers are poets who, when they feel compositionally stranded in a poem, avoid what is easy. Such poets may not yet have found the poem's true subject or the structure that will best serve locating it. But they know that the problem has to do with "the pressure their movements exert" (ibid., 149). As they write, they're "both pressing down . . . with their entire weight (that is, everything they can bring to bear on the subject). And they're walking light, employing the appropriate skill for the task" (ibid., 150).

Most poets, Dunn says, become ice travelers only rarely. Dunn is most obviously such a traveler himself when he explores risky yet ordinary territory—the complications of lust, love, sex, marriage, betrayal. And he does so most convincingly when he employs a persona: the kind of generic *other* generated in a point-of-view voice so set apart from Stephen Dunn *the man* that we would feel uncomfortable assuming such a voice is that of the poet, be it in first or second person. (Besides "The Reverse Side," see such poems as "Sleeping with Others" (*IB*, 84–85), "The Soul's Agents" (*EE*, 36–37), and "After" (*DH*, 66), to name a few.) Alternatively, he may use third person, focusing on a protagonist who is insistently not Stephen Dunn, as in such poems as "Achilles in Love" (*IB*, 66–67), "Poe in Margate" (*LV*, 67–68), "Mary Shelley in Brigantine" (ibid., 91–92), and "Please Understand" (*WG*, 171).

When Dunn wishes to have us believe his speaker is indeed himself, he lets us know early, as in "Five Roses in the Morning," (*IB*, 78) which has as its epigraph the date "March 16, 2003," a detail that underscores the probability of its being a poem in the poet's own voice. Or, as in "Imagining Myself My Father," (*L*, 52–53) the title itself prods the reader into the comfort of the belief that speaker and poet are the same person. In "The Refuge," an example of another way Dunn lets us know *he* is speaking the poem, he includes details that have the semblance of such veracity:

> I had come with my sister-in-law,
> nephew and niece, a familial gesture, not exactly
> my style. My brother was back on the couch
> watching football, my wife cooking. (*L*, 81)

One cannot be certain, of course, that such details mark the poem this way; in at least one other poem, Dunn's speaker speaks of his two athletic sons (the poet has only daughters). And of course there are poems—for example, "The Unsaid" (*LV*, 45) or "Best" (ibid., 53)—in which a speaker's identity does not matter.

"Cruelties" is a poem of the poet-as-speaker category—Dunn speaking as himself—and yet its final gesture presents a clue to the question of identity in other Dunn poems:

All day long, my former love, I've been revising
a poem about us. First, a gentle man
spoke it, then I gave the Devil a chance.
But you always knew my someone else
could only be me. (*IB*, 80)

But such Dunn-as-speaker poems are rarely those filled with wisdom lines. Perhaps this is because, as the poet says himself, the goal of a good poem is "annihilation of the self, or at least self-consciousness" (*WLN*, 149)—impossible when one is writing as himself.

Is one of the keys to Dunn's success as a poet in part enabled by his ability to deliver truths in an unabashed voice, no matter which point of view he uses, provided that that voice not seem to be the poet's own? The advantage of letting the poem's musings belong to a persona allows the poet to push farther out on the ice. If, during the process of creating the poem, the poet speaks as an *other*, there will assuredly be less chance to worry over sounding pompous, or seeming to be a know-it-all or appearing superior to his reader. A persona can be smarter than the poet. Or stupider. What has the poet to lose? And, too, once a poet adopts the voice of someone other than himself, he is free to explore without embarrassment and without holding back. Risks taken are the risks of the other. He may be out on the lake while the ice beneath his feet is melting, but the sun isn't that hot and he can put just the right amount of pressure on the ice—he can walk lightly as possible but still walk—if he wears someone else's lightweight shoes.

"Deprivation is the mother of beauty, / a wittier man might have declared," Dunn states in "Aren't They Beautiful?" (*WG*, 169). But of course in stating what this wittier *other* might have said, the speaker both denies his alliance with this other and at the same time—because, after all, he's claiming to know and speak the wittier one's witty remark—claiming it for himself as he quotes and simultaneously denies allegiance to it!

In "The Perfect Life," Dunn personifies the eponymous title and has his speaker respond to it. Here is the entire second stanza:

The perfect life was never quite present,
so could never be faulted, and seemed
to keep just enough of its promises
to keep me committed. In this way it resembled
one of those beautiful strangers
made of smoke and thin air, the lovely trouble
I've often foreseen, but still wanted to lie down with.
(ibid., 167)

The speaker's purpose here and in the rest of the poem is to analyze that perfect life as if it were a presence—a personality, a form of being, nearly human, perhaps—but a presence that teased people, flirted with them, inviting them to believe in its existence. The speaker, as the stanza above demonstrates, had been duped by that presence, and in the poem he, now a man who understands the corrupt nature of that presence, argues with it, admonishes himself for believing in its good intentions. Here is how the poem closes:

Later on—oh the perfect life doesn't like the sound
of history—later on, amid the regret, the heartbreak—
amid such words I now permitted myself to say,

I nevertheless remember a clearing by a river,
the camaraderie there, the small fires and the dancing,
and looking up into the lambency of the night
how I believed that all of it was ours. (ibid., 167)

By "all of it," the speaker means the promises of a future implied by the presence of that "perfect life" that lingered so that the speaker "wished [himself] further into it" even "[telling] others / . . . how it might feel to have our desires / matched, then satisfied, every day of our lives" (ibid., 167).

Stephen Dunn would likely agree that writing only autobiographical poems is not only limiting, it is boring. In the introductory essay to the second edition of *Walking Light*, he suggests that one way to write a meaningful poem is by suppressing what he claims to be "unnecessary impulses" in order to "[make] freedom more possible" (*WLB*, 3). What are these "unnecessary impulses"? While the poet cannot know the answer to this question until "the poem has found its destination," at the very least he must suppress what Dunn calls the "false freedoms" of both "indulgence and solipsism" (ibid., 3). In other words, the poet must at least avoid confessional outpourings and instead allow the imagination to rule. "It is the imagination's task," he says, "to accommodate unruly impulses, to eventually make them feel inevitable. Poems should shimmer with a necessity, or otherwise be 'holidays of the mind'—romps for the serious, trips to worlds that resemble our own" (ibid., 3).

One might believe that "What Men Want," the final poem in *What Goes On*, is autobiographical since it contains facts about Dunn's actual father and brother. But assuming we have made such an assumption, about midway through the poem the speaker says, "I want no one / . . . to suspect / that what I choose to reveal / is my way of withholding" (*WG*, 194). Does this mean that what the speaker reveals is factual? Or is Dunn playing us? If we suspect the identity of the speaker to be Dunn himself, we're now given evidence that corrupts our assumption. The poem closes this way:

> *Just be yourself*, [my father] once counseled.
> Who would want to know me then,
> I thought, who would forgive me?
>
> I've always needed paper and pencil
> in order to speak as little as I should.
> After the power to choose
> a man wants the power to erase. (ibid., 195)

Here, as elsewhere, Dunn's speaker is a man who occupies the territory of the "in-between," staking claim to a place without definite answers to the philosophical questions posed or assumed. No matter what point of view the poet takes, he evokes a person who, as in his poem "The Hours" from *Different Hours*, prefers "the enigmas of early morning // and the neither-here-nor-thereness of dusk" (44).

In his desire to be an ice traveler, Dunn takes particular kinds of risks—as evidenced in his use of abstract language, incorporation of wisdom lines, careful choosing of point of view, and his sometimes subtle adoption of the voice of a persona—each intended to help bring as much weight as possible to bear on his poems without the poet falling through.

Implication

A Pastiche

Judith Kitchen

In the decade between 1991 and 2001, I reviewed work by Stephen Dunn a total of four times for the *Georgia Review*. Looking back, I found many recurring threads but none so omnipresent as Dunn's technique of implication—both of self and reader. The following is a pastiche—new commentary combined with paragraphs and sentences freely lifted from all four reviews—but with a recombinant DNA all its own. The three specific poems mentioned here are ones that seem to me still to contain the essence of Dunn's methods of entanglement.

Stephen Dunn has consistently been a spokesman for the suburban middle class—in short, the poet who represents so many of us. Building on a persona—an ordinary man, speaking rather openly about his life—the poems quickly establish an intimate, familiar voice. He might, he suggests, have struck up an acquaintance with you on the commuter train.

For all their surface accessibility, Dunn's poems are nevertheless subtle and complex. They give us wit and wisdom in equal measure, playful banter between epigraph and poem, serious dialogue between epigraph and poem, serious encounter with idea and concept, and a grand, expansive love of life. The speaker of these poems, who honestly admits that desire has often come before duty, is attracted to a kind of recklessness, an abandonment of the self to excess. The poems become a performance, a way of holding the reader at arm's length by seeming to tell all, intentionally leading us through the tunnel of self-implication as though the poet could speak our secret thoughts.

Never willing to settle for the "simply moral" (*DH*, "Irresistible," 86), for what Dunn calls the "virtue" (ibid., "A Postmortem Guide, 119) of the seldom tempted, he comes naturally to the multifaceted implication of self and reader alike. What is at stake in his poetry is how to live the one life we're given with integrity, with humor and exuberance and, yes, grace.

Landscape at the End of the Century explores the disparity between our public and private lives. "Should we tell them / very little, or none at all?" ("Little Essay on Communication," 59), Dunn's speaker asks, making his reader complicit in his wily mask, marking his reader as someone who has also loved in "good silence" well into the night. Good silence is perhaps the driving force behind the fourteen-page-long poem, "Loves" (*LE*, 81–94), that ends the collection. Organized in paragraph-like stanzas, "Loves" opens by establishing a fictional confidant, a reader (almost a lover) who understands the speaker thoroughly. And then the speaker holds his accomplice to an enforced secrecy.

The poem is ostensibly a catalogue of what the poet appreciates: people, food, movies, flowers, basketball shots, gambling, baboons, and newts ("surely evolution has a sense of humor"; ibid., 86), oddities such as shifting from second to third, the ocean in winter, spires, tuxes, hornets, leaving and being left. Dunn piles love upon love, working out his own preferences against the backdrop of history by listening always to the noisy, knowing voice in his head and the unforgettable voices of the past with their alternative visions:

> In spite of their lack of humor
> I love Thoreau and Jesus, Marx,
> Malcolm X. I love their obstinate courage,
> Hunger Artists all . . . (ibid., 87)

He then counters with Shakespeare and Picasso, Dickinson, Becket, Frost: "wise dark players / among entropy and the ruins."

In fact, "Loves" takes the risk of going too far, becoming repetitive and losing impact, but Dunn covers that base, too. Very early in the poem, he states, "I love that a list like this / must always extend itself, / and must exclude, slash" (ibid., 82). The poet extends and excludes, offers up contrary opinions, weighs his best moments against his worst, worries away at what makes for individual taste. Sometimes Dunn indulges in characteristic pairings: "I love the way sorrow and lust / can be companions" (ibid., 84). At other times, his loves show a kind of ornery contrariness: "But never to have betrayed, admit it, / is a kind of lethargy or rectitude, / a failure, pure" (ibid., 82). But always the poem plays itself out under the shadow of a seemingly offhand remark: "I love that there's a secret / behind every secret" (ibid., 85). In the end, the poem becomes so inclusive and so intimate, so funny and serious, that the reader must bow before it—and be included in the list.

"Loves" is both personal and political, moving easily from one realm to the other, a synthesis of inner and outer worlds. Always at the center of this tour de force is the fictional "other"—a device of Dunn's own making—and the poem ends by confessing to his invention:

> Here is where loveliness can live
> with failure, and nothing's complete.
> I love how we go on. (ibid., 94)

There's something redeeming in our efforts to "go on." There is horror in the world, true, and complacency is never benign, but Dunn alleviates our guilt at not feeling guilty enough. We are not absolved, but the hurt is tempered with real—and human—affirmation.

Dunn's poems always flirt with their own dark interiors, so it is not surprising to see that flirtation become something like romance. The speaker is encumbered by the complex, even perverse, ways of the heart and, far from making us feel self-conscious, the poems reverberate with a kind of "aftershock"—the surprise that keeps surprising.

Interspersed within poems whose ostensible (and yet very real) subjects are as varied as epileptic seizures, movies, imagined and real lovers, remembered motorcycles, and a tiger raised by goats, Dunn gives us intermittent confessions. Even these seem to glide off the tongue couched in the "he" and "we" and "you" that deflect the poem from direct self-examination. Those admissions sound like the "agile tongue" (*L*, "Imagining Myself My Father," 53) he imagines for his salesman father or the missing half of the man who gives only partial attention to everyone. These are the lines we learn to say because they sound intimate in a world of so much alienation.

Loosestrife explores the disparity between our public and private lives. To do so, the speaker often pokes fun at himself, sees himself as being ludicrously (and hilariously) ineffectual, and often seems to be preparing for an ultimate solitude. The title poem (*L*, 89–96) is named for a flower Dunn knew (he reports) before he knew its name. In other words, it once served as pure image. But in the poem it functions as only one of a list: "loosestrife, goldenrod, pixie moss" (94). Whatever other associations it may have accumulated for the author, or whatever associations it carries for the reader, are defused. That list, along with pitch pine, crowberry, and black oak, serves to demonstrate the natural, more harmless side of the suburbs. There are others to reveal the darker side: the shooting place where a hunter can pick off farm-raised quail, pickup trucks with rifle racks, a brush fire out of control. That list masks an uglier side of society: right-wing politics that penalize the poor, abused children, gang warfare, slums. Combining "loose" and "strife" in ever-widening circles, "Loosestrife" surveys a moral landscape and finds it wanting.

"Loosestrife" is built on a discursive, even anecdotal, voice. The speaker notes, and lets us know he notes, the ironies of his condition. His is a commentary. The daffodils are not merely daffodils; they are flowers that didn't know better than to come up before the last frost. Just beyond the frame of the "postcard" where he lives—mottled sky and osprey swooping low—is the broken glass in the schoolyard. He begins a halfhearted dialogue with Pascal, whose "We wander in times not ours" (ibid., 92) has struck a sympathetic chord. In the ten sections of the poem, Dunn recalls "the winter winter never came" (ibid., 93), the nebulous seasonlessness of the soul that culminated in the bombing in Oklahoma City. If the poet is looking for revelation, he realizes there is no "truth" in the senseless destruction of lives: "Far away, men were pulling bodies from debris, / a moan the sweetest, most hopeful thing" (ibid., 96).

But even as Dunn pulls us deeper into a shared tragedy, he fends us off with a self-conscious voice that moves from the vagaries of weather to the vagaries of language, savoring the doubled sound and near mistake of the phrase "the winter winter never came" (ibid., 89). Remember, he reminds us, this is only a poem.

So how are we to read it? The images serve to clarify and particularize the external landscape. We have no doubt that we are in the suburbs of South Jersey, not all that far from Atlantic City, driving past the yard sale on Clarks Landing Road, on down Chestnut Neck toward Red Wing Lake, looking for number 575 on a mailbox or, if we can't find that, for Sinton's apple orchard and the shack with three cars in front. The interior landscape remains elusive. The attitudes in "Loosestrife" reside in the voice and the way it questions itself, but it's a voice we trust only so far, a voice that brushes the surface but refuses to dig down. The genius of Dunn's voice is that it knows this, and so there is something else at stake. The emotional terrain is so far underground, so close to the core of the earth, that it burns with a restless energy. It wants out.

But Dunn is too cagey even for that. When a student asks him why he's stayed in South Jersey, he replies, "Because it hasn't been imagined yet" (ibid., 96). But the answer does not suffice, and Dunn knows that, too. He worries it over in his mind, trying to find a workable—and worthy—response.

> I should have kept talking until I'd gotten it true.
> Something about what the mouse doesn't know
> and the owl does. Something intolerable
> like that, with which we live. (ibid., 96)

Each of us has, at one time or another, retreated to the lonely internal space Dunn is willing to explore. In the face of such essential loneliness, Dunn's keen wit is keener, his wry irony more ironical.

There must be some significance to Dunn's recurrent use of the word "lone" as a modifier. His interior world is repeatedly withheld, as if at base there's a man defending his privacy. In fact, the poems depend on the reader's recognition of individuality. They carve out a space that is completed only by its underside.

And so a paradox is constructed: the reader becomes aware that the writer is aware of his own ploy—simultaneously confiding and fending off, establishing an intimacy based on the admission that he is using intimacy to ward off further intimacy. Distance becomes part of Dunn's performance as he ironically calls attention to it, comments wryly on the personality traits that court it, noting when—and how—it gets in the way of true connection. Thus he forms a complicit bond with the reader, one that is oddly appealing precisely because the reader is later made aware of his or her own linguistic evasiveness. What isn't said is always invoked by what is being said.

Different Hours explores the disparity between our public and our private lives. The book jacket text reads, "Dunn explores the 'different hours,' not only of one's life, but also of the larger historical and philosophical life beyond the personal." Certainly a poem title like that of "Oklahoma City" (*DH*, 113–14) alerts us to communal experience. In fact, such a title raises—before the fact—red flags: of exploitation, of the possibilities for expected response, or false insight, and of the poet's appropriation of the subject matter. Dunn manages to avoid the pitfalls precisely because this *is* personal. He begins with dry observation:

> The accused chose to plead innocent
> because he was guilty. We allowed such a thing. (ibid., 113)

The story is immediately individualized with an "I" that seems as much an observer as a participant in the communal "we." The speaker is on his way to a party, listening to a survivor's account on the car radio. Life goes on—"not one of us wouldn't be smiling" (ibid.)—and, in this case, the party's banality accentuates the import of the larger issues. The difference here is the *way* in which Dunn is personal. He has always pointed the finger at himself, but here he seems a bit more willing to implicate others as well. The poem circles and circles, moving from the inconceivable event to the all-too-conceivable self and back, as though trying to find the "something large" (ibid.) that it admits outright will always be missing. And still the poem probes for an answer.

At work here is what I would call a deliberate deflation. The event in all its horror is undercut by the fact that it is being reported, then re-reported at the party, reduced to small talk even as it occupies the center of attention. The speaker, rather than imagining the victims, the devastation, the aftermath, is fixated on the perpetrator:

> Oklahoma City was America reduced
> to McVeigh's half-thought-out thoughts.
> Did he know anything about suffering? (ibid.)

The echo of Auden at least suggests that the masters know more about suffering than does McVeigh; poetry is, after all, thought-out thoughts. But that would be far too obvious for a poem by Stephen Dunn, and so we are forced to turn to the last stanza, where he notices two young women whose world was "not wholly incongruent" (ibid., 114) with the world of the speaker. "I had no illusions, not even hopes, / that their beauty had anything to do with goodness" (ibid.). Although the poet describes his own disillusionment, the "I" here has become generic as we face our own dark honesties. Under Dunn's subtle direction, we implicate ourselves.

How has he accomplished this? With orchestral legerdemain, the poem alternates between the world of the party (which ironically contains the world of ideas) and the world of half-thought thoughts (which overlaps with the physical world of pain). We are never in one place for long. Instead, we are forced to see the event in a context, and it happens to be the context in which most of us find ourselves most of the time: we participate peripherally, as observers, and we try to make sense of it. Rights and wrongs eddy in these stanzas, become an alloy of competing loyalties and conflicting ideas. The hole at the center of rationality is set against the rationalism of the Constitution. Science, religion, politics: nothing will serve up an answer. Nothing is transformed.

We're happy enough to watch someone implicate himself but less willing to walk out of a poem fully encumbered. Yet, under the right circumstances, we appreciate the weight of obligation—and that is what gives Dunn's poems their satisfying quality. The significance here is the mesh in which we see our lives and their often-unacted-upon insights so deftly reproduced.

We often think of a poem as being either private or public. But Stephen Dunn manages—over and over—to make his poetry do double duty. By combining the serious with the humorous, the silly with the profound, he moves easily between a personal (and interior) world and the shared space of politics, ethics, and philosophy.

Dunn's poems almost always manage to mean more than they say. My suspicion is that Dunn's inner landscape is even darker and more honest than his guileless speaker is willing to reveal—an idealess, imageless, almost wordless space in which he knows that the fragile body prays to an absent God and goes unheard. If we glimpse that space at all, we do so at an oblique angle, as in Dunn's tribute to silence: "I say the nothing it hears" (*L*, "Homage," 67).

Works Cited

Various passages have been used, with permission, from the *Georgia Review*:

Kitchen, Judith. 1991. "Under the Umbrella." *Georgia Review* 45, no. 1 (Fall): 603–6.

———. 1995. "Fourteen Ways of Looking at Selecteds." *Georgia Review* 49, no. 2 (Summer): 509–11.

———. 1996. "A Convention of Things." *Georgia Review* 50, no. 4 (Winter): 784–87.

———. 2000. "In Pursuit of Elegance." *Georgia Review* 54, no. 4 (Winter): 777–80.

Part Eight

Double-Teaming

Stephen Corey

Smart, sensitive, and sly, Stephen Dunn seems an unlikely candidate for equating capital-L life with a game—not even his lifelong favorite one, the one in which one of his teams caused a blip on the screen of college athletic history, the one in which he was still known as Stevie as he entered adulthood. All those poems in all those books over all those years don't give us a cosmology, which is really just a fancy term for a strategy with rules and boundary lines; Dante and Dunn begin with the same letter, but the notion of circles and levels is so porous and fluid for the latter writer that a reader may be hard pressed to find or even speak of entry and exit points, positions plus or minus, winning and losing, knowing or not.

One must be cautious when encountering something like "Defeats" and "Acceptance," the last of the forty-five "prose pairs" constituting Dunn's *Riffs and Reciprocities*. At the culmination of this most overtly philosophical of Dunn's many books, "Defeats" opens this way:

> Those failures of nerve, not of skill, are the worst. The tentative shot. The safe position we took in the argument. Double defeats, really; where we end up on the sorry side of the score *and* our character's in question. . . . (*RR*, 110)

That "shot" can be so many things, literal or metaphorical, that we have little right to play the biography game, to jump to that guard—we'd call him "point" now, but the term had no currency in the late 1950s—who had the long-range eye, had *the* shot on that Hofstra team when it reached a pinnacle of success not matched before or since. Winning is not all, but neither is losing. "Defeats" continues:

> Better to be overwhelmed and have no excuses. Even when a series of defeats sends us to the bottom of ourselves, at least there's a chance we'll locate some bedrock of dignity, a place below which we won't go. Then we can begin the long climb. Maybe we'll have learned something that can be converted into victory. Or a reason to endure. (ibid., 110)

Paeans to losing are easier to conjure on the heels of a winning-and-more season, and analogy is often easier to stomach than straight-up actuality: if we make "the bottom of ourselves" the division or conference cellar rather than the dark night of the soul, climbing in the standings—or failing to do so—feels less imposing. But would Stephen Dunn try to slip us that game-of-life stuff?

If we allow ourselves to think so, we could have more than an acceptable level of fun with a poem such as "Halves" from *Local Time*, a collection that preceded *Riffs and Reciprocities* by a decade—and was a decade closer to Dunn's basketball days of glory. A basketball game at the college level is divided into halves—so, yes, we get day/night, young/old, and silence/speech as countermeasures in the whole of this poem, and we are told,

> Soon the equally mysterious world of women
>   and men, of momentary
> common agreement and wild misunderstanding,
> will impose itself naturally on the simplest event. (*LT*, 24)

So why can't we take the thought that "we were balancing // two delicate and always vanishing halves" (ibid., 25) as a reference, in part, to that fleeting time on the hardwood? And when we hear at poem's end "the alarm, and the body rises / to yearn for what is here and gone" (ibid., 24), why should we be kept from the alarming quality of the game buzzer—a beautiful symphony's final chord for the winner, a buzz saw cutting into the heart of the loser?

Still, here be monsters for an overzealous reader, who before the poet knows it may turn to "Cut and Break" from *Everything Else in the World* and think, "Dunn is even putting critical basketball terms into his titles!" Note that these "terms" initially refer to the practical work of stonemasons building a wall at the speaker's new home—"new" as in he's taken up residence with his new love after having "torn apart" his marriage. In the literal labor, these masons "had to cut and break // before they could make anything whole" (*EE*, 86). But the speaker is seeking reconciliation and justification as he ponders the masons' so-solid creation, and he tells himself "my love had a way of finding me / wherever I was. And soon I'd meet a man / whose decline in tennis matched mine" (ibid., 87). So, now, life continuing to go by as it tends to do, the game the man may have taken up to assuage the diminution of his abilities in his earlier sports love is in turn diminishing. The young guard who feared the "tentative shot" was also the player who had to "cut" and "break"—that is, take aggressive action—to succeed; the middle-aged tennis player must "cut" shots to "break" service—and to avoid being broken.

Overzealous reading? What if we leave behind such seeming stretchers of analytical storytelling and turn to a realm of poetic reality and plain speaking, one where

> It's probably a Sunday morning
> in a pickup game, and it's clear
> you've begun to leave
> fewer people behind.
>
> Your fakes are as good as ever,
> but when you move
> you're like the Southern Pacific
> the first time a car kept up with it,
>
> your opponent at your hip,
> with you all the way
> to the rim. Five years earlier
> he'd have been part of the air

that stayed behind you
in your ascendance.
    On the sidelines they're saying,
He's lost a step. (*DH*, "Losing Steps" 63)

Sunday morning. The guys ought to be in church, and . . . oh, the court must *be* the church. And that seemingly innocent "begun to leave" is like begun to go out of this world, to die, and that slowing like the old train makes "you" a part of the past unable to live up to (or in) the present, to say nothing of the future. And that "ascendance" (which can also be spelled "ascendence," if you're not in the market for the dance of life) is something Mr. Alighieri would certainly play around with—but this is the twenty-first century, so maybe "you" is just jumping.

The narrator can hear those sideline whispers, but we can't tell whether "you" catches them. However,

In a few more years
it's adult night in a gymnasium
streaked with the abrupt scuff marks
of high schoolers, and another step

leaves you like a wire
burned out in a radio.
You're playing defense,
someone jukes right, goes left,

and you're not fooled
but he's past you anyway,
dust in your eyes,
a few more points against you. (ibid., 64)

Isn't the narrator talking to and about himself, which is why he is smarting from that dust, perhaps can smell that burned wire and "hear" the silence it creates? That crappy old gym isn't much of a church, nor does all this awareness seem to do a damned bit of good while the hero is slipping from not getting ahead to getting left behind.

Then comes the third and final section of "Losing Steps"—a poem published first in the *Georgia Review* (for which I work) prior to its appearance in the Pulitzer Prize–winning *Different Hours* (2001):

> Suddenly you're fifty;
> if you know anything about steps
> you're playing chess
> with an old, complicated friend.
>
> But you're walking to a schoolyard
> where kids are playing full-court,
> telling yourself
> the value of experience, a worn down
>
> basketball under your arm,
> your legs hanging from your waist
> like misplaced sloths in a country
> known for its cheetahs and its sunsets. (*DH*, 64–65)

More time has gone by, and what we thought the speaker seemed to have learned in section two is receding rather than advancing: he doesn't know enough to be playing a game like chess, knows only his whimsically passionate belief that he might somehow outsmart both the world and time.

In the opening scene from John Updike's harshly brilliant early novel *Rabbit, Run* (1960), the "aging" Rabbit Angstrom—he's twenty-six—insinuates himself into a back-alley game being played by a half-dozen "real boys." Rabbit whips up on them, even when it's he and one boy against the other five, but the victory is unseemly and even sleazy feeling. In the very act of trying to replay his past,

Rabbit recollects the swift arc of an athlete's rise and fall: "They've not forgotten him; worse, they've never heard of him" (1960, 9).

But I think of this other literary basketball game for its circumstance, not for its tone. Stephen Dunn's much-more-aging protagonist has a gut faith in himself that we can admire, a forward-leaning hope (tempered by the self-deprecating sloth image) rather than a backward-looking sense of loss.

Also in *Riffs and Reciprocities* is a pair titled "Faces/Bodies" (*RR*, 64–65). In "Faces,"

> High school reunions are the proving grounds. Say, one's twenty-fifth. So interesting to see how character can overcome bone structure. Pretty, handsome, cute—how those attributes, those intimidations, once seemed permanent. No need to mark the many ways faces go bad. Or the sadness, for example, of remaining cute. Time is good only to those who survive its accidents, who manage to befriend it. Yet what advantages they have, the ones who start so well. They are the panthers and leopards created by an unjust god and allowed to move among the hyenas and goats. Sometimes, at any rate. We never knew how intelligence could insinuate its way into eyes and mouth, could become a kind of glamor. We never knew one could grow a face. . . . (*RR*, 64)

Those panthers and leopards here, those cheetahs in "Losing Steps"—do they take us back to the "Defeats" with which we began, those "failures of nerve"? No, they go more to "Acceptance"—and note that Dunn uses the singular here. What acceptance? Well,

> Certainly not of things as they are. Certainly not of a cosmology that posits we're insignificant, though of course we are. And aren't some of us less insignificant than others? The personal is what matters—this defeat, those mundanities, a few triumphs. And then the expansion of what personal means: another person's tragedy, a country's collapse. The larger the personal becomes the greater our helplessness. Better to be furious at one thing, become radiant

> with purpose. Better to love links and rhythms than all-embracing answers. . . . (*RR*, 111)

That "you" in the closing lines of "Losing Steps" is furious at one thing, is radiant with purpose—as is Dunn, there in behind the "you": the poet of five decades and fifteen or more books, the lover of links and rhythms in his lines and sentences.

In "Bodies," hard upon those panther and leopard faces, Dunn begins with "The good zoo of them, the names we could name them if we dared to begin!" (*RR*, 65). The "good" here, likely as not, doesn't include the self: "Difficult, after a while, to love one's own—its inconsistencies, the classic diminutions, the terror of having only one" (ibid., 65). This is particularly true, I think, if that one body has been deployed in arduous physical activities increasingly less possible, however sharp or gradual its turning away from the stronger and finer points of movement. Updike's Rabbit is cowed by the passage of youth and time, but Dunn concludes "Bodies" with this assertion and these emphasizing italics: "If bodies had epitaphs, I'd want mine to read: *It rattled its cage. It wouldn't be appeased*" (ibid., 65).

In his poem "Mon Semblable" (*NS*, 229–30), Dunn begins with

> I like things my way
> every chance I get.
> A limit doesn't exist
>
> when it comes to that.
> But please, don't confuse
> what I say with honesty.
>
> Isn't honesty the open yawn
> the unimaginative love
> more than truth? (ibid., 229)

And he closes that poem:

I'll say I love you,

which will lead, of course,
to disappointment,
but those words unsaid

poison every next moment.
I will try to disappoint you
better than anyone ever has. (ibid., 230)

So, I am back to my opening question about what claims Stephen Dunn might be willing to make concerning basketball and Life. Answer: of *course* he might choose to equate the two, given that he is smart, sensitive, and sly. He is always dealing with—and isn't every strong poet, whatever his or her overriding vision?—"the expansion of what personal means."

In "Relentlessly Interesting," an interview included in this book but originally published as part of a lengthy feature on Dunn in the *Georgia Review*, Dunn responds to a question about his relationship with books during his high school years by saying, "It's amazing that I had time to read them. I was devoting most of my time, it seems in retrospect, to playing basketball." Then, a moment later, "My secret life was books; my overt life was that of an athlete." Could we possibly think that when the great wheel turned to place books—their writing as well as their reading—on top, in full light and sight, the other life or lives would go away?

No, we must think just the opposite. However mysteriously obsessions may develop, they seldom go away; a certain amount of shifting may take place, but obliteration is the exception. We may read the athlete—Dunn's sensibility and knowledge and body awareness—into the poet, Dunn's poems, anytime we are moved to do so. We will misread some moments, some details, but the game plan will be a solid one. As we were told back in the early days of our learning to play the great American game, the hoop has a much greater diameter up close than what the eye perceives from court level, and the double-team properly executed can be overwhelmingly successful.

Works Cited

Updike, John. 1960. *Rabbit, Run*. New York: Fawcett World Library.

Mount Holyoke, 1992

Pam Houston

The year was 1992. My first book of short stories, *Cowboys Are My Weakness* (2005) had come out in January from W. W. Norton to a better reception than anyone could have, in a million years, imagined. I was still in graduate school, a creative writing PhD program where I was making $4,500 a year teaching comp, but I was suddenly being contacted by magazines, writer's conferences, universities, all offering me work. I'd been invited to teach at the Mount Holyoke Writer's Conference, which took place that year in early June along with Jack Driscoll, Gerry Stern, Linda Gregg, and Stephen Dunn.

Four days before I was meant to go to Mount Holyoke, I was out planting tomatoes in my garden when the phone rang. When I heard my father's voice on the line I knew it had to be bad news. My mother was the only one who ever called, and she called often, and she would fill my father in in little bursts during the conversation while he kept his eyes trained on whatever golf tournament was on TV.

She had died in bed, the night before, right beside him. She had complained of feeling poorly at about eleven, and he had asked her if she wanted to go to the hospital, and she had said no, and they had gone to sleep, and when he woke up the next morning she was dead. She was eleven years his junior, active, athletic, young for her age. She was an anorexic and an alcoholic and was taking Vioxx, but if there was anyone who knew how lethal a combination that was in those days, it wasn't us. She had been and would always be the good parent. None of us, me least of all, had expected that she would die first.

I was in Pennsylvania early the next morning. We buried her the day after that. My father and I were both in shock, I see now, and we had never really learned how to talk to one another. When I was a child, I was afraid of his anger and his occasionally violent outbursts, the most serious of which left me with a broken femur when I was four years old. In the years since I'd been old enough to "take him," as one close friend put it, I had made no effort to understand his conservative values, and he had made no effort to understand why I had dedicated my life to the arts.

On my second morning in Pennsylvania, I went around town collecting menus from restaurants that offered delivery, and educated him in using the washing machine, the dryer, and the dishwasher (he was shocked to discover that if you put glasses in the dishwater right side up they wind up full of water.) On the third morning, I loaded up my mother's now redundant car and drove to Holyoke as if this detour home had always been part of the plan.

It was only when I saw the giant bouquet of lilies that W. W. Norton had sent to my Mount Holyoke dorm room that I realized it was probably strange that I hadn't cancelled the teaching engagement. I am a workaholic from a family of workaholics and our first commandment was always that if you have been hired to do a job you show up on time and ready to give it everything you've got. My father felt the same way about work, and would never have suggested I stay and help him get his bearings. "No one had cut off our legs" was one of his favorite expressions, and I was in the classroom, ready to go when the conference began.

The great Carol Houck Smith, my editor, and, also, of course, Stephen's, was also in attendance that week. It is only at this moment that I realize what amazingly good timing that was, to have my surrogate mother on hand the week after my real one passed away. To say nothing of Stephen, and Gerry, who Carol also edited, and Jack Driscoll; all broad-shouldered soft touches, all men well acquainted with the labyrinths of grief.

The next morning, out of the blue, my father showed up in Mount Holyoke, the first of several drop-in visits over the next decade and a half until his death. These visits always occurred at writers' conferences, usually somewhere lovely (Squaw Valley, Taos, Provincetown) never at my home, and always without warning. He would show up in one or another Cadillac convertible dressed in yellow slacks and a fleur-de-lis tie, expecting to be fed and watered and included in the parties. But this time, no one raised an eyebrow, no one asked if I had known he was coming. The conference simply absorbed him and made him feel at home. Stephen and Jack played tennis with him each morning. Gerry entertained him with stories of the old neighborhoods of New York. I don't know if my father realized how lucky he was to be in the company of men who were so particularly articulate in the language of sorrow, who were so skillful at offering solace absent of pity, but none of their kindnesses were lost on me.

I had gotten to know Stephen and Gerry because of Carol. It is commonly known that her writers were her family, and she loved to pull various groups of us together at the conferences she attended. She had introduced me to Stephen's poetry when we first started working on "Cowboys" together, three years before, and I had devoured his poems, reading the books so many times I could recite many of them from memory. I read "Decorum" (*NS*, 24–25) at the beginning of every class I taught; I read "Something Like Happiness" (*NS*, 19–20) to my fellow PhD students, mired as we often were in Foucault and Derrida; I read "The Woman with Five Hearts" (*NS*, 17) to all potential suitors to gauge their reactions; and I read "Some Things I Wanted to Say to You" (*NS*, 21–22) to everyone I loved. I believed that Stephen had written "To My Friend in Love with the Wrong Man Again" (*NS*, 120) for me, even though we had not yet met when he wrote it, and "Missing" (*L*, 50–51) was surely written from the point of view of, not of the woman I was, but the one I wanted to be. I had debated for hours with the poet Jane Hirschfield about the emotional bent of the last line of "From Underneath" (*LT*, 74–75). I had talked at length with Stephen Dobyns about the "abstraction poems" he and Stephen had written as a kind of game to play together: "Happiness" (*NS*, 220), "Tenderness" (*NS*, 211–12), "Kindness" (*NS*, 215–16), and so on. I mention all this by way of pointing out that I was fluent in Stephen's work, more fluent than he might have expected a barely thirty-year-old short story writer to be, and I say with all humility, I think he was at least a little charmed by my fluency.

It is easy to see now that at Mount Holyoke that summer, everyone was looking out for me in ways I may have been too much in shock to fully recognize at the time. Carol came to my room every night and asked me to tell her stories about my mother. Jack Driscoll sat with me for an hour while I showed him the stills I had brought from her Broadway—and more often—off-Broadway days. Gerry Stern teased me endlessly about everything, including my habit of showing up at events with my hair still wet. And though I assured him it was because my hair has always been too dry to tolerate a blow drier, he insisted I did it only to be sexy, something I think of to this day every time I walk into a public space with my hair even slightly damp. I hadn't asked for any of this care, would have said I didn't need it, but no one ever asked if I needed it—they just showed up for me day after day.

Which brings me to the remarkable thing Stephen did that week: he allowed me to choose all the poems for his reading, not only which poems he would read but also the order in which he would read them. I asked him if I could do it, and after laughing a little taken-aback sort of laugh, he agreed.

It's hard for me to understand, twenty years and a whole writing career later, not only why I made the request, but how on earth I had the nerve to do so. I was a baby writer, who'd had unexpected success with a book that had, of all things, the word "Cowboys" in the title, and Stephen, at that point, had published eight books of poems. I had immeasurable admiration for his poetry and poetry in general, having been a graduate student at Utah in the days of Larry Levis and Mark Strand, who each in their own way suffered no fools.

Maybe something in me understood, in spite of my denial, that losing my mother would untether me from the earth in a way that would take years to comprehend, and choosing Stephen's reading gave me, in that instant, some small measure of control. Maybe I was looking for approval from someone vaguely parental, in the same way that, when I was ten, I would memorize all the individual player stats of the Philadelphia Phillies to try to impress my dad. Maybe I thought, as I have so many times when life deals a blow, that a deep intimacy with a particular body of literature would save me.

Stephen didn't ask me why I wanted to choose his reading. He didn't ask me who I thought I was, or what I thought I knew, or whether or not I'd considered that there might be new poems he was dying to try out on the crowd. He didn't ask me if I was finally losing it, as anyone might, four days after the unexpected death of her mother.

"I would be gratified to see what you came up with," he said, in his most gentlemanly undertone, and so I sat at his sunny table and made a playlist for his reading, which he studied thoughtfully before tucking it into the front of his book.

I don't believe my father had ever read a poem in his life, prior to his arrival in Mount Holyoke that year, but he attended Stephen's reading in the chapel, where Stephen read all the poems I had requested, in essentially the order I requested them. I couldn't be entirely sure because he had the only copy of my list. He ended the reading, as I had asked him to, with the poem "Loves" (*NS*, 275–87).

When the reading was over, my father said, "You know, I never would have thought of poetry as much of anything at all, but the way he put things together was so powerful. I was," and at this he sounded frankly bewildered, "actually moved." I did not ask him what he thought I had been doing with my life for the last two decades. I did not invite him to come live with me in Colorado so that we might read literature together and make up for lost time. I bought him a copy of *Landscape at the End of the Century*, and had Stephen sign it for him, to take when it was time for him to go back home alone.

In a Different Hour

Collaboration, Revision, and Friendship

Lawrence Raab

Many years ago—and I really don't want to remember exactly how young we were—Stephen Dunn, a friend but not yet a collaborator, was traveling from New Jersey to Yaddo, the artists' colony in Saratoga Springs, New York. He stopped for the night at our house. During the course of the evening, I recall bemoaning the fact that I hadn't written a poem—maybe not even tried to write one—in over a year. I had writer's block, I announced, as if it were an identifiable disease. I had not yet learned the wisdom of William Stafford's famous, or infamous, remark that there is no such thing as writer's block; all you have to do is lower your standards.

Of course Stafford didn't mean you ultimately aim for less. You just have to give yourself a break to get started, and accept whatever occurs to you because "something always occurs" to us, as Stafford says in his essay "A Way of Writing" (1978, 18). Let the act of writing carry you beyond your first inevitably dull words, to better words, better sentences that may give you access to something waiting in your mind "ready for sustained attention." This is the writer's daily work—putting some words down, then rearranging them, adding, then subtracting, looking for a shape, a focus, "the poem's informing principle," as Stephen Dunn puts it in his wonderful essay "The Good, the Not So Good" (*WLB*, 38). If that's inspiration—and I like to think so—it's *earned* by the work of writing, not given as a gift of the gods, like an autumn leaf fluttering down significantly on the poet's head.

Those are some of the things I didn't know when Stephen and I and my wife, Judy, were having dinner. "Writer's block blah blah

blah," I continued. (I was about to spend some time at Yaddo also, arriving a few days after Stephen.) "Well," Stephen said amiably, "when you get to Yaddo, do what I do—write a new poem every day." I didn't know Stephen did this; the idea seemed inconceivable, even appalling. "I can't do that," I declared.

"Yes you can," Stephen said.

"But how?"

"You just do it."

I knew that was true, but what a strange truth. You tell yourself to do it and you just do it. So I followed Stephen's advice, and that summer we started showing each other a new poem each day. Over the years, we developed rules. We could continue to revise a poem, but only for another day, to avoid getting stuck on it. Then a harder rule: a draft of the poem had to be done by lunchtime. Of course almost all poets need trustworthy readers, but we were compressing the process radically. After lunch we'd work more on the poem, play tennis, then have drinks and show each other what we'd done, then work some more, and maybe look at the poems again later in the evening.

At times, what I'd come up with by noon was something I could see promise in, even believe was already a poem, shiny and perfect. Most often, whatever we had at those moments were pieces of language that were just beginning to assert their power over us, just starting to ask to be honored as "poems." In daily life, they would have found their way into the manila folder called "Notes" and perhaps languished there. But in those weeks at Yaddo, it was all work in progress at its earliest and most perilous state. Later I often couldn't believe I'd shown Stephen the incoherent mess I'd cobbled together that morning. But we learned how to manage these moments—Stephen and I—what to be particular about, what to suggest, and how to find opportunity in the apparently incoherent. "This poem," I recall Stephen saying many times, "needs to make another move. Maybe half-way through."

"What sort of move?" I'd ask, and he'd usually say he didn't know, it was, after all, my poem.

"Just go somewhere else."

Infuriating as this advice could be, it has stayed with me as a writer and as a teacher. When you think you're stuck, I tell my students, just go somewhere else. You believe your poem is about this beggar on the streets of Manhattan, but maybe he's there only to take you to a different place. So after the line about his raggedy pants (or maybe before that rather pallid line) write: "Meanwhile, in Argentina. . . ." Why Argentina? Because you haven't been there. But if you don't like South America, go to Paris, or back to the room you lived in as a child, the one with the monsters in the closet, the one you had to leave when your parents divorced, and you cried, or refused to cry—whatever truth the poem needs.

Yet how easy it can be at noon at Yaddo (or MacDowell, our other haven), and at such an early, tender moment in the life of the poem, to be dismissive, or know-it-all, or the opposite: too full of a kind of praise that hasn't yet been earned, inattentive to the wildness the poem might only have begun to hint at. We learned to be *appropriately* critical, meaning helpful, respectful of the whole endeavor, but insistent as well. Maybe once a summer Stephen would read a poem, nod, and say, "Yes, you got it." How much better my sandwich tasted after that!

That first summer at Yaddo after my "writer's block," I wrote twenty-nine poems in as many days. Stephen probably wrote the same, maybe more. (Sometimes he'd sneak in a really short one to make the numbers add up.) But it was good to be competitive, as is inevitably the case with Stephen. In the afternoons we played tennis. Stephen always won. Sometimes I'd suggest his victory was a sign that my poem that morning was better. He'd say it was my turn to buy a new can of balls for tomorrow's game.

I think of this as "collaboration" rather than just "criticism" because of how quickly our poems would confront each other's sensibilities, how much we would risk and how much we would borrow, or steal, from each other. "You can't write a serious poem about space aliens," Stephen once declared, suggesting that what I'd done that morning was doomed. But I kept on and yes, Stephen finally said, "You got it." Years later, he also wrote a successful poem about aliens, which I was very critical of for a long time.

We'd try to make things harder (or more playful) for each other by coming up with assignments; some we'd both do, some were designed for the other person. Here are two short ones Stephen gave me a few years back: (1) Write the poem that can't be written; (2) Write a poem called "Against Compassion." I did both. The second ended up being called "Against Compassion," and the first "The Poem That Can't Be Written." Here's one assignment from the same group that I couldn't do: Write a poem in which every fourth line obstructs where the poem appears to be going. Great assignment; too much math.

Sometimes, when we failed to get into a colony together, we'd find other ways of meeting for a couple of weeks. Once I rented a house outside Peterborough since Stephen had gotten into MacDowell and I hadn't. Sometimes we'd e-mail each other from home, making sure we responded as quickly as possible. For a while, we sent each other lines from our own earlier poems that hadn't worked out—to be used, changed, or ignored. Every so often I'll see a poem of Stephen's and think, "Isn't that a line I wrote fifteen years ago?" It pleases me to wonder, as if it were evidence of another self I didn't know I had.

We also published a chapbook of "actual" collaborations called *Winter at the Caspian Sea*, poems in which we wrote alternate lines, folding the paper over so that only the second of the two lines could be seen, in the manner of the surrealists' "Exquisite Corpse" game. Everything was done quickly, and no revisions were allowed; our motto, if we needed one, would have been Robert Frost's "Play's the thing." Our aim was to allow for as many surprises as possible. The second collaborative method we tried was designed like this: Each of us would write four lies (and yes, that's "lies," not "lines"), one of which had to be more elaborate than the others, on an agreed-upon subject. We could use both lists, but we gave ourselves only fifteen minutes to write the poem. Why lies? To avoid the ordinary, to move the material as quickly as possible into metaphorical territory. One pair of these poems was about the sky, the other about silence. Here are the first nine lines from the two poems based on lies about the sky. From "Sky":

> At night among the stars we see
> the ever-present animals and heroes,
> which preceded us. The gods
> we placed there have fallen,
> and the sky is thinner now
> without them, lighter than
> an invisible hand. It's amazing
> we can touch it, that it's as close
> as it is far.

And from "The Other Side of the Sky":

> When God was waiting
> to be invented, the sky
> was thinner. You
> could have touched it,
> then turned away
> without the fear of being seen,
> gone back
> to your father's house
> where everything was quiet.

In the chapbook, we didn't identify whose poem was whose. Reading them now I'm not sure. I like not being sure.

This was "play" and we kept it that way, while also believing that the beginning of any poem was also play. I want to give one example of an assignment triggering a more consequential poem. I know some of my assignments provoked poems from Stephen, but he's too good at covering his tracks. So I have to settle for one of his assignments and one of my poems. This is from a list of six assignments he gave me last summer at Yaddo. One assignment mandated the inclusion of Muddy Waters, Aretha Franklin, and Glenn Campbell, and had to begin "In the secret, dark corridors of Cedar Rapids," which, except for the specificity of Cedar Rapids, already sounded like a line of mine, and not a very good one (which Stephen probably knew). The assignment I finally completed was the most outrageously complicated of any of Stephen's assignments over all the years (so far), and so intricate that I finally saw the only way I could respond to it was to steal it and turn it into the poem it already almost was.

First, the assignment:

> Write a poem from the viewpoint of someone who used to be in love with an imaginary woman. Your speaker is only sure that he wishes to have power, wishes to control the terms of his life. His stutter, or other handicap, keeps getting in the way. You'll need an adjective for bedroom, and an adjective that makes the forest he keeps returning to seem run-down, a kind of bad neighborhood. Then an adjective before "path," which changes the meaning of it. The imaginary woman should appear at some point, throwing everything into question. Think of your poem as an examination of an obsession, and perhaps the sadness of being cured of it.

My poem is called "A Difficult Assignment," and appropriately it was published in an issue of the *Cortland Review* devoted to Stephen's work. I see now that I failed at the end to find the adjective that would change the meaning of "path." In fact I never looked for it. The poem didn't seem to need it. Perhaps the adjective's absence is a secret sign of my resistance to the assignment's authority. Or perhaps it's something only Stephen and I—and now you—know is missing.

A Difficult Assignment

for and after Stephen Dunn

You'll need an adjective for bedroom,
another that makes the forest you keep returning to

seem run-down, a kind of bad neighborhood.
Then an adjective before "path," which changes

the meaning of it, as if you weren't going to end up
where you planned. Or the opposite—

you can't help where you're going. And where
would that be? It's up to you, but remember,

in all of this you should be alone
although at some point a beautiful woman

must appear, throwing everything into question.
That's when the false note rings true.

Maybe she has something to say about Cedar Rapids
or Muddy Waters. She's imaginary,

she can say anything you want. Yes,
how much she desires you is one kind of beginning,

but another might involve looking carefully
at the flowers at the edge of the forest, asking her

their names, then suggesting you don't care
where the path leads if that's where she wants to go.

All that I've been describing—and there's much more, since we've been doing this for over twenty-five years—results in making poems easier to begin and harder to finish. We each keep the other on track, changing the meaning of "path" as we go.

Hard as it is to write poems, sometimes it seems even harder to write about them. These days in particular, criticism appears to have turned into the consideration of mere subject matter, or the dismissal of content in favor of clever but impersonal games. The critic finds it more and more difficult to talk about language, about tone of voice, about the attitude that uses and transforms the subject. So both Stephen and I have become poets who write in a "plain" style and produce "quiet," "accessible" poems about "every-day life."

Tack on an apparent moral and you come close to what Robert Frost discovered was his way to fame: the pretty postcard of snow falling into a dark woods watched by a man who doesn't want to be seen; the desire to choose one road over another, even when both are exactly the same; the bravery of standing up for the tearing down of walls even as you yourself set out to mend them. These, I believe, are three of the greatest poems of the twentieth century. And they became famous because readers could love them and leave out their complications. They're designed to both pat the reader on the head and spin him around until he's dizzy, maybe even lost enough to find himself. They include woods and roads and stone walls—all the *stuff* of a Frostian landscape—but they're *about* what they've hidden, the broken drinking goblet from the children's playhouse under a spell so "the wrong ones can't find it, / So can't get saved, as Saint Mark says they mustn't" (1969, 379) Where did *that* voice suddenly come from?

Dunn, like Frost, is widely and rightly praised for his accessibility and for his deft use of "ordinary" materials. Yet in the best Dunn poems, as in the best Frost poems, perceptions are deceptive and accessibility is a tactic, luring the reader into a complicated, provocative, and sometimes terrifying moral landscape. "The ear does it," Robert Frost famously wrote in a 1914 letter. "The ear is the only true writer and the only true reader." Nobody working today has a better ear than Stephen Dunn—an ear for the insinuating revelations of American speech, and an even better ear for how the colloquial, the everyday, and the recognizable can become what we call "poetry"—memorable speech, sentences that are hard to get rid of.

> And somewhere a philosopher is erasing
> "time's empty passing" because he's seen
> a woman in a ravishing dress.
> In a different hour he'll put it back. (70)

About these lines of Stephen's maybe I once said, "Is 'empty' really the best word?" Or: "What about another adjective—'red,' perhaps—before 'dress'?" Maybe I said, "Why are there always ravishing women in your poems?" Maybe I just said, "Yes, you got it."

These four lines are the end of the title poem of Stephen's collection *Different Hours.* A lesser poet would have used the moment to choose sides, suggesting the triumph of the physical world over abstract thinking. But Dunn knows better. What engages him is the continuing tension between beauty and circumstance, between the truth of the world and the truth of what we want it to be. At one moment we are overwhelmed, and then we think differently. We change our minds; we revise our lives. The revisions of thought—and the subsequent transformations of the imagination—are Dunn's central subjects, and his poems are enactments of those concerns. The reader is not told what to think: the reader is seduced into the process of thinking, as if by a good friend who believes deeply in the value of disagreement.

Then a beautiful woman in a ravishing red dress walks past. You're sitting in a sidewalk café drinking coffee. Once she might have seen you, turned, maybe smiled. Now she continues down the street into her own particular future. The sky clouds over. A little wind flaps the striped umbrella above your table. Maybe it will rain, maybe not. Time passes like this—empty *and* ravishing. You're desolate, then amazed.

Works Cited

Frost, Robert. 1969. "Directive." In *The Poetry of Robert Frost: The Collected Poems.* New York: Holt, Rinehart, and Winston. 377–79.

Stafford, William. 1978. "A Way of Writing." In *Writing the Australian Crawl: Views on the Writer's Vocation.* Ann Arbor: University of Michigan Press. 17–20.

"Let Things Darken as They Will"

The Revision Process

Lisa Honaker

If, as Stephen Dunn has said, it is his "habit of mind to resist," to question existing truths and expectations, to mistrust even his own ideas and words, revision is more than good poetic practice: it is the principle that defines his poetry. Dunn's contention that a good poet must have an attraction to the blank page, to the freedom and possibility it presents, makes revision the logical consequence of that attraction.

His decision to make revision the focus of *Stephen Dunn: Poems, A Retrospective*, a manuscript exhibit of his work mounted at the Richard Stockton College of New Jersey in 2010 and again in 2012, provides greater insight into how his habit of resistance translates into craft at the same time that it gestures beyond it. Featuring wall art created from scans of manuscripts mostly culled from the (then) yet to be published *Here and Now* (2011), this exhibit presented revision as a live process—not only the formal practice of distillation we might expect of a mature poet but a continual effort after dislocation as well.

Drafts of individual poems from the exhibit—numbering from two to more than fifty—show us a process about which it is difficult to generalize. All of the poems undergo significant change between their first and last drafts. Dunn makes large-scale revisions, going well beyond adjusting individual words and phrases (although there is plenty of that) very late in the process, with poems undergoing frequent changes to endings and titles, their very shape and implications shifting in even their "final" drafts.

To see Dunn's revision process is to unsettle our vision of his poems as "finished," to undo the decisions about language and form he has made and reinstate the choices that craft has made invisible. We are able to see published poems as themselves provisional—the idea implicit in this essay's epigraph, which, we might note, puts no time limits on revision.

Decades pass, for instance, between Dunn's composition of "Full Circle on a Half Turn" in 1964 and the complete makeover it undergoes to become the title poem in *Here and Now*. His work on this poem gives us a vision of the first draft as both a launching and reference point for revision. The 1964 piece is a love poem, though it demands that we put that love in quotation marks and attend to its darker manifestations. The poem describes a relationship, now seemingly past, in which the speaker finds himself in the grip of an attraction, the romance of which is undercut by a focus on its debilitating effects:

> You were the careful one. As definite
> as sky. The one who'd tiptoe
> into passion and cut it in half
> with your mind. The innuendo of ice
>
> behind the iris. Clear-day
> skating on your eye. Stare-me-
> down to a blink anytime
> you wanted. You were mine
>
> in the sense an object owns its owner.
> I was the run-amuck. As tentative
> as sky. The one whose passion multiplied
> geometrically in the round. Underbelly,
>
> (a word reserved for animals),
> I played guitars. Tamed by your
> ability to catch my breath. My
> nervous eyes unable to fix. I became
>
> rational to the point of lethargy. Wild as death.

2008's "Full Circle," the first of eleven drafts, is Dunn's return to this subject, signaling its relation to this earlier poem through its title and through a further reference to that title in the body of the poem. This later version is so different from its predecessor that it is initially hard to see it as a "revision" of that poem at all:

> Thee and Thou: dead words
> evocative of an old, unequal relationship
> I once needed to break off.
> Back then, though, I admit to loving
> the language of reverence, and still
> sometimes miss its ornamental stateliness,
> its Sunday clothes.
>
> But now I want
> something more mutual, like lust
> felt at exactly the same time.
> At least I want the Thou in my life
> to desire me, and our language to be alive,
> slanged into truth,
>
> indicative of both of us
> having arrived full circle
> after a scary half turn. Here and Now
> are lovely, simple words.
> I want all the playgrounds in town
> to be open until dark,
>
> and when the dark comes
> with all its grandeur and bearing
> with it its ancient fears, I want
> for none of us to be its supplicant,
> but perhaps to exult and boogie in it
> all the way home. (June 2008)

In this revision, Dunn looks back at that earlier draft's conception and language of love, and redefines both from a new, somewhat more mature vantage point. No longer focused on the differences in character, which we see in the first version's oppositions between "the careful one," whose icy nature gave her the whip hand in the relationship and the speaker himself, "the run-amuck," this new version seeks something more mutual, something that defies our preconceptions and expectations about what it means to fall and to be in love. Though Dunn has the speaker in this fresh draft admit "to loving the language of reverence," he associates with the past and that "old, unequal relationship / I once needed to break off," he now wants "our language to be alive / slanged into truth." Such a dynamic puts into stark relief the earlier poem's "object owning its owner" and the inherent inequality and stasis of that phrase.

While we see no revisions as wholesale as those in this first 2008 draft in those that follow until the fall, the changes we do see record Dunn's ongoing efforts to move the poem's language beyond existing frames of reference and description. In fact, the poem becomes "Here and Now" and gains a dedication "to Barbara," in its fifth draft, signaling a shift away from the orientation offered by the 1964 poem (though references to it remain in the body of the work), insisting on immediacy and specificity, on a present that demands a living language. In the sixth draft, the speaker proposes something

> part Motown,
> part Williams, perhaps a dash
>
> of King James, slanged and elevated
> into something we can call our own—
> the greatest story as yet untold,
> tender and seemingly hopeless

"Part Williams" has replaced the fourth draft's "part Ecclesiastes," and Dunn continues to revise this bit of lively, charming wordplay for several more drafts. But in the poem's tenth version, Dunn deletes this portion altogether. A living language, the language of mutuality, this revision suggests, will not and cannot be an amalgam of allusions. Dunn, like his speaker, must move beyond their comforting appeal to get to what he's after: something as alive and as propulsive as "lust felt at exactly the same time."

In the context of such demands, it makes sense that in the final two drafts, Dunn also dismisses the celebratory dances he played with over the course of his revisions. By the final version, gone are the "boogie" (draft 1), the "moonwalk" (draft 2), and the "rumba" (drafts 4 and 6 through 9) as well as the playgrounds "open until dark" and the childish pleasures of "finding our way home," "on lamplit streets, without retribution, / kicking a can, stepping on cracks" (draft 11). The need to publicly "exult" is gone. There will be no more bravado, no more already articulated images of delight in new love. In the version of the poem that appears in *Here and Now*, the closing lines define a more private, less proscribed vision:

> Let night come
> with its austere grandeur,
> ancient superstitions and fears.
> It can do us no harm.
> We'll put some music on,
> open the curtains, let things darken
> as they will.

A quiet confidence informs these lines, proceeding from a receptivity to, rather than a defiance of, what will come. The speaker and his partner have arrived home. Whatever happens after they "put some music on" remains immanent, beyond enunciation.

While it takes forty-four years for Dunn to reach "Here and Now," the path to "Connubial" is considerably shorter—a matter of months rather than years—with Dunn returning to the more elusive text of the original draft, ultimately rejecting its expansion and elaboration, even its two title changes. In March 2008, Laure-Anne Bosselaar and Dunn exchanged e-mails in which they discussed the verb tense in "Connubial," this "amazing short poem" he sent her:

Because with alarming accuracy
she'd been identifying patterns
I was unaware of—this tic, that
tendency, like the way I've mastered
the language of intimacy
in order to conceal how I felt—

I knew I was in danger
of being terribly understood.

Bosselaar asks why Dunn has used the past perfect tense, and he replies,

> In one version I had it in the present tense, but for me two things are accomplished by the way I have it now.
>
> One (and curiously), the action seems more immediate because "she'd been" suggests recently, as opposed to "she identifies patterns," which suggests what she does all the time. I want the speaker's realization ("I knew . . .") to directly follow what she HAD BEEN DOING, not what she always does.
>
> The second reason has to do with sound. I like the pattern of d's throughout, especially how "understood" glances off of "mastered." The present tense feels flatter. (29 March 2008)

This version (and the revision Dunn refers to here) enhances the speaker's appreciation of a relationship whose intimacy both surprises and slightly scares him. Then, between June and September 2008, leaving these first eight lines unchanged, Dunn changes the poem's title from "Connubial" to "Along the Way" and adds the following fifty-one lines:

So I went into the forest with a bucket
I hoped to fill with wild raspberries.
I was prepared to endure
birdsong and the beauty of tall trees,

all the alienating tranquility a forest
has to offer someone like me. That she knew
I had no interest in wild raspberries
was exactly the point. I'd pick them
and place them at her feet. I'd please
and confound her.

But I found myself drawn to the sound
of laughter, and veered toward it,
and soon a young man and woman
were proving how interesting nature
can be. They'd begun the old comedy
of becoming decent—a hasty
putting on and a tucking in.
Meanwhile her bra, hanging from a bush,
made its clear white testimony.

What should I have have [*sic*] done?
Bowed with a grin? Hurried on?
It would be a lie to say I hurried on,
but I did take steps in another direction,
and soon their laughter resumed
along with sighs and gaps of silence.

I kept moving past wildflowers
and mossy fallen tree trunks,
past the many things
I wouldn't have seen had I gone straight
for those raspberries.
Were these the pleasures
of taking the wrong path?
Or the fundamental rightness
of the wrong path? There I was,

thinking the language of fortune
cookies, which if spoken attracts

> the people who used to say "groovy"
> and now say "cool," its false hush
> hush [*sic*], wisdom
> which only a belly laugh can correct
> with a belly laugh, but n [*sic*]
> to what was expected of him, language that carried with it
> that hush of holiness
> No, he was evidence
> that a holy man doesn't speak
> in a hush of holiness. The lovers
> that very moment—I was sure—
> were saying a language beyond
> all argument—Oh baby and Oh God—
> the truth, incontrovertible,
> rising up from within them.

The raspberry-picking expedition works as an example of the patterns or tendencies Dunn describes in the poem's initial six-line stanza, its calculated thoughtfulness somehow akin to the "language of intimacy" his speaker admits to having "mastered." The speaker's awareness of a similar sort of calculation in his response to the forest locale—the expectation of truths revealed through quiet meditation—addresses audience expectations of poetry that takes nature as its theme and setting as well. The couple having sex in the woods interrupts these expectations, presenting a surprise that echoes the speaker's own in the early lines—when his more controlled relationship to intimacy is found out. The couple also exists in contrast to the speaker's self-consciousness. Though initially surprised, the lovers get back to business once the speaker is out of sight. He can hear them "speak" a more direct language of intimacy, one without that layer of calculation and self-awareness.

In a move so sweeping Dunn doesn't even bother to correct typos in the new material or put the revision on a new sheet of paper, he deletes the raspberry-picking expedition from the poem's final version. Having scratched out "Along the Way" and replaced it with

"Nuptial," he simply notes in the margins that the first eight lines "ended up being the entire poem." At some later point beyond the drafts we have, he changes the title back to "Connubial."

Removing the raspberry expedition and its randy couple from the poem returns the focus to the speaker's relationship with the woman who has found him out, by whom he has been "terribly understood." This terrible understanding marks something new, then, a change in the language and, presumably, the habits of intimacy the speaker has developed. While the title change to "Nuptial," with its connotations of weddings, suggests the ceremonial importance of this change, the change back to "Connubial" invokes a more personal vision, focusing our attention on the relationship between a husband and wife without the rites or rituals. The speaker, it seems, has met his match, but the couple will go on to define this new intimacy themselves. The finality of the poem's last word, "understood," gives way. Dunn's decision not to provide further commentary on the speaker's usual habits enhances the sense of discovery that lurks beyond this understanding.

Dunn puts a more gradual, if just as transformative, process on display in his revisions of "Evenings Like This," a poem in which the speaker examines the contradictions of an evening spent enjoying a sumptuous upscale meal with "old leftie" friends. Dunn takes this poem through forty-five drafts and ten title changes from June to September 2008, expanding it to over twice its initial length, and even turning it into a prose poem at one point. With several late drafts focused on the poem's conclusion, the "final" version undergoes additional substantive revision in a 2010 draft that expresses the limitations of art and language.

The first draft, "Discreet Charm of the Incoherent Life," invokes the Buñuel film, with its "bourgeois" and its upscale dinner party conceit, as the speaker takes us from appetizers to dessert in thirty-three lines:

> No need to put out our best dishes or placemats
> not with these friends, though we have

and—to brighten the conversation—dimmed
the dining room just enough to let in,
what might need to be cloaked in order to be said.
I poured the wine. We clicked our glasses and spoke
some words. Not a single click or word rang wrong.
Amazing, the four of us, our compatible differences,
our evenings often in search of a playable tune.
One night the art of humane dishonesty,
another on varieties of listening.
Tonight, it seems, one of us is heading toward
arguing the need to interrupt, without apology—
the importance of how an idea must be resisted
before the moment of its currency is forgotten.
But here comes the carrot soup with a dollop
of sour cream, and the salad with pine nuts and a touch
of garlic and an airy scent of French countryside
lightly dressed. All of it is too beautiful to eat,
but we've learned how to eat the beautiful
as we've learned how to have a good time
now and then while we know others in the world
are sharing a single small bowl of rice.
Then comes the scallops wrapped in bacon,
dappled with sesame seed. We make these things
to please the ones we love, and the conversation turns
to conservation, ways to save and be saved,
and it almost seems possible, to live lives like this,
strawberry swirl cheesecake for dessert,
then out in the dark to the town meeting to protest
the onslaught of wind turbines and slag heaps.
But not before another toast, another round of saying
what we mean and forever hope to mean to each other.

By the thirty-fourth draft, the poem, now called "Colloquy at the Base of Savage Mountain" after many title changes, has more than doubled in length to seventy-three lines, as conversation and observation have taken their place among the courses. It has also become a poem in which the conflicts are much more overt, with the speaker making far fewer references to the group as a whole and expressing less amazement at and more judgment of the couples' "compatible differences." In fact, the phrase "compatible differences" disappears from later drafts entirely.

By the thirty-seventh draft, as though the narrative elements of the evening's drama have overwhelmed the form, Dunn divides the piece into five prose-poem paragraphs. In the fortieth draft, he changes the form yet again, creating twelve six-line stanzas. The return to a more measured form actually exacerbates the poem's tension, bottling up the contradictions that we've known from the first draft are a regular feature of dinner with these friends, in whose presence the speaker becomes preoccupied with the idea of what it means to live a comfortable life in a world where wealth and opportunity are so unevenly distributed. While Dunn gives these inequities greater specificity through details of a larger Appalachian setting ("where strip mining and slag heaps / uglify the nearby mountains, and where / the already poor will lose their jobs / if the problem is corrected") as well as the couples' self-conscious references to these inequities ("here's to an evening as exquisite as Eugene Debs / insisting on fair wages"), he is just as keen on presenting the ways in which the two couples manage the inconsistencies and disturbances such thoughts and realities create within the foursome and what it means and costs to manage them.

Much of the energy of revision, from the first draft onward, is focused on negotiating the ending in which these questions might be resolved—or not. Throughout Dunn's revisions, the speaker either avoids or seeks a confrontation that will upset the balance necessary to the evening, the friendship, and, perhaps, the life he lives. Dunn moves back and forth between conciliation and judgment over and over, up to and including his last two drafts. Here are the last three stanzas in the poem's forty-fifth draft, which Dunn had originally identified as final:

> In my silences, I admit, judgments reside.
> I can only hope they're seldom perceived.

Jen says, as I was about to say, I'm feeling
a widespread sense of decency, aren't you?
I'd like to agree with her, this woman
who's too good to be true, but *widespread*

makes me think of the night sky,
all those vacant spaces. *Widespread?*
I say, let's try to name names.
Jack breaks in—Where is, he says to me,
that shameless, store-bought cheesecake
called Strawberry Swirl, I'd like some now.

I recognize his tone, know what's up.
This is how our evenings go, always someone
poised to prick a mood, or attempt to find
the delicacy to stop just short
of going too far. Widespread decency,
I say good and loud, Yes, it's everywhere.

Dunn opts here to have the speaker play his part in maintaining the balance necessary to bring the evening to an amicable conclusion, while acknowledging the discomfort and effort it requires. The speaker neither agrees nor disagrees with Jen's comment about "feeling a widespread sense of decency" but muses (in a revision of a line in an earlier draft), "Soon someone else will have / to find the delicacy of how to stop just short / of going too far." The hesitancy built into those lines has the effect of slowing the speaker down, giving him time to make the adjustment necessary to preserve the peace.

Yet in the actual final draft of the poem, which has metamorphosed into "Evenings Like This," Dunn revises those final lines completely, deleting his speaker's conciliatory move:

As I was about to say,

Jack says, ever since Obama, I'm feeling
a widespread sense of decency, aren't all of you

I'd like to agree with him, but widespread
suddenly makes me think of the night sky

and large, empty spaces. More like pinpricks
of decency, I want to say, isolated little outposts,
but here comes Barbara with the shameless
store-bought cheesecake called Strawberry Swirl,

which, for a while, tends to end all arguments,
through there was a time we'd have renounced it—
back then when evenings like this were emblems
of excess and vapidity and a life that made us furious.

This new version stops short of spoken agreement or disagreement. The temporary resolution of the evening's conversational skirmishes materializes not with the speaker but with dessert. The speaker never responds aloud to Jack's (not Jen's) question to the group about "a widespread sense of decency." Removing the speaker's feeling that he must smooth things over in the end, Dunn's new conclusion intensifies and further internalizes the conflicts characterized more blithely throughout the poem with toasts: the speaker's "Let's drink to privilege . . . / the privilege of evenings like this" and his "Here's to an evening of contradictions, / I say let's never live without them."

We can see in this new conclusion the language of idealistic oversimplification, a continuation of the mocking judgment Dunn has had the speaker make about earnest "old lefties" Jack and Jen throughout the meal. Yet we can also read the lines as a kind of mourning for the "furious" idealism that none of the characters, including and especially the speaker, with his focus on language and the well-turned phrase, can muster any longer. While earlier in the poem the speaker tells us that Jen has "accommodated mixed feelings, walked / through squalor as often as the rest of us / to reach some golden center of a city," in this final draft the speaker himself is part of the "we" speaking that "old leftie" language in the end. If, as he believes, the "sense of decency" is not widespread, his own preoccupation with language impresses upon him even more forcefully the intractability of the very real problems outside his doors. No amount of store-bought cheesecake will change that. Revision here again calls our attention to what language cannot do or contain, revealing in craft its own limits. Perfection, we see, is not the goal—or the point—of this or any of Dunn's revisions.

There's no crying in poetry, Dunn tells us, because "there's still time to revise." Though his comments are playful, their implications, as I hope to have shown here, articulate the only idea, perhaps, to which Dunn is willing to commit. Thus, revision becomes another lens through which to view his career, a way to understand his craft *and* his productivity (which shows little sign of abating). It shows us the individual manifestations of Dunn's desire for another blank page, a desire that persists not just through every volume but within every poem.

Part Nine

Gods That Bite, Dogs Who Forgive

Peter E. Murphy

Stephen Dunn and I have been friends for many years, and over that time, in addition to talking about poetry, we've spoken quite a bit about religion and the spiritual. Underscoring our friendship are a few differences: I am a Baha'i by faith; Stephen is an atheist. Stephen loves dogs while I can't stand the beasts. When it comes to these two things, I really think that Stephen Dunn is just dyslexic.

While he has made a career of doubting, Stephen writes about God, religion, spirituality, heaven, angels, and the soul more than just about any other contemporary American poet. Here's just a random assortment of titles across his oeuvre: "Outline for a Religious Story," "Resurrection," "The Afterlife," "The Guardian Angel," "Between Angels," "The Retarded Angel," "The Sacred," "Dancing with God," "The Soul Boat," "Heaven," "Because You Mentioned the Spiritual Life," "Saints," "Religion," "The Death of God," "The Soul's Agent," and "Talk to God."

In his poem "At the Smithville Methodist Church" (*LT*, 53–55), he writes that he wonders if he should tell his child that

> the Bible
> is a great book certain people use
> to make you feel bad? (ibid., 53)

and later in the poem admits,

> Evolution is magical but devoid of heroes.
> You can't say to your child
> "Evolution loves you." The story stinks
> of extinction and nothing

exciting happens for centuries. I didn't have
a wonderful story for my child
and she was beaming . . . (ibid., 54)

Dunn's concerns continue in other poems, and in the title poem of his book *Here and Now* (41–42), he continues dogging the deity:

There are words
I've had to save myself from,
like My Lord and Blessed Mother,
words I said and never meant,
though I admit a part of me misses
the ornamental stateliness
of High Mass, that smell

of incense. Heaven did exist,
I discovered, but was reciprocal
and momentary, like lust. (ibid., 41)

Near the end of this poem he writes,

I learned, in time, to let heaven
go its mythy way, to never again

be a supplicant
of any single idea. (ibid., 42)

Is Stephen Dunn an agnostic? Is he an atheist? What does he believe in? What does his god look like? Certainly not like the heavenly father of his Catholic upbringing. Once over a meal of red meat and baked potatoes loaded with butter and sour cream, I said, "As a Baha'i, I don't believe in the same God you don't believe in." Stephen choked. He's written, however, in half of one of his prose pairs in *Riffs and Reciprocities*, "Religion" (27), that "to love Christ you must love the Buddha, to love Mohammed or Moses, you must love

Confucius and, say, Schopenhauer and Nietzsche as well[. . . T]he sacred cannot be found unless you give up some old version of it." I told Stephen that he couldn't get much more Baha'i than that.

One thing is certain. He is a not an atheist. He cares too much about God. Who else would he argue with if God didn't exist? In the prose poem "Advocacy" (*RR*, 23), he writes, "[I] have opposed what I most believed, testing if what I believed was true" (ibid., 23). What Stephen has opposed most is dogmatism. Stephen's arguments are not with God. It's with humans who use God, as I have already quoted, to "make you feel bad."

Stephen Dunn's "heaven" is located in the physical world or, as he famously quoted from a student paper, the "doggie-dog world." The idea of a material heaven, a sacred, secular place, is located throughout his work. In his essay "Poets, Poetry, and the Spiritual" (*WLB*, 159–74), he writes, "Before self-consciousness, gods and demons spoke and had to be consulted" (ibid., 164). In Philip Pullman's *His Dark Materials*, humans possess souls called *dæmons* that exist in the form of animals outside the body. Children's dæmons change with their mood and interest, but this shape-shifting stops at puberty when the soul is fixed for life. Stephen's dæmon, I am sure, would be a dog, perhaps a black lab or an Irish setter. This is evidenced by his unambiguous, dogmatic belief in dogs that thrive throughout his poems.

Unlike real dogs, however, Stephen's dogs rarely snarl, growl, bark, or bite. Perfect beings, they can do no wrong. They are omniscient, faithful, and undemanding gods who rarely intercede in the world of humans, but when they do, it's to remind us to be moral, be good, and to tread the righteous path.

In "Don't Do That," the narrator is spiteful and seeks revenge:

> I felt like a wild thing, ready to mess up
> the party, scarf the hors d'oeuvres. (*HN*, 47)

However, the Rottweilers, Rosie and Tom, become his conscience, scolding him not to misbehave:

But the dogs said, No, don't do that,
calm down, after a while they open the door
and let you out, they pet your head, and everything
you might have held against them is gone,
and you're good friends again. Stay, they said. (ibid., 48)

My theory, as I've said before, is that Stephen is dyslexic. If you switch the word "dog" with the word "god," it becomes:

I felt like a wild thing, ready to mess up
the party, scarf the hors d'oeuvres.
But the gods said, No, don't do that . . .

This is the divine voice that that Stephen listens to over and over. Change "dog" to "god" in the poem "I Come Home Wanting to Touch Everyone" (*WL*, 64):

The gods greet me, I descend
into their world of fur and tongues.

It also works in reverse. Here's "Dancing with God" (*BA*, 56–57) as "Dancing with Dog:"

Dog was a wild dog . . .

Dog held me close
and I felt for a moment
I'd mistaken him,
that he was Death . . .

Stephen Dunn is not an atheist, and in fact, may not even be an agnostic. His dyslexia, his blind spot clearly proves, despite himself, Stephen believes in dogs. I wonder if he's heard this old joke:

Have you heard about the dyslexic, insomniac agnostic?
He lay awake all night wondering if there was a dog.

Scattered Notes on a Coherent Poet

Kurt Brown

I've always thought Stephen Dunn to be one of the wiliest of our poets. He is a poet of ideas, not just passions. A poet whose passion *is* ideas embodied as people in complex, unromantic relationships—or relationships that remain unromanticized. His method is to pose, then puncture, common wisdom. He proceeds by rigorously refusing to adopt any emotion or position that has not been dispassionately examined. In this he is a provocateur, revealing our fondest pieties, our borrowed, stale beliefs. Dunn's revelations pertain, mostly, to everyday life, to people in ordinary circumstances who cheat, lie, betray, and deceive even sometimes themselves, but he never excludes himself. He knows what self-betrayal is.

I think he borrowed his line from Dr. Williams, though I can't be sure of that. Perhaps he adapted it from Wallace Stevens drawing on Dante. Whatever the case, he has made his style his own. He trims the fat off everything he writes, and the final product is shapely and exact. Like most leading poets of his generation, he knows the uses and effectiveness of humor. And, like Woody Allen, his humor comes with a price. Life is serious. That's what makes it so funny.

Dunn has been a presence in American poetry now for over forty years. His influence has been carried forward by thousands of students, and his work has garnered the many prizes it deserves. Participants in his workshops both desire his comments and dread them. He is direct and honest. He will not say, "This is wrong," but "I think I'd reconsider the opening . . ." or "Perhaps the poem would be better served without that last line." He has that attribute shared by all great teachers: he can put his finger on weak spots in a poem the first time he hears it or reads it. There is no hesitation. He won't accept anything faulty, but he knows how to act in public. He's tactful and rigorous. This is why he is so reliable.

Like his moves on a basketball or tennis court, the moves in his poems are subtle and deft. He can size up an opponent—or a problem—and find a way to solve it, and his solutions are inevitably satisfying and elegant.

There is a moment in many of Dunn's poems when an unexpected reversal in attitude occurs, when the poem turns back on itself, on what it has just been asserting, to declare (in essence), "Reader, I thought it was so, *but* my ensuing experience has taught me it was otherwise." This self-correcting instinct is everywhere evident in Stephen's poetry. That small conjunction, "but," whether voiced or not, is the fulcrum on which many of Stephen's poems shift the balance between what we are supposed to believe and what, if we are candid and self-vigilant enough, we truly do believe and secretly know. It is the sign of the genuine, the authentic, the unequivocal in poetry that we sorely need—now as much as ever before.

In an era of mass persuasion and increasing self-delusion, this is political poetry in the most fundamental sense: lines that reveal how we behave, who we truly are.

Desire is Dunn's main subject, sexual desire to be sure, but all forms and manifestations of desire in general. He is not a Buddhist about it, but he knows that desire is the root cause, the motivation, the prime mover of almost all human action and consequent experience. The trick is not to deceive ourselves about our desires, which his poems state, in one way or another, over and over again. The soul, the spirit, the ego is not quiescent but tossed on a sea of longing. What we choose, and what we do about choosing it, is all. This is a reductive way of looking at Dunn's poems, but it provides a general frame through which to view his work.

If I had to choose one word to characterize Dunn's poetry, I would choose the word "sly." I do not mean that, in his personal life, he is sly. I mean to suggest that he is more than clever or resourceful, but adept and crafty about how he constructs a poem, how he shapes his thinking in order to convince the reader of the veracity of what he has to say. He entices by being adept, cunning, playful, and mischievous in a charming (roguish) way in order to lead us to a truth, a self-recognition, that might otherwise remain concealed or not owned up to. Dunn slyly disarms us, before we even know it, and forces us—pleasurably—to confront our own foibles and self-deceptions.

For years, though I loved reading his work and respected what he had achieved, I felt that Stephen (and a number of other of poets in my generation) lacked a certain kind of ambition: the drive to produce a monolithic, world-defining work, such as Milton or Dante or, even in our time, Pound or Eliot or Crane sought to write. Stephen has not chosen the path of overweening ambition but the steady accumulation of knowledge about the real world that adds up, in the end, to the kind of epic portrait of America I thought might be accessed directly in a single act of poetic bravado. The literary landscape is strewn with the careers of such poets while Dunn is still writing relevant, penetrating poems into his seventies, and shows no sign of stopping. It is necessary to understand what kind of poet you are at the beginning of your career and to proceed accordingly. Dunn seems to have known this instinctively, and he has never wavered.

I suppose it is possible to view Dunn as a moralist, but one who makes no prescriptions. He never preaches. He simply observes human behavior and represents it as accurately as he can.

Another trait of Dunn's poetry is the subjunctive mood: would, could, seems, and if, perhaps, possibly, and so on. There is a sense, too, in a large number of the poems that one is trapped in one's life but finds ways to accommodate pleasure and satisfaction without the attendant lies often necessary to effect that conclusion. Like the perfect couple who turn out to be tragically wrong for each other, Dunn's poems refuse surface appearances and dig deeper to find more difficult, harder truths. Not perfection, but consolation of sorts.

The epigraphs Dunn chose for his *New and Selected Poems, 1974–1994* reveal his sensibility and the nature of his work. The first one is from Van Gogh: "The best way to know life is to love many things." This seems straightforward enough, and many poets would leave it at that: a positive adage, a satisfying view of how to proceed with the difficult business of living. But Dunn follows this, immediately, with a quote from W. H. Auden: "The greater the love, the more false to its object." This is the reversal, the self-correcting instinct so characteristic of Dunn's consideration of anything we might say about the world. Whatever we say—whatever *he* says—must be immediately qualified by the possibility of its opposite. There are no absolutes in Dunn's poetry, and excess is always balanced with restraint and second-thinking.

It's an art in itself: the poet of wisdom trying everything in his power not to appear wise. That's where qualification comes in, and second-thinking. Wisdom may finally consist of avoiding opinions altogether, especially the authoritative kind.

There is the almost total lack of imagery, at least of the conventional kind. When a concrete image does appear, it is often a substitute for an idea or an abstraction yoked to a concretion in order to make the abstraction stand out in higher relief. "No ideas but in things" is another New Jersey poet's dictum, not Dunn's. He might reply by reversing that assertion altogether: "No things, but as occasions for ideas." Dunn's poetry may look conventionally concrete, but it is radically abstract, a species of contemporary meditative poetry in which people are enmeshed in ideas, their lives lessons in morality without the moral, every action a precept, every gesture an adage. What keeps this kind of poetry from being dry and dull is an incisive wit, the power of its perceptions, its pervasive humor and uncompromising honesty, and Dunn's ability again and again to hold a mirror up to manners.

Dunn's poetry is not descriptive but perceptive. Only insomuch as the objective world corroborates the subjective world in some important way is Dunn interested in it at all. He has little use for a red wheelbarrow, in and of itself. In a way, he's a spiritual poet interested in the inner, immaterial world of the mind and might be viewed as a contemporary follower of Bishop Berkeley rather than Thomas Hobbs.

Dunn may be a poet of ideas, but that doesn't mean he's a philosophical poet. Philosophy doesn't interest him as much as people, and how they act and interact in their daily lives. If he's a philosopher at all, he's a decidedly practical one.

Lying is an important element—even a major subject—in Dunn's work. Or, to put it in a more positive light: invention, fabrication, fiction. In the most practical sense of all, invention is often simply more interesting than fact, than truth. Lying, of course, is related to truth—whatever that might be—and truth to belief. These ideas appear and reappear in Dunn's work as leitmotifs. He worries over them like a dog worries over a bone. Finally, it's a question of reality: what is it? A question of epistemology: what can be known, and how can we know it? Everything is up in the air in Dunn's poems. *Just when you think* this, he often suggests, *then* that *happens.* Reality is elusive, or maybe it's not there at all. Just a matter of context, belief, and circumstance out of which we construct something we call a life.

Five Sketches of "Tenderness"

Brian Turner

What follows are five sketches, or meditations, on Stephen Dunn's poem "Tenderness" (*BA*, 41–42). It's a poem that ages well. It's a poem I continue to circle around, reading by reading, each circuit an engagement with nuance and subtlety. For some, these sketches may hint at some form of resolution in the aggregate, if not in the individual. My intent here is to lean away from this impulse—to sketch, to circle, to recognize possible layers of meaning within the poem, and not to offer a conclusion, to revel in the mastery of the difficult art before me.

The Blues

It's long past midnight and we're sitting in a diner somewhere in Edward Hopper's America, there in one of the vinyl booths near the back, drinking coffee. Steam curls over the cups in the yellow light of old paint and countertops and diner talk that rises in thin columns and flattens out against the ceiling above us all. The speaker in Dunn's poem tilts his head back and lets out a long exhale of held breath, the heavy kind of sigh that seems as though it's made of oxygen from some other time. And I'm not sure what makes him talk to me now. Maybe it's the way the man sitting at the far counter angles his head to watch the red-haired woman stub out a cigarette in the ashtray between them. Maybe it's the auburn color of her dress, which leads the eye naturally to the muted amber paint glowing in the closed door beyond. Or maybe the reflections of the couple in the pane of glass behind them does it—some sense of a past made visible in the present.

I don't know. I can't tell you why he begins talking about the idea of *tenderness*, but he does. And when the poem rises out of him, it does so in a voice that's made of different times fused together. It's a bluesman's voice. The rough voice of someone who's been there and knows. The voice of someone who has been through the broken times and leans in close to tell you how it is, how it was, how it could never be anything other than this. That's the voice I hear in Dunn's "Tenderness." Intimate and close. Stripped of ornament and verbal flourish. A voice that allows us to "overhear" the speaker's train of thought.

When the speaker in "Tenderness" says, "It's a word I see now / you must be older to use / you must have experienced the absence of it," I hear an echo of Robert Johnson singing "I went down to the crossroads, fell down on my knee." I hear an echo of the blues singers of old and how they often used the past tense—when set in light of the present—as a kind of call to authority.

Don't get me wrong. This isn't some parlor trick. This is the real deal. This is wisdom poetry, the poetry of the sage, blues poetry. Dunn's poetry. And I'm drinking my coffee. I'm hearing him out. Even when the woman in the auburn dress leaves with the man who closes the door behind them, even as they disappear into the rain-dampened streets of the city, their reflections will remain in the glass beyond the counter. Dunn knows it. And because he's crafted a poem to lead us to the past, a poem that somehow also tells us about the present, a poem that defines the word tenderness twice over, we do, too. We see how the lovers run their fingers through each other's hair. How they touch one another with their hands made of light and sorrow, barely visible. How they do this *because* of the world. *That* tenderness.

The Space

Of course, there is no overt setting for the poem. The speaker isn't given a backdrop and Hopper's painting is my own attempt at providing context and landscape for the speaker's voice, as well as the impetus behind the poem.

Let's put aside, for a moment, the simple fact that most poets would be thrilled to have one of their poems discover this (even if we don't factor in the added pun of "Oh" in this case):

Oh abstractions are just abstract

until they have an ache in them.

And the poem would resolve there—its focus more toward creating a conversation on the aesthetics of the craft, a poem focused on creating a discursive, subtextual dialogue with the reader on the nature of the romantic in literature than searching for what happens to us when we try to connect with another human being.

The key word here: *abstractions.* "Tenderness" works almost completely as abstract sketchwork, save for the particulars, the specific details in the second and third stanzas, and even these are open to the reader to add the necessary details.

Dunn allows the reader space to construct the poem within. He doesn't force the setting or the backdrop by following the standard writing credo of *Be specific: it's all in the details.* For example, the poem catalogues the thinnest sketch of a series of moments, saying, "all / I knew / were back seats and a night or two // in a sleeping bag in the furtive dark." When I read this, I'm transported to California and I'm nineteen again. It's 1986. Summer nights with a dark green Ford Galaxy 500 parked on the dirt frontage road by the orange groves in the San Joaquin Valley. The "sleeping bag" takes me to the California coast, to the breakers curling white in the darkness of 3 a.m. as our bodies glowed in the ice plant dunes and the salt-tinged air roped our hair into hard tangles we'd try to undo hours later in the awkward morning light. Those hours would turn into years and still the tangles would never completely come undone.

The thing is—and this is part of the genius of this poem—Dunn realizes that the details are contained *in the reader, in us.* The craft in this poem goes against the grain of contemporary verse, against conventional wisdom, and defies the approach of most poets writing in what many might consider a fairly conventional narrative style. The heartbreak, the wisdom, the sad and necessary medicine of looking back—all of this will be constructed from the reader's own memory.

The sketchwork art of this poem is in its ability to *suggest.*

And, if the reader doesn't connect with the speaker, if the reader simply listens in and "overhears" this poem's inner soliloquy, well, the tragedy rests within the thirty-four-year-old woman's story as well as within the poem's subsurface—*the unsaid.*

The Medicine

When I read the poem this time, I'm somehow sitting in a hospital on the third floor, I think, in the ICU. A bright window to my right is half-filled with the tops of cypress trees shifting in the wind. The speaker of the poem wears the patient's thin blue robe and sits propped up against a couple of pillows on the hospital bed. A television plays in the far corner of the room, but the sound is on mute. I think it may be a documentary about the man's life, a narrative that would explain a great deal about the man talking to me, but he only gestures toward the television once or twice as he speaks to me with his rough voice.

"I can't remember / ever saying the exact word, tenderness," he says, looking out at the trees beyond us, "// though she did." And when he pauses over the word with memory guiding him to its definition in experience, he says, "What silk and deep balm / it is." Tenderness. He seems to be circling around the word the way the circuits of memory often lead back to the same moment or series of moments. And although this could be perceived as an inexorable return to sadness, a deep-held recognition of the tragic in this world and in the speaker's own life, I also see the return of memory as a kind of balm in itself. It isn't a poem of despair; it's a poem that circles back to an old lover once again, only this time with a well of empathy that's grown much deeper as the years have passed by. The balm of *tenderness*, the pure medicine of it, lies in its ability to remind us of our own empathy.

The Ruins

Part of what I learn in Dunn's "Tenderness" is this: Live long enough, or hard enough, or both, and you'll carry a version of the word *ruin* in your own hands.

And as I reread the poem, I keep circling around the idea of damage as a source of maturity, fracture and brokenness as a source of necessary knowledge—that we need to search the ruins in order to live more fully in this world, to appreciate beauty and the finest of rare gifts available in this world. It's disturbing. I'm not saying that it doesn't ring of truth; I'm simply trying to recognize the hard fact of it. That we learn through pain. And I'm wondering if there's a parallel corollary here with the old adage on the comedic: *All comedy is rooted in pain.* What does this tell us about the recognition of beauty, love, and tenderness?

The Unsaid

As I reread the poem, I also keep cycling back to the bluesy call and response of it, how our minds do this in looking back through the years we carry within us, the sadness we carry within sometimes made more beautiful and resonate over time while also, often, amplifying the original. Over time, that which was once hard to live with is now nearly overwhelming. Pain becomes tragedy and the tragic becomes beautiful. The speaker's deep recognition of this process places this poem squarely in the ranks of wisdom poetry—poems that show us how to live in a world constructed among ruins.

Part of the poem's unsaid territory, the silently referenced, is the speaker's own pains, losses, desires, and the complications of intimacy. We sense years of loneliness. Alleyways and rain-washed streets smeared in neon and oil. Liquor stores. Newsprint. Ashtrays. The songs of heartbreak on the jukebox. Nothing to match the empty days behind and the empty days ahead. National Biscuit long after the joke has soured. National Biscuit when there's no longer anyone to share the joke.

The unsaid promise of the poem—its nod toward the future—is a lover's promise: here is what I carry in my hands, these are the years, these are the struggles and heartbreaks, and, if we are to become lovers, these are the hands I will touch you with, these are the fingers I will try my best to draw through the hard tangles of your hair, this is the knowledge I will bring to unravel the tangles until they fall loose from the very tips of your hair. Again, part of the genius of this poem is that the materials, the specifics, the details reside within the reader. So, by extension, the poem teaches us to recognize the ruins within us and how the pain we carry within us is, in part, transformed into the love we share with those we care about most. And, to bridge the gulf, we can also recognize this in the hands of our own lovers when they touch us, when they draw their fingers through our hair, when they kiss us, when their fingertips whisper the word *tenderness* onto our skin.

The Quarrel

Gerald Stern

Sometimes Stephen gets it so right that it's almost unbearable. Sometimes it happens in a single poem and all else beside that poem is shattered and useless. And he gets it right in different ways.

In his poem "Don't Do That" in *Here and Now*, it's as if he reached a point where convention, artificiality, light thinking, dull habit, and what dear Thoreau called conformity are all so suddenly, so finally overwhelming that he must step out of the picture and off the page to what is elemental, brutal, and frightening. Here's the poem:

Don't Do That

It was bring-your-own if you wanted anything
hard, so I brought Johnnie Walker Red
along with some resentment I'd held in
for a few weeks, which was not helped
by the sight of little nameless things
pierced with toothpicks on the tables,
or by talk that promised to be nothing
if not small. But I'd consented to come,
and I knew in what part of the house
their animals would be sequestered,
whose company I loved. What else can I say,

except that old retainer of slights and wrongs,
that bad boy I hadn't quite outgrown—
I'd brought him along, too. I was out
to cultivate a mood. My hosts greeted me,
but did not ask about my soul, which was when

I was invited by Johnnie Walker Red
to find the right kind of glass, and pour.
I toasted the air. I said hello to the wall,
then walked past a group of women
dressed to be seen, undressing them
one by one, and went up the stairs to where

the Rottweilers were, Rosie and Tom,
and got down with them on all fours.
They licked the face I offered them,
and I proceeded to slick back my hair
with their saliva, and before long
I felt like a wild thing, ready to mess up
the party, scarf the hors d'oeuvres.
But the dogs said, No, don't do that,
calm down, after a while they open the door
and let you out, they pet your head, and everything
you might have held against them is gone,
and you're good friends again. Stay, they said. (47–48)

There is tradition in this poem. Catullus and Horace both went to boring feasts and Eliot drops his lines "In the room the women come and go / Talking of Michelangelo," but the events in this poem happened yesterday, tomorrow; they are our own mild hell. The speaker already—maybe in anticipation—has brought some "resentment" to the gathering along with his Johnnie Walker Red. He says he "held [the resentment] in / for a few weeks," and one can only imagine the slights he suffered and the bores he met. Maybe in this case it's the cheap invitation suggesting you "bring-your-own if you wanted anything hard," and we might guess that the speaker is not interested in sipping some sugary white wine to get through the evening. The poem is anti-bourgeois, in the old sense, anti-academic, anti-polite, I would say anti-civilized if you considered "little nameless things / pierced with toothpicks on the tables" as a sign of civilization. The speaker calls himself a "bad boy," but he is really almost ferocious. He "toast[s] the air," he "[says] hello to the wall," and he undresses "one by one" the group of women "dressed to be seen." Seen, I guess, not touched.

I love that he feels at home with the dogs, the brutes, and with them only. And I love that they are Rottweilers, with their great jaws, and that they have such sweet names, and that he—the speaker—knows just where they are in the house. They don't even bark at him, civil as they are, and of course they don't eat food from toothpicks. Dogs aren't wild, though, even if they have huge jaws and adore bloody food. One could even say they are partly civilized themselves and thus sick, or sickly, even as their masters are or their mistresses. But they are used here—in the poem—only as symbols in the classic model of the civil and the anti-civil. They don't, for example, actually talk, even if they lick. And their advice to the bad boy to "stay" and "calm down" is itself civil, *civilized*, advice, not brutal and wild. They are, if you will, even more "advanced," more civilized, than the tooth pickers downstairs; they are that *without* the aid of Johnny Walker Red, which makes the "bad boy" less of a "wild thing" than the poem, on its surface level, might indicate. Stephen knows this and uses it—symbolically and metaphorically—and he knows that if he wanted to be a truly "wild thing" he would choose to be a gorilla, say, or a dragonfly. But that's not his poem. As it stands, he gets all the use he needs of the raw material in the house to make his point. Indeed, his fluent, superbly tuned voice shows who is the civilized one in this deeply moving and heartfelt poem.

Stephen is eternally discriminative, but he is not a Puritan, though he claims—as always though with tongue in cheek—that he is, particularly and specifically in the opening poem of *Here and Now* called "The Puritan and the World" (19–22). "I also knew," he says, that "a little was plenty / and more than I deserved." He claims he "was guilty / long before any verdict," and gave to the world "a closed-mouth kiss." He wants the world to be "held accountable" in all its abundance. He realizes it is not puritanical, the world, and he explains, he discovers, that he *is* his discriminations, and "that's how I discover / what I love (*sometimes . . .*)." Frost says he had a "lover's quarrel with the world," but Stephen has an *angry* lover's quarrel, it seems to me—he who takes especial pleasure, after the wind topples the empty trash cans, "in returning them to the curb, / securing their lids."

I think it's accuracy that's at stake, linguistic and moral. It's as if Stephen is a piano tuner, one who responds to the difficulty, the inability, of language to express the reality—who, at the same time, is responding, reacting, to the illusions, false images, false paths, confusions, of existence itself. In the good tradition, he is blind, his gorgeous ear and his tuner telling all. And when you say, "That's it, you've got it," he looks at you with his milky eye and goes back to work. Nor is it the light touch of a Polish virtuoso we are measuring, but the balance of heaven and hell itself.

Those who would nail him down like to talk about reticence, irony, civility, scorn and restraint—as a counterpoint to precision, discrimination, loneliness, wisdom and grace. It's as if he can't bear the trivial and the petty, as if those things—and dullness and falseness—were morally outrageous, even if *tokens*. And when he lets himself go, as in "Don't Do That," there is a terrible power afoot.

In "Aren't They Beautiful?" one of the new poems in *What Goes On: Selected and New* (168–69), the very title is loaded: tense, bitter, sarcastic. He is walking—as he often is—with a woman who, in this case, rubs him the wrong way, although he may be "in a mood" and anything would do it, or anyone. They are looking at, maybe passing, some foxglove—digitalis—and he's being slightly upbraided, I would say even scolded, for not noticing them, let alone giving a lecture—as I might—on how they help urine flow and have powerful effects on the heart—I mean by ingesting the leaves as they are ground down, not just looking at them. He—Steve, the speaker—only thinks of them as "purple things" and tells her it's a "nice name" but is wary about that word "beautiful," and though he acknowledges that such a word is only a beginning, "an honest way in," he longs for the kind of beautiful "a troubled soul might see, / give me *that* kind of beautiful," he says. But even then he hears "the sanctimony in it" and only says, "Until you asked, . . . / I saw nothing, almost nothing"; altering Stevens, he calls "deprivation" "the mother of beauty," but he is desperate as he struggles to find not just the adequate but the precise words. In response to her (persistent) questions, "What do you see now? . . . / you're staring right at them," he replies, in frustration, rage, and hopelessness:

> *The lies of daylight, the failure of language,*
> *God the vicious, hiding behind another veil.*

Is it too extreme to say his quarrel is with God?

The Voice of Stephen Dunn

Essays by Stephen Dunn

Poetry Now, and Some Thoughts on History, As if, Maybe, and No

On the advice of some friends, I watched *I Am*, a documentary made by former Hollywood comedy director Tom Shadyac about how to improve the world. As with many utopian notions, the thinking behind it remains annoyingly ahistorical throughout, with just token depictions of war and rallies against it, civil rights marches, and such. Occasionally, we see Nazis mechanistically parading—all this without much commentary by the voice-over, which at other moments recommends that we love each other, do good deeds, etc.

Periodically, the movie gives us excerpts from interviews with some of the genuine heroes of the past century—Martin Luther King, Nelson Mandela, Howard Zinn, Gandhi, Desmond Tutu—to support its viewpoint. No mention of the bad guys, Hitler or Stalin or Mao. Not once is the word evil mentioned, not once are great writers like Sophocles, Hawthorne, or Melville evoked or discussed. The human heart is devoid of darkness. And we are presented scientific evidence from the natural world that all things are interconnected, from which only positive conclusions are drawn.

Not only did the movie make me long for Hobbes and Marx and Nietzsche, for analyses of history and human nature that run counter to the documentary's viewpoint or at least would acknowledge other world views; I would have especially welcomed Camus' idea of a "relative utopia," which he defined as a philosophy free of all messianic elements and devoid of any nostalgia for an earthly paradise.

The genuine heroes I've listed above are emblems of vision and bravery. Each effected important changes and was able to galvanize large movements. Most of them were charismatic figures. Yet Hitler and Mao were charismatic figures who galvanized large movements.

Cruel and tyrannical as were their methods, they, too, believed they were improving the world.

They were wrong, of course. But their singular Nietzschean will to power, and their sway over the many who followed them, seemed to also support the movie's main contention that in essence our natures are fundamentally cooperative: we're driven to get along, and the will toward good in most of us is so strong that we will follow a charismatic embodiment of it, blindly, almost anywhere. What the movie never brought up is that this aspect of our natures is always appealed to by tyrants: the world will be a better place if we purify it of differences, let's all be equal, let's rid the world of property owners and share the land. The movie would have us ignore mass graves, religious zealotry, the dangers of the true believer. A lot of folks joining together, cooperating with each other, are required to wage war as well as to seek peace. History is a graveyard of cooperation and good intentions.

At some point in the movie, somebody asks the Dalai Lama what the world most needs. The first thing he says is "critical thinking," which the movie proceeds to ignore. Good thinking, it seems to me, involves saying *no* or *maybe* before saying *yes*; that is, holding out for the more satisfactory yes and then maybe doubting that one, too. It means a constant measuring against notions that have come before, which means Euclid giving way to Einstein; the world according to Genesis yielding to the world according to Darwin; and, in a different sense of influence, Walt Whitman opening the way for Allen Ginsberg.

Of course we admire the people who try to make things happen, to effect change, especially those who work against injustice and the limitations of the past. But as much as these people remain significant, one wonders if effectiveness will almost always sacrifice truth for the realization of its goals. The well-told partial truth, we are often reminded, deflects attention from the raw truth beneath it. Those of us who write know how easy it is to hide behind felicities. We also know that to suppress is not necessarily a bad thing; it can lead to transformation, to another way of saying something.

If poets improve the world—and they must not write with that intention—they do it gradually, over time. However, in certain historical circumstances, we can imagine how Shelley's contention that poets are the unacknowledged legislators of the world might yield to Auden's counter-proposition—that it's really the secret police who are the unacknowledged legislators. But even in the face of repression and hardship, good literature—I choose to believe—corrects by seeing well, by getting things right. A visionary is someone who sees the unseen interconnections, identifies them, gives them accuracy's radiance. The visionary, in other words, is someone who sees the present as it is.

The visionary, for my purposes here, is the poet—who lets into the poem the strange, the unmanageable, and tries to create a livable environment for them. The result need not be pretty. What's beautiful in a poem, for me, is often a balancing act of factors—the ugly, say, under a sunset—so that the stuff of the world is delivered in its variety and complexity.

In Robert Frost's essay " . . . content with the old-fashioned way to be new," which is also the introduction to E. A. Robinson's *King Jasper*, he recounts a conversation with a young man who says, "Whereas we once thought literature should be without content, we now know it should be charged full of propaganda." Frost says to him, "Wrong twice," but the young man pushes his case: "Surely art can be considered good only as it prompts to action." Frost replies, "How soon?" and goes on to say we must be tender to our dreamers. And then, "We shan't mind what they seem, if only they produce real poems."

How soon, indeed.

Aren't our lives mysterious? To register what it feels like to be alive in a particular moment in history is an enormous and noble task. Yet we need to remember the noble doesn't rule out, say, the profane. And that *serious* and *solemn* need not be compositional cousins. And that there are many other ends apart from instruction to which poets aspire. Some of us will be content to dazzle, to make words frolic and sing. Others will want to oppose the aesthetic that preceded them. Paul Valery wanted poetry to be a holiday of the mind. Wallace Stevens wanted to make his imagination yours. Great poets (and I would count Stevens among them), like Shakespeare, Dickinson, and Eliot (we each can make our own lists) will aspire to all of the above.

Most of us who write know that the genuine can emerge from the arbitrary, seriousness from play, profundity from resistance. Most of us know that poems *should* get away from us. We long to feel as though we're flying, or on fire, having gotten beyond our original intention. My compositional pleasures involve giving myself permission to say what I've found myself saying. Completing a poem is often a matter of stitching and arranging, of rewriting line 2 to make sense of that startling wildness I found myself achieving in line 18. The purpose behind such stitching and rearranging should be veracity, and to move the reader to a different way of regarding a landscape, or a night at home.

Frost again, from his essay "Poetry and School": "Practice of an art is more salutary than talk about it. There is nothing as composing as composition."

A while back, not too long ago, we found ourselves in the era of French criticism and the "unreading" of literature. And a lot of bad poetry. We learned how to deconstruct, which was valuable, but to construct anew was a different matter. Poems written out of theoretical conviction, I came to learn, will likely read as such.

Most poems driven by a postmodern sense of language's indeterminacy are, at best, interesting. At worst, they're self-indulgent. The poets who bought in to the (albeit correct) notion of language comprising signifiers seemed to feel that they didn't have to try very hard to make sense. "What was the point?" they seemed to be saying. This could be substituted for that, that for this. For a while it seemed we got a lot of inventions from intelligent people refusing to let us in on their concerns. But if language is indeterminate, all the more reason to work hard to make it yield sense. I've chosen three poems from *Poetry*, a journal that since the turn of the twenty-first century has become more interesting for its prose than its poetry, but has tried under its current editor, Christian Wiman, to forge a certain aesthetic with the latter. In its pages, the hijinks of language often take precedence over the possible revelations that can come from working and deepening a subject. Here's an example by Atsuro Riley that strikes me as the literary equivalent of a two-year-old throwing food from his high chair. It's called "Chord" and was one of the lead poems in the December 2007 issue. To be merciful, I'll quote only its beginning:

> *Come the marrow-hours when he couldn't sleep,*
> *the boy river-brinked and chorded.*
>
> *Mud-bedded himself here in the root-mesh; bided.*
> *Sieved our alluvial sounds—*
>
> Perseverating fiddler-crabs pockworking the pluff-mud;
>
> (perforated) home-bank gurgle and seethe . . .

And on like that ad nauseam for two pages. The poet is in love with his arch vocabulary and his alliterative indulgences more than he is with his poem. In fact, he mistakes these things for his poem. He's a word thrower, leaving the reader with a mess of language that clutters and overwhelms. This reader is not inclined to pick up after him. To paraphrase Roland Barthes' apt sexual metaphor: the text must prove to me that it desires me. Of course, there are many ways a text can demonstrate such desire, but I'm sure the above isn't one of them.

In the same issue, a poem by a different author seems to have created a you/he dramatic situation, then drops these governing pronouns as if they've never been introduced. My guess is that Fiona Sampson doesn't know or care that she's raised narrative issues and therefore promises. She gets involved with her language play instead.

The poem remains evasive throughout—a "Why should we care?" poem if ever there was one. This is how it begins:

The Lodger

You could figure it as a trapdoor,
blur and hinge and
                              down
into the unconscious of this stranger
moving around your garden like a trap—
making all the greens unstable
as the warble of nausea come bang up to greet you.
Bang to rights
is how he'd like to have your house.

I find "this stranger / moving around your garden like a trap" indecipherable. Like a trap? Moreover, would a "warble" result in a "bang," especially if that warble were "a warble of nausea"? Then, this—after a four- or five-line interval—is the poem's conclusion:

    Meanwhile the unaccustomed heat.
Meanwhile, a sky tunneling upward—
sense of proportion—golden section
of elder hedge; then the disgraceful paddock gone wild.

Its many imprecisions aside, "The Lodger" provides fodder for those who believe that the author is dead, or might as well be. The best I can say is that this author is someone who likes words. This text desires no one; I'd say it's not even interested in itself. It invites autopsy more than examination.

I don't wish to indicate that the editors of *Poetry* publish only poems that frolic aimlessly with language or use language as some kind of smoke screen for their authors to hide behind. I could cite several poems in which the editor's love of sound and syntax lead to the publishing of better work. Here is the first half of one from the December 2009 issue, by Hailey Leithauser:

Delirium

Such green, such green,
this apple-, pea- and celadon,

this emerald and pine and lime
unsheathed to make

a miser weep, to make his puny
bunions shrink; these seas

and seas of peony, these showy
tons of rose . . .

As the poem goes along, though, it can't hide its effort, its arty elbows:

greedy bee to bid
the bully hearts of cops

and bosses sob,
to tell a stubby root unstub, a rusted

hinge unrust, the slug unsalt;
to stir the fusted

lungs to brim, the skin to sting,
the dormant,

tinning tongue to sing and hymn.

We sense that the author is a wordsmith and a talent, perhaps strongly influenced by Hopkins. Yet if that talent were tempered some, it could better serve its subject. I'd welcome, for example, at least one straight, unfancy line, like "Glory be to God for dappled things" or "And for all this, nature is never spent," to help locate and position the poem's concerns. The language in "Delirium," however rich, remains monotonic. No one move or choice seems more important than another; the poet's need to compose by one startling phrase after another levels the poem's effects. A more sympathetic reader might, I suppose, say that "Delirium" is in the business of delivering its title. I might agree with that sympathetic reader.

A good counter-poem to the one above, I think, is "The Price" by Anne Stevenson, from 1977's *Enough of Green*, which has the same virtuosity of sounds but also a fidelity to insight and, in general, to sense.

The Price

The fear of loneliness, the wish
to be alone;
love grown rank as seeding grass
in every room,
and anger at it, raging at it
storming it down.

Also that four-walled chrysalis
and impediment, home;
that lamp and hearth, that easy fit
of bed to bone;
those children, too, sharp witnesses
of all I've done.

My dear, the ropes that bind us
are safe to hold;
the walls that crush us keep us
from the cold.
I know the price, and still I pay it, pay it—
words, their furtive kiss,
illicit gold.

In an essay entitled "The Unified Dance" (*Poetry*, March 2007), Stevenson says,

> Language, like the human mind, consists of a conscious and an unconscious element, and what "real" poetry can do, even when it looks like prose on the page, is to reproduce the hidden music we are all born hearing but lose as we grow up. The danger today lies in pursuing novelty beyond a point of no return, of technically "making it new" until we no longer hear anything but the virtual pulse of a spoiled, over-mechanized civilization that is destroying its childhood as it ages, boasting the while of its progress.

Earlier in the essay she says, "The best poetry—great poetry—happens when sound, rhythm, and image bring about a mysterious feeling of wholeness that somehow draws mind, body, and spirit together into what both Yeats and Eliot envisioned as a unified dance." "The Price" not only has the feel of a unified dance, but in it we are treated to an exploration of something recognizably human—the loneliness in marriage and the words that approximate it—a price the speaker is willing to pay for such loneliness. "My dear" grounds the poem, suggests an addressee, if not an urgency in its telling. By comparison, "Delirium," rather than capturing some lost, hidden music, merely seems juvenile.

Anna Moschovakis' *You and Three Others Are Approaching a Lake* won the 2011 James Laughlin Award. In a long section called "The Human Machine (Thirty Chances)," she seems committed to arbitrary spatial arrangement and various fracturings of her narrative. Yet she uses these "experimental" techniques to great advantage. The entire book is written in extended, patterned parts. Here are the *twenty-seventh* and *twenty-eighth* movements (the author spells out and italicizes these numbers), which I've separated with asterisks.

> No, in a shed   under
>
> the machine
>
> holding a candle
>
> A man will wake up

in the middle of the night

    that candid hour

after the exaltation of the evening

and before the hope of   dawn

        will see everything in its   colors

except himself

the language

of obvious

            things

                the conclusions

the part

before

*****

Shall we call it intelligence?

Human Machine: I do not say that the reason is always
entirely right, but I do say that it is
always less wrong than the heart.

When I see a poem laid out on the page like this is, I'm immediately suspicious. But not only do the white spaces slow us down, they isolate important phrasing ("the language / of obvious / things" is my favorite), and we sense the virtues of composition by field that

Charles Olson wrote about. On closer inspection we can see how her syntax, broken up this way, contributes to a mysteriousness meant to draw us in, one that extends and invites various readings. What a good surprise "candid hour" is after "holding a candle" just three lines above, but it might not be if the poem were conventionally lineated. Throughout most of Moschovakis' book, I feel in the presence of a poet trying to find new ways of delivering perceptions. She defamiliarizes, and through patterning makes a coherent whole out of the odd and the amorphous.

"For poetry makes nothing happen," writes Auden in his elegy for Yeats. The quote is often left at that, but to be fair to Auden's meaning it shouldn't be. The sentence continues:

> it survives
> In the valley of its making where executives
> Would never want to tamper, flows on south
> From ranches of isolation and the busy griefs,
> Raw towns that we believe and die in; it survives,
> A way of happening, a mouth.

As "A way of happening," residing beneath most consciousness, poetry survives—even for those not disposed to it—subliminally. To accomplish this effect, sometimes poets need to be unreasonable, if reason is defined by executives or by certain critics. All of our great heroes were unreasonable in the face of powers that defined the world wrongly for them. If asked, they probably wouldn't claim heroism for themselves. They might say their motive was unhappiness. Or a consciousness they couldn't deny once they had acquired it. Or justice.

I Am perpetuates sweet lies. It possesses all the dangers of naïveté delivered with sincerity and earnestness. One issue that the movie raises, albeit unconsciously, is whether one can offer truths that don't entertain their opposites. I'm not sure of the answer to that, but I do feel, along with Joseph Brodsky, that evil "tends to appear in the guise of good," and that "nothing can be turned inside out with greater ease than one's notion of social justice, civic conscience, a better future, etc." To feel good about ourselves is difficult as we uncover and formalize what's before us. To get the world right is not necessarily sanguine, just as "getting in touch with our feelings" is often to learn we're despicable.

As if thinking liberates the possible, while moral certainties confine it; a good poem might employ a combination of the two. A student of mine wrote, "Left by Fate at the altar years ago, Lust had an ax to grind." I told her the line would be more plausible as "she acted as if her lust / had an ax to grind," though I added that nothing but deletion could save "ax to grind." Moral certainty may exclude flights of imagination, yet at the same time be an invitation to ingenuity, the way strict form can. Another student, compelled by assignment to write a love sonnet about a failed relationship in which the moon somehow would be involved, completed his poem with this couplet—

> I gave you a diamond. It should have been a pearl.
>   It should have been a stone to hang above the world

—creating a loveliness, I think, that couldn't have been arrived at without the constraints he freely accepted. *I Am* put no obstacles in the way of its original position, so never underwent the pressure that leads to discovery. Neither did it need any *as ifs*, because it rarely risked saying anything outrageous or exotic.

In a poem, I want to behave as if what I say matters, even though few may be listening. That means trying to be as clear as possible, which doesn't obviate difficulty. We say what we can straight out until we no longer can. Our lives, and the world itself, are messy. At some point we must reach for analogue to approximate what we're after. We move into the often murky, often crystalizing, world of metaphor.

But we must not be wholly happy to be there, nor for our moments of apt phrasing. We need to know that a poem is the sum of its effects, and that sum can be a metaphor, too. Wisława Szymborska cautions against such writing when she says, "The fear of straight speaking, the constant, painstaking efforts to metaphorize everything, the ceaseless need to prove you're a poet in every line; these are the anxieties that beset every budding bard." However, she goes on to say that such impulses "are curable if caught in time."[1] If a poem's surfaces are compelling, I don't mind difficulty—but I don't seek it. Deliberate obfuscators, I think, are cowardly, afraid to enter the world of meaning and its attendant possibilities of failure.

Saints and radicals wish to go all the way, and very good poets are willing to go as far as the going is useful to their poem. Tact, as Cocteau said, consists of knowing how far to go in going too far. Saints and radicals scare us because they go further, their very presence asking us to be better than ourselves. However, if they were writing poetry, the single-mindedness they bring with them would be a hindrance. The poet resides in the world of ambiguity or ambivalence, qualities that makes one hesitate, reconsider. Not many activists are also successful poets.

The poet's test of bravery may arise in politically repressive countries where poets are taken seriously—think of Osip Mandelstam and Nazim Hikmet, for example. My guess is that those men wrote out of the same motives some poets in the United States do—to make sense of their world, and their involvement in it, and/or out of anger and a sense of injustice. Their personal is political, their bravery is to publish, and they take their quieter place alongside the Nelson Mandelas and the Gandhis of the world. It's a lie to say that slogans like "Love one another" could save anyone from the crazies out there. But to behave toward each other *as if* love mattered is a notion to which I respond with a guarded *yes*.

I came of age twice: once in the passive late 1950s, the Eisenhower years, and again in the late sixties, in graduate school. Drugs

1. From Szymborska's column "How to (and How Not to)," originally published in the Polish journal *Literary Life*, translated by Clare Cavanagh and available on the Poetry Foundation's website at http://www.poetryfoundation.org/article/178592.

and rock 'n roll, sex, politics, protest marches. Watching this section of *I Am*, I had no feeling for the fifties, but did have some for the sixties. We were all so alive then, though the movie also reflected our self-righteousness, our frequent stupidities in the name of progress and high-mindedness. The movie made few distinctions, congratulating its maker on changing his life, and a generation on being itself.

Still, *I Am* brought back a sexy, heady time—Bob Dylan replacing crooners like Pat Boone, Richie Havens making us feel the blues for his baby down by the San Francisco Bay. I started then to long for words that helped define my experience. I memorized Theodore Roethke's "In a Dark Time," with its brilliant first line: "In a dark time, the eye begins to see." Later in that poem, his "Which I is I?" made me feel sane, not confused. William Meredith wrote his poem to Nixon, "A Mild-Spoken Citizen Finally Writes to the White House," during the Cambodian bombings; it was a masterpiece of artful chiding from which I learned the usefulness of tactical praise. Some of us dared to speak of our souls and about the unspeakable. The surreal infused the real, absurdity became a kind of clarity—and for proof, all we had to do was read the headlines. Russell Edson's nuttiness made perfect sense, as did Bill Knott's imagistic eccentricities. Beckett, Ionesco, and Pinter, too, regularly came to the rescue. The tragic world was funny. And was not. The clown hid his tears, but you knew he had to be weeping.

In the postmodern climate (which I hope has now faded into the past), all assertions seemed to have quotation marks around them. Multicultural poems and novels, welcome in many ways, were put next to *Moby-Dick* and "The Wasteland." Distinctions were discouraged. Critical thinking was what you brought to a few books of criticism. The poems written in this spirit, like many of the faux-surreal poems of the 1970s (I confess to being guilty of several), often felt disingenuous—offering a posture rather than a vision. A mature intellect challenges its assertions, is willing to let the poem be in dialogue with itself by exerting a counter-pressure, an internal resistance in its attempt to tell the truth. Of course not all poems seek *the* or even *a* truth. We don't ask a beautiful bowl to be anything but beautiful, don't ask what it means. And some poems wish to explore possibilities of meaning by confounding our sense of it.

John Ashbery, to mention just one confounder, comes to mind in this regard. In among the blurrings and invention for invention's sake, his poems have been gradually teaching us how to read them, as Stevens' poems did, for some of us, a few generations earlier. Ashbery's great poem "Self-Portrait in a Convex Mirror" is ambitious and difficult, and rewards the attention we might give it. For a while I was inclined to say, with some annoyance, that Ashbery writes about nothing, but now I realize it's a nothing that is seen in this convex mirror—strange, remote, and intimate—as is the face in Parmigianino's self-portrait. In the forty-some years since that poem was published, Ashbery's work has become, if anything, more elusive, more resistant toward conventional interpretation. Yet his fractured narratives, his refusals to give us what we want, are born out of a way of seeing, a world view. Still, I must say that most of his poems and their opacity don't offer me what I want from poetry—to be moved from one way of regarding experience to another, along with some sense of how it all feels.

Gifted inventors like Dean Young, Mark Halliday, and Tony Hoagland, along with the wonderfully inclusive Albert Goldbarth and Frederick Seidel, to name just a few, remain in need of their Clement Greenberg or Randall Jarrell. These great critics identified strengths not easily identifiable, wrote persuasively about them, and elevated what was overlooked or misunderstood into our consciousness. Instead, we have William Logan, whose bile always muddies whatever insights he might have to offer, and Helen Vendler, who seems quite brilliant when writing about dead writers, but less so when writing about contemporaries.

Surely there's nothing wrong with experimentation, except the boredom we must endure while waiting for a genius to emerge who will show us the value of the same experimental techniques. We await him or her. The Greenbergs of the critical establishment identify for us the Jackson Pollocks and the Paul Klees. Greenberg's comment about certain experimental visual art—"all surprise without satisfaction"—could easily apply to any creations that are trying too hard to be new.

I began this ramble by invoking a film, and I seem to be ending it by invoking painters and art critics. So be it. Loving the wildness and play of Pollock and Klee, I'll conclude with a prejudice I share with a different but no less excellent artist, Edward Hopper. Please substitute "poetry" for "painting" in his assertion that "Painting will have to deal more fully and less obliquely with life and nature's phenomena before it can again become great."

I can think of arguments against that statement, and some art that might render it narrow and foolish, but sometimes we just have to dig in, have to declare what we want to be ours.

Here are two contemporary poems, one by Lawrence Raab and the other by Donald Justice, that risk being serious in ways I admire, much like those I admire in Anne Stevenson: by offering clear voices in service of complex attitudes and ideas, each with its own formalities. Each poem is historical in the gestures it makes toward a prior literature upon which it depends. I'm not sure of their greatness, but I am sure they take on their subjects in ways Hopper would like.

The Sirens

After a while we just got tired of singing.
One morning out there on the rocks
with not a ship in sight, we all felt it—

a certain weariness, a *malaise*,
if you will. We felt it together,
sympathy having become

one of the finer aspects
            of our nature. We've drifted apart
since those days, yet we're happy

being remembered as impossible
to resist. The stories used to claim
we knew the future—*all things*

which shall be hereafter upon the earth,
as our song put it. Everyone only assumed
we were beautiful. But we were, and are,

though not unlike so many other
women now, those who promise much less,
but let you live. It was a relief

to give up our powers willingly.
That didn't happen often in our world,
where the gods kept on amusing themselves

with their meddling, and the hero
plowed ahead, lashed to the mast,
dying to be tempted. Did we enjoy the clamor

of shipwreck? The cries of the disillusioned?
It was our job, our particular talent.
We weren't supposed to want anything else. (Lawrence Raab,
from the *Massachusetts Review*, Summer 2012)

There Is a Gold Light in Certain Old Paintings[2]

1.

There is a gold light in certain old paintings
That represents a diffusion of sunlight.
It is like happiness, when we are happy.
It comes from everywhere and from nowhere at once, this light,
And the poor soldiers sprawled at the foot of the cross
Share in its charity equally with the cross.

2. PENDING: Reprinted by permission of the estate of Donald Justice.

2.
Orpheus hesitated beside the black river.
With so much to look forward to he looked back.
We think he sang then, but the song is lost.
At least he had seen once more the beloved back.
  I say the song went this way: *O prolong*
  Now the sorrow if that is all there is to prolong.

3.
The world is very dusty, uncle. Let us work.
One day the sickness shall pass from the earth for good.
The orchard will bloom; someone will play the guitar.
Our work will be seen as strong and clean and good.
  And all that we suffered through having existed
  Shall be forgotten as though it had never existed. (Donald
  Justice, from the *New Yorker*, November 24, 1997)

I, like Stevens, or like any lover of what preoccupies him, would like to make my prejudices and tastes yours—for a while, anyway, until each of us replaces them with a different manifestation of what feels lovely and true. In the meantime, there is fine work being done in America. Let's try not to get too discouraged by the plethora of mediocrity we find in abundance. Every century abounds with it. We read wishing to be startled into alertness—which means we begin with a certain kind of boredom, anticipating very little. Then, voila! One or two out of fifty is a lot. I put them in my notebook. I try to remember to reread them in those inevitable moments of despair.

Forms and Structures

The shortest essay I ever wrote, maybe the shortest essay anyone has ever written, was called "Little Essay on Form." It went like this: "We build the corral as we reinvent the horse." Later, I added: "Craft is what nails the gate, helps formalize the space, and keeps the horseshit out of the picture. It leaves us with the necessary."

I was rather pleased with my epigrammatic self, yet knew if I were to continue in that reductive mode I might be on my way to silliness. Metaphor pushed too far is always on the verge of collapsing. That's why the exquisite metaphor or simile pleases us so. It goes to the precipice, dangles, survives. It has in it a recklessness, a groping in thin air toward an unknown correlative. Eliot has Prufrock say, "The evening spread out against the sky . . ." How so? Well, "like a patient etherized upon a table." You can't get much more successfully reckless than that. I take that back. Maybe Frank Gehry has. Or any number of less famous architects that you know about, and I don't.

Which is to say that the imagination plays a large role in the creation of structures or forms, even in relatively fixed forms like the sonnet. Either we're working within chosen confines, our details pressing up against boundaries and those boundaries pressing back, or we're seeking those confines which will hold in place our wanderings. Or both. Each presents its own demands and opportunities.

I want to read you a poem that wandered toward what I think are its necessities. I also want to read it because it probably accounts for why I've been invited to speak to you today. Some years ago I was lucky enough to be at The MacDowell Colony with your own Catherine Ingraham. She was clearly the most interesting person there, and one day she told me a story about Peter Eisenman, an architect who had designed the Wexner Center at Ohio State University in which there is a column that hangs down mid-air and does not connect with the ground. As often happens at artist colonies, at least for me, snippets of conversation heard at meals get appropriated, stories get happily stolen and/or transformed. And that's exactly what happened. I went back to my studio, and wrote "The Stairway," which is based on Catherine's story, but creates different terms. It's written in free verse, which means it's a poem that was seeking its formal properties as it was composed.

The Stairway

The architect wanted to build a stairway
and suspend it with silver, almost invisible
guy wires in a high-ceilinged room,
a stairway you couldn't ascend or descend
except in your dreams. But first—
because wild things are not easily seen
if what's around them is wild—
he'd make sure the house that housed it
was practical, built two-by-four by
two-by-four, slat by slat, without ornament.
The stairway would be an invitation
to anyone who felt invited by it,
and depending on your reaction he'd know
if friendship were possible.
The house he'd claim as his, but the stairway
would be designed to be ownerless,
tilted against any suggestion of a theology,
disappointing to those looking for politics.
Of course the architect knew
that over the years he'd have to build
other things the way others desired,
knew that to live in this world was to trade
a few industrious hours for one beautiful one.
Yet every night when he got home
he could imagine, as he walked in the door,
his stairway going nowhere, not for sale,
and maybe some you to whom nothing
about it need be explained, waiting,

the wine decanted, the night about to unfold.

In mediating what Catherine told me about the architect, I became aware, perhaps by mid-poem, that I was writing an ars poetica. That is, I knew that the architect's creation was suggestive of working habits and perhaps a sensibility that were analogous to mine. The architect builds a stairway that is beautifully useless. In so doing, he has removed himself from the world of art as commodity; his creation is its own reward. In the telling, I was as concerned about the selection and phrasing of details, their tone, and the pacing of them, as I was about the story itself—which I was reinventing as well as reconstructing. The architect's stairway is ownerless, one of those creations so magical he can't claim it as belonging wholly to himself. The house that houses it, however, is solid and practical; it draws little attention to itself (not unlike my poem's block form). It is a vehicle for the suspended stairway, nothing more. I let the architect dream of one person who would perfectly understand what he had made, to whom no explanations were necessary, though I don't remember making a decision in that regard. I suppose by this time her story about the architect was sufficiently my story; I felt no allegiance to what Catherine had told me; I could extend things as I so felt. Ah, *to be understood,* the refuge and solace of the artist, especially one who can't make a living from his work.

I don't wish to romanticize either poets or architects. The architect, more often than not is designing buildings in tandem with others, is in the habit of working out effective compromises. He understands "that to live in this world {is} to trade / a few industrious hours for one beautiful one." The poet generally has more freedom to be wild, reckless, but if he's a good poet he wants that wildness harnessed; he's simultaneously seeking limits. Shortly after the first hot rush of composition, he will have brought to his work the cold eye of the problem solver. It's trench work after that.

Robert Frost's "Stopping By Woods on a Snowy Evening" is a poem—with its iambic tetrameter and rhymed quatrains—that has more conspicuous formalities than mine. His solution to the rhyme pattern in his famous last stanza is one of the poem's brilliant moves, a move that was made possible because of the poem's established regularities. Before I read the poem to you, here's what Frost says about the making of it, as reported in Reginald Cook's book, *The Dimensions of Robert Frost.* If it had a title, it might be called, "Structure as a series of commitments."

"I can have my first line any way I please," Frost says, "But once I say a line I am committed. The first line IS a commitment . . ." He goes on to say how he could have written the next line so that he'd be working in couplets, and worried then that he'd have to have couplets all the way. But no, he says, he was dancing, he was free. Then he found himself writing, 'He will not see me stopping here,' the poem's third line, and felt uncommitted, or perhaps he'd written a line that he knew would be seeking but had not yet found what it might be committed to. "For the three rhymes in the next stanza," he says, "I picked up the unrhymed line in the first stanza" ('He will not see me stopping here'), which began for him a way of interlocking his stanzas. "Every step you take is a further commitment," Frost concludes, and disarmingly admits, " For my poem is a commitment to convention." He then offers what we've come to understand as a characteristic Frostian counter-thought: "The interest is the quarrel with those commitments."

Frost had established a pattern he could break away from, and the timing of the break serves to accentuate the poem's emotional import. In essence, the structural unfolding of the poem becomes a link to its content—the commitment to "promises," to leaving, to staying awake. His poem is an example of how strict form can facilitate ingenuity and a deepening of concerns.

Compositional sloppiness, on the other hand, delimits possibility. W. D. Snodgrass sought to demonstrate this in a sequence called *De/Compositions.* He wanted to to have some instructive fun with well-known poems like Frost's by tampering with their diction and metrics, and he did. Here's Frost's poem, and then Snodgrass's. Let's call Frost's the carefully made house. The other, as you will see, will fail inspection.

Stopping by Woods on a Snowy Evening

Whose woods these are I think I know.
His house is in the village, though;
He will not see me stopping here
To watch his woods fill up with snow.

My little horse must think it queer
To stop without a farmhouse near
Between the woods and frozen lake
The darkest evening of the year.

He gives his harness bells a shake
To ask if there is some mistake.
The only other sound's the sweep
Of easy wind and downy flake.

The woods are lovely, dark and deep,
But I have promises to keep,
And miles to go before I sleep,
And miles to go before I sleep.

Passing by Woods During a Snowfall

—de/composed from Frost

Who owns these woodlands I don't know
But they live somewhere else and so
They won't mind that I've come out here
To see the lovely falling snow.

My horse must wonder why we're here
On back roads though no one lives here
Next to a forest and a lake
Where it's so cold this time of year.

He gives his windblown mane a shake
To ask which way he ought to take
But I'm enchanted by the sweep
Of wind and whispers of snowflake.

The woods lie clad in beauty deep
But Man has schedules he must keep.
I've got to go home now and sleep;
I've got to go home now and sleep.

I don't want to spend a lot of time on what I trust is obvious, but from the clunky first line that begins the de/composition all the way to the abominable last quatrain we feel—I'll put it nicely—in the presence of a writer who exhibits throughout that he values content more than the handling of content. Let me also put it less nicely. As the poet's tin ear suggests, Snodgrass is imitating someone who probably hasn't read very much. Nothing in his history of reading or writing would make him wince when he wrote, "The woods lie clad in beauty deep / But Man has schedules he must keep."

Snodgrass's burlesquing of Frost's poem is deliberately broad. But just think how the smallest of alterations might ruin a good line. "And ten miles to go before I sleep, / And ten miles to go before I sleep." Not only would "ten" provide an extra syllable, and thus break the iambic flow, but we'd be left thinking about specific distance rather than the "miles" that could represent a lifetime.

The best practitioners take great care with the smallest of things. The worst seem to think that there's an intrinsic value to what they've found themselves doing and saying. Certainly the carpenter who poorly frames a door doesn't go around saying how well it shuts. Sloppiness embarrasses him. But I've heard many would-be poets defending the equivalent of a poorly made door. They actually believe that how they feel about something is important. Beginning poets take note, and for all I know, beginning architects: the artisan never believes that how he feels is more important than how he executes.

If I can wander back to the corral for a moment, it's easy to see it as a fixed structure, but the implication of my one line essay is that it doesn't fully become what it is until the experience that occurs within it is made vital by transformation. Different degrees of ambition, of course, create different challenges. So I can imagine that even an empty corral could be made interesting, say by someone who saw it as a structure within a structure, whose aim was to explore a vision of an entire ranch and its interrelationships. He'd have more space to formalize, more horseshit to hide. The fun might be just beginning.

"The maximum amount of wildness the form can bear," is what poet Donald Justice wanted from an ideal poem. You might think he had in mind a poem like "Howl," but more likely he was thinking of poems by Emily Dickinson or Weldon Kees. Nevertheless, "Howl" seems to qualify nicely as an example of Justice's statement. Wouldn't the New York and Bilbao Guggenheims also qualify? Said differently, form is the pressure the artist puts on his material in order to see what it can bear. Its primary aim is paradoxical—to exclude and accommodate. It wants to make room, for example, for odd shapes and strange companions. But it's an assassin to the superfluous, or any failure of precision. Essentially, form's job is to help reveal content. It's in the business of heightening, subordinating, arranging. It controls rates of disclosure, degrees of importance. It guides the eye.

Or maybe form's job is to be a thing unto itself.

Frank Lloyd Wright said, "The small house is the architect's greatest challenge." I suspect that poets who have experimented with, say, heroic couplets or the haiku, would know exactly what he meant. Any error is magnified. Like Snodgrass's de/composition or, say, a failed bungalow, there's this terribly conspicuous thing in front of you. Wright seems at his best when he could bring his imagination not just to the design of a particular house, but to how it would fit into a neighborhood, become both a part of and an extension of its environment. I'm thinking in particular of his "Fallingwater," which happens to exist just fifty miles from where I live.

The small house may be the architect's greatest challenge, but the large, ambitious structure should be handled by the architect or poet as if it presented the same problems. Of course, the viewer only wants something splendid to admire and think about. Anyone who has looked hard at Notre Dame or the Taj Mahal or tried to get a sure handle on, say, "Paradise Lost" or "The Waste Land" knows the opportunities for exploration in structures to which form has given the feel of permanence. The larger the structure the more the opportunities. And depending on where you're standing in relation to them—physically, psychologically, historically—such structures take on different properties. Their coherence is an invitation into their mysteries, and permits rather than restricts speculation. That which is sloppily constructed, on the other hand, permits more viewpoints than are useful.

A master of forms, that very scrupulous and mischievous "sculptor" Andy Goldsworthy is in no such danger. He contends that "All forms are to be found in nature," and adds, "by exploring them I hope to understand the whole. My work needs to include the loose and disordered as well as the tight and regular." He believes that he's "in collaboration with nature," which is a useful, necessary fiction for him. What he actually does is impose on nature what is inherent in it, until what we're looking at is a semblance of nature. More than anything else, what we're looking at is a Goldsworthy. The maker of memorable things always leaves behind his signature.

Looking at almost any Goldsworthy construction, I'm reminded of these lines from Wallace Stevens' "Anecdote of a Jar."

> I placed a jar in Tennessee,
> And round it was, upon a hill.
> It made the slovenly wilderness
> Surround that hill.
>
> The wilderness rose up to it,
> And sprawled around, no longer wild.

Art gives us a vantage point, a way of seeing. The jar formalizes the wilderness just as the man-made corral might focus the observer's eye, make the ranch itself less amorphous.

In many ways, Goldsworthy's work reminds us that art is *not* like what we recognize as experience, but rather is a fully realized arrangement of gestures and moves, an imitation of experience, an enactment, which moments before did not exist. Such is my double pleasure with it, and with the work of great poets like Stevens as well. It intensifies something previously half-known or half-seen and is an object in its own right.

Goldsworthy is also a wonderful exaggerator. For example, he extends a crack line in slate so far that we see that there are actually crack lines in slate! In so doing he points to what we come to realize is a structural insight. We feel in the presence of a fine excess (emphasis on the adjective), which Keats called poetry.

Though Goldsworthy's work tilts toward the underlying patterns in the natural world, it also borrows its symmetries and discordancies from the history of art and architecture. We see this in the pyramids he makes out of rocks, in any of his various arches, in the surreality of his ice sculptures. He surprisingly transforms the known, then further defamiliarizes it by doing something else to it—in one instance by placing a dead heron's feathers and cut stone in among stacked branches, or, in another, by building a giant, moon-like snow ball into the bare branches of a tree. Pure mischief. It is beauty happening by the permission he gives himself to construct it that results in the vitalization of landscape.

But I've mostly been talking about form as if achieving it was more or less rational. Isn't there always something secretly propulsive about how the best art gets made? Let's call it "the unknown agent x," which is what Nabokov called the most influential force that molds a human being. Heredity and environment, he says, take second and third place to it. This unknown agent x has formal or structural implications as well.

"Prudent Triangle," a poem by the Yugoslav poet Vasko Popa, might be a paradigm for what mysteriously drives a poem. It is translated by Charles Simic.

Prudent Triangle

Once upon a time there was a triangle
It had three sides

The fourth it kept hidden
In its burning center

By day it climbed its three peaks
And admired its center
At night it rested
In one of its three angles

Each dawn it watched its three sides
Turn into three fiery wheels
And vanish in the blue of never return

It took its fourth side
Embraced and broke it three times
To hide it again in its old place

And again it had only three sides
And again it climbed each day
To its three peaks

And admired its center
While at night it rested
in one of its three angles

Perhaps the triangle is prudent because, although it has a fourth side, an agent x, a side that is active all day long, "at night it rested/ in one of its angles." The triangle knows when not to be active, knows when it's better off "admiring its burning center." At some point, therefore, it has distance, aesthetic distance, which of course is analogous to Popa's participation in his own poem. Surely, "Prudent Triangle" invites other readings, but for my purposes in this talk the way the triangle behaves is emblematic of structural fluidity.

The fourth side is the agent of heat. It's a propulsive force, altering our conventional understanding of the triangle. By day, the triangle's three sides "turn into three fiery wheels/and vanish in the blue of never return." (The triangle just "watches" this happen, implying that what it has set in motion has imperatives of its own.) Then the triangle takes its fourth side and breaks it "three times/to hide it again in its old place." (Here the triangle is active and full of intention.) I take this as a metaphor for the poem's energy, the energy that is a combination of the poet's intentionality and the poem's vibrant, increasingly insistent demands.

The triangle (and, by extension, Popa) is the orchestrator of its mysteries, sometimes admiring its elements from afar, sometimes watching as its parts seem to act by themselves, sometimes very close and involved, embracing and breaking. As with my corral metaphor, it would be wrong to push Popa's little "Once upon a time" fairy tale too far, but it does point to this: a discussion about a poem's form is often incomplete unless it identifies its main propulsive forces, which are likely linked to its central concerns.

Let me conclude by saying that the greater the artist the more he or she is able to accommodate the unruly, the serendipitous, the discordant—in a sense, the unmanageable—and create for them a livable environment. To do this, it helps to know something about commitments, small and large. Though form seems to presume a reining in, it also should be a permission to be expansive. We need a Walt Whitman for every Emily Dickinson. A Louis Kahn for every Philip Johnson. But when we're speaking of form we need to remember at least two different kinds of nobilities. One is represented by the stairway whose stairs no one will ever use and by Goldsworthy's often evanescent structures. The other is represented by all those poems and buildings that attempt to frame and house what's human. I want my structures to be habitable with doors that open into spaces that intrigue. I want them to cast a light on what is there, but not easily seen. For a poet to forget that one of his jobs is to explore what it feels like to be alive in a particular place and time is the equivalent of an architect forgetting that houses are to be lived in. Form has a curious integrity; it wishes to serve. It only sometimes wants to be only itself.

Intraview and Interview

Brief Answers to Unspoken Questions

An Intraview

STYLE. It's like a doctor wishing to have a bedside manner: if it sounds rehearsed, it has been. Some writers think they can will it. When that happens, every effort feels like effort.

No, I don't think the writing teacher in this respect is much different from the physician: the person under examination would like us to keep our private lives out of our diagnoses.

A poet of domestic life? Seems rather reductive to me, even though domestic life is an enormous subject, especially if you believe, as I do, that it has its mysteries. But to unearth things is not enough. You need to find a choreography for them. The detritus of a day, e.g.—not unlike imagining those creatures making their way toward us in *Night of the Living Dead* . . . slowly, awkwardly. Opportunities for movement, for undreamed-of sympathies.

This is what I know about teaching: if you kiss one gorgeous student, you're likely to kiss another. I've always tried to kiss someone else.

I agree: to listen well is an act of curiosity and respect. It presumes that someone has something to say. But I know it's not enough to be a good listener. The best listener listens, à la Wallace Stevens, "with the innermost ear of the mind." Then what he says in response must reflect the quality of his hearing.

I'll answer this way. My favorite dog cartoon is this one: two dogs meet on the street, and one says to the other, "They always call me good dog. They never say great dog."

Well, here's what I used to hold dear. A truth is most comfortably received when preceded by an indefinite article—*a* instead of *the* unlocks the noun, makes the truth feel credibly small. Now I think that to make assertions using indefinite articles mostly serves to keep us from making fools of ourselves, and yet, sometimes, don't we have to risk this? Aren't the most memorable statements asserted boldly, like Flannery O'Connor's "The truth will make you odd," or André Gide's "It is with noble sentiments that bad literature gets written"? Actually, there are many things other than truth that are dear to me. The tone with which something is said, for one. My fear is Stendhal's: "I may have expressed only a sigh when I thought I was stating the truth."

The lesson of Scheherazade: The king doesn't need a reason to fuck me. He does need a good reason, however, not to execute me. Every reader is a potential tyrant. Make sure the page gets turned.

No. A fiction is a beautiful thing. Unmediated and untransformed experience is a form of ugliness. It sprawls. You can see its underwear.

Hero is the wrong word. I'd say I've often been a protagonist; that is, someone on the verge of learning what everyone else knows about him.

Well, you have to be careful with what you say to certain students. I said to one young man, "You can't go around comparing the yearnings of vampires with your own criminal desires. You're a guy, not a genre; there's less expected of you." He didn't think that was funny, which worried me.

Occasional mischief always seems more interesting than earnestness of any duration. But what if I were to say that there are issues of design and scope to consider, of how and where things fit, not to mention the indulgences of mischief, the poignancies of something actually meant. Oh, I see . . . I'm proving your point.

No, I loved those writers who addressed my daily sense of dislocation. Beckett and Cervantes and Kafka—those serious comedians. Then, later, Roethke. Rilke. James Wright. The list is long. I used to read to be introduced to myself, and to otherness; I used to read in order to feel normal. Now I'm more likely to read to see how a writer got from one place to another, to try to locate the secrets and magic of how something gets made.

Good taste? Nothing narrows what we're able to see and invent more than good taste. Then again, I have to say I've enjoyed many a narrowing.

Sure, I usually find myself rearranging what I've started. I'm fond of those good bad movies in which tornadoes rip through trailer parks, leaving lives and furniture strewn about. I'm the mayor who tells the reporter it's time to rebuild, who's fascinated by the odd, jigsaw-puzzle logic of how things might be put together again. Of course, the stakes become different if, say, my aunt lives in one of those trailers. Lament complicates reconstruction, as it should. I might not want to improve that broken rocking chair, which was hers. Lament just might want me to leave it there next to her son's one shoe and his overturned tricycle.

Special effects? I hate them. It's the fault of *Star Wars*, a good movie. After *Star Wars*, lots of dazzle, things somersaulting at terrible speeds. Fewer and fewer depictions of people destroying their lives normally. I hate fireworks. I hate parades. Give me backroom betrayals, or a quiet lie that makes a family cascade downward or, through unlikely courage, transcend its fate. I never have a good time on the Fourth of July. I refuse to wave to anyone riding in an open car.

Here's something that I'd say to writers: At least have the decency to claim your unhappiness. Don't leave it lying around the house, bleeding like that. Make something of it.

Yes, yes, but sometimes the soul is so sick it isn't able to open the door.

What I mean to say is that my soul stays shy when it hears someone spill the beans.

My influences? *Claire's Knee*. Things half-seen. The impossible shot. The need to make my life appear more interesting. More interesting than what? I come with a magnifying glass to the ant farm.

Oh yes, I've had many plans. But "everyone has a plan until you hit them," said Mike Tyson. Careful now, don't automatically discredit what the discredited have said. One punch from him in his prime, and the last chapter of your memoir would need to be rethought. That is, if you were still capable of thinking. When the verdict is in, I often ask myself how we keep on going.

I'm so tired of defending atheism. The burden, of course, is on the believers. Me, I believe in love at first sight more than in the existence of God. I believe that if you call someone and she answers, she's there.

Really, the obfuscators are cowards. So what if language can only approximate? Some writers approximate better than others. Count me as someone who tries to be as clear as he can about what it feels like to be alive while knowing the heart itself resides in the dark.

Oh, there are all kinds of great sentences. Joyce's "A frowsy whore with black straw sailor hat askew came glazily in the day along the quay towards Mr. Bloom" is one of them. "There was an old woman who lived in a shoe" is another. And then there's Mussolini in 1934 saying, "We have buried the putrid corpse of liberty"—a reprehensible well-turned phrase. Compare it with Eisenhower authorizing the Normandy invasion in 1944: "Okay, let's go." Context raising simplicity to eloquence.

No, I'm a hedgehog *and* a fox. Sometimes I see the world through a single lens. Sometimes the world overwhelms and brims over. I need to widen my glance as often as I need to narrow it. I love Tolstoy, I love Dostoyevsky—vast and contradictory. Let the fun begin.

Why would I? I'll remind you to look up the definition of self-indulgence.

We are responsible for what we invent; God's loneliness is ours. That's my latest position. From now on, when it comes to God talk, I plan to be merciless.

I'll tell you a pretty story; maybe then you'll understand.

Now, now, I often tell myself, no weeping. There's still time to revise.

Relentlessly Interesting

An Interview with Stephen Dunn by Laura McCullough

from the *Georgia Review*

LAURA MCCULLOUGH (LM): Let's begin with *What Goes On: Selected and New Poems*. I get a clear sense throughout the collection that the character of the poet has been formed by his forebears poetically, intellectually, and personally. Do you live with such ghosts?

STEPHEN DUNN (SD): I live with many ghosts, yes, who tend to daunt more than haunt. Frost is one of them, Stevens another. Roethke. Donald Justice. I seem to be returning to Stevens most of all these days. Of course I don't write like him, but he's a model of what R. P. Blackmur called "erudition," by which he meant someone intensely aware of effects. There's a kind of harnessed wildness to Stevens which continues to intrigue and inform me. He's a great blender of dictions, a master of rhythm and pacing. I think of "The Idea of Order at Key West," for example, as a model of how to blend direct and lyrical speech, and especially of pacing. How you pace is how you hear your own poem, your own tonalities. But then there are my other influences, odder ones I don't much talk about but should—like Jean Shepherd, to whom as a teenager I listened on the radio every night, from 10 to 11, in New York City. A great storyteller, as was my maternal grandfather.

LM: Storytelling seems to be one of your favorite subjects—the how of it, and the various ways we fail our stories as well. Could you talk about that a little?

SD: It seems I've always "storified" my life, largely because I was quite sure that my actual life was uninteresting. A little embellishment always seemed to help. Good stories, good poems, are successful illusions, voice and "fact" in cahoots. And then there's the issue of why anybody should care about what you're saying. My sense of social obligation is to never tell a story in public unless it's going to please or be poignant. I quickly tire of people who tell stories merely to impart information. I find myself waiting for something that they have no intention of delivering.

Of course, the stories I tell in my poems are designed to be overheard.

I love the storytellers who are either quite sure of where they're going, and therefore choosing their details with a certain intentional relish, or are delighting themselves as they wing their way forward, seemingly astounded by their own bravura performances.

Poems, narrative or not—shouldn't they be relentlessly interesting? It's like telling a good joke: you trust there are going to be allurements along the way, as opposed to the long, bad joke where you're just waiting for the punch line. That's unbearable to me. I know that Shepherd was a positive influence in how to sustain interest as one goes, as was my grandfather, and maybe the most significant person to me in this regard was my friend Sam Toperoff, who was the only literary person I knew until well into my twenties. A great raconteur.

I've written about Sam in my essay/memoir "A History of My Silence." In it I recall a late evening after a road game—we both played basketball for Hofstra—when I went to Sam's hotel room, where he was talking to Dick Pulaski, another teammate. Like Sam, Dick was five years older, having been in the army before starting college. Pulaski was a philosophy major, and Sam was, if not the brightest person in the college, certainly the most brilliantly idiosyncratic. They were talking about *Moby Dick*, and it was the best conversation I had ever heard in my life. For one thing, I didn't know you could be funny about serious things. I just sat there. They didn't address me or expect me to speak. If I was famous for anything then besides my jump shot, it was my silence. For many years, I was quietly taking in, storing up. I wanted to speak about books the way Sam could.

LM: The most common perception of silence is that it is an act of withdrawal and being passive; your silence, as described here and in your essay, seems to be the exact opposite.

SD: Well, maybe. Chosen silence is fine, but as a young man I often found myself with more painful manifestations of it. A tongue-tied-ness. A self-consciousness in the face of superior knowledge or superior style. The silence that debilitates. I can think of a fairly recent relapse—a weekend in Napa Valley with Charles Simic, Mark Strand, Daniel Halpern, and Robert Hass, all of whom are quite gifted at talking about wine, when I found myself without comparable language, and without an escape hatch. It wasn't their fault, but there I was, back in my old childhood silence. Painful.

LM: Perhaps this is what happens when people are aware of authority in their presence, but it's stunning to hear you talk about other major poets this way. I can't imagine they felt that you should have been silent.

SD: No, they were fine. They were having a good time. I'm only offering the story as an example of a silence of mine that didn't have redeeming qualities. As you know, I do know how to talk now, and I do get by in the world quite well. [laughter]

LM: Let me change the subject to poet-as-teacher, something you've written about in your book of essays and memoirs, *Walking Light.* Some poets who teach are variously rigorous, even harsh, while others tend to be more nurturing. You have had a long career as a teacher. What is your thinking about how best to teach creative writing?

SD: Have them read everyone. And about their own work—tell them the truth, and try to keep them alive at the same time. Most of them, that is. For some it's more merciful to suggest they be social workers.

If you've been around and teaching as long as I have, you come to realize that if you were in the business of making poets, you would have to quit your job. There are students of mine, like yourself, who have gone on to do significant work, but not many. Mostly, teaching writing means making people better readers, more attuned to discernment of what's good, and teaching them how to be discriminating with language. That's what I'm mostly doing, and I'm reconciled to that. Those of you who have surpassed those expectations—well, I couldn't be happier with that, and how much I might be responsible for your growth is at best uncertain.

Regarding nurturing, I don't think it is a useful thing unless it arises out of severity, out of saying credible things. On the other hand, you don't want to kill people; as everybody knows, the smallest criticisms of a work are taken personally. But, finally, I'm not interested in fostering self-esteem. I'm interested in the poem. If the writer's allegiance is to the poem more than, say, to self and self-discovery, well then she has a chance.

LM: Do you find any difference in the ways those writing fiction and those writing poetry accept criticism?

SD: Accept? I don't know, but poets have a better chance of hearing more reactions to their work. Often with poems, because you can write several over a short period of time, there is a greater possibility of redemption. One doesn't work, another does. When you have a story and it's not working, and you've worked on it all semester long, that's a different issue. Also, a poet or would-be poet may be able to pull off what looks like a poem now and then, even if he or she is not particularly well read, but I think that's almost impossible for fiction writers. If you don't have shapes and models of good writing as part of your wherewithal, your failures are going to be everywhere evident. (Actually that's true for the poets as well.) The last several years of teaching fiction to undergraduates have been enormously frustrating for me because the students had read so little. Their errors were not redeemable.

LM: What qualities are you looking for in a student?

SD: I've said this before: a certain humility before the enterprise and enough balls and gutsiness—gumption—to get through the likely neglect that awaits, even if you're very good.

And they have to love their tools, or learn to love them. They have to be in love with sentences and lines. If they only talk about their work, and they don't talk about writers they love, I'm already in worry mode. But, you know, student work is one thing. What we need to keep in mind is the larger goal. As readers, we want to be enthralled and enlightened. As makers—that is, as illusionists in search of formalities and structures that hold our little worlds in place—we need to exceed ourselves, we need to be in the business of trying to make something memorable. All the student stuff is apprenticeship; it's practice. Finally, you give yourself over to your art if you wish to be an artist. I really don't think there are shortcuts.

LM: I've heard that Li Young-Lee asked Gerald Stern, "What does it take to become a great American poet?" and Stern said, "Read five books of poetry a week for the next ten years." Would you say that's apt?

SD: Well, do that . . . do whatever will enlarge you. But of course that sounds like just the beginning of an answer to an enormous question. I'm sure Gerry could have happily elaborated further. He might have said, "Be someone on whom nothing is lost," or, more Stern-like, "Distrust the language of power," or "Behave like a Jew." Maybe Gerry was saying we should read enough so that we can develop not only influences, but a critical sense. One of the things I can't stand to hear readers say is that they liked something because they could relate to it. That means they're happy with stasis; they've been congratulated on something they've already thought.

LM: Right. Affirmation, not discovery . . .

SD: When I hear potential writers talk about writers they admire, it would be very nice to hear them say Proust or Yeats in addition to some good contemporary. I remember liking what a woman writer—I can't remember her name right now—said in an interview about how important Dostoyevsky was to her as a writer. The interviewer asked her, "Well, do you think your own work measures up to his?" The woman laughed and said it was enough for her to be pointed in his direction. I like that a lot.

LM: May we talk about your history as a reader and a thinker? How did you come to be a writer?

SD: A crooked path. Some luck. Perseverance. A fear of embarrassing myself.

LM: Tell me about what you were reading as a teenager—say, at ages 15–17.

SD: All of Maugham. All of Hesse. Salinger. Ayn Rand. (Yes, I admit to having been an enthusiast.) *Moby Dick*. Some Hemingway (the Nick Adams stories). No poetry at that time. A book called *The Amboy Dukes*. And *God's Little Acre*. The "dirty" books of that era. *Peyton Place*.

LM: Where were you getting these books?

SD: I don't really remember. Maybe the way books suggest other books. Maybe because I was aware of how much I was unaware of, I listened very acutely to what those who seemed to know what they were talking about alluded to. I really can't remember. Maybe—and this is one of my longtime motives—I wanted to be someone I'm not, someone better than I am. I do remember, for example, telling someone I had read *Ulysses* when I hadn't, and then of course reading it so I wouldn't be a liar. Maybe I became a serious reader in order to catch up with my lies.

LM: You weren't getting books at school or at home?

SD: No, I probably was learning about them from a few smart girlfriends. It's amazing that I had time to read them. I was devoting most of my time, it seems in retrospect, to playing basketball.

LM: Were you embarrassed by your dual life of books and sports?

SD: I didn't think of it as a duality. My secret life was books; my overt life was that of an athlete. My two important high school girlfriends were cheerleaders. All the smart girls at Forest Hills [NY] High School at that time were cheerleaders. They were the cream of the crop, and I think they all went to first-rate colleges.

LM: You were reading all kinds of books because you wanted to be smart enough for the girls?

SD: Something like that.

LM: So, the most serious person I know had limits to how serious he wanted to be?

SD: Well, of course. Probably what I was most thinking about at that time was sex. *Thinking* about it being the operative word. (Not to say that sex isn't serious.) Even after I had grown into my so-called seriousness, I valued dumb days, days of avoidance and aimless play. I still do.

LM: You told me once that one of the most important books in your young life was *The Brothers Karamazov*. Is that right?

SD: *The* most important. It took on so much. I remember identifying with almost every character, being pulled one way and the next.

LM: So you're still in the land of moral complexity?

SD: I'm in the land of moral complexity even when I play ping-pong.

LM: In *What Goes On*, *storification*—a word you've coined and used for years—seems to be a major theme in the poems. In reading the *Selected and New*, I find you seem to have taken great care with the way the poems speak to each other. There are elements of a kind of novel, of a character taking shape over time.

SD: Well, that is something you can inform me about, because I don't know about that.

LM: Then how were you making those selections?

SD: I chose the best poems I had written, in my judgment, from each book.

LM: Some of the omissions are interesting. You chose to leave out, for example, "The Telling of Grandmother's Secret" [*Georgia Review*, Winter 2005], which in many ways I think is interesting in relation to "What Men Want," the last poem of the book.

SD: I guess that's true—I don't remember making a decision about that.

LM: In conversation once, you told me that when one has reached a certain age, there's a very large wealth of unsynthesized data from which he can continue to draw. Your poems seem so clear in their suppositions and their arguments, but are you also suggesting that you're composing with less consciousness?

SD: Yes and no. The truth is that most poems don't occur in any orderly way. Often I've stitched two or three poems together, have rearranged entire sections, have abandoned an original intention for the sake of pursuing something that just dawned on me mid-poem. I love that you think the new poems seem so clear in their suppositions and arguments. If so, they are victories over a sloppy mind, testimonies to what Stevens calls "the power of the mind over the possibilities of things."

LM: I don't want to lose one little thread concerning the grandmother poem. If I'm hearing you right, in terms of selecting poems, being merely interesting is no longer enough?

SD: Yes, that can never be enough. There are lots of instances of "interesting" subject matter that lack the felicities of phrasing and music and form. Maybe *interesting* should be redefined to mean "all the parts of a poem serving their subject" or something like that. Levertov's definition of form comes to mind: "the revelation of content." Just a personal aside: in recent poems I've been more conscious than ever of finding the right word by ear, so sonics also take their place in creating what constitutes "interesting."

LM: To return to the poem "Grandmother's Secret": at the end, the speaker is walking toward his home and says something like, "I've only just begun to know what I . . .

SD: feel.

LM: Yes, that's it. Given that you are seen as a poet of reason, this is a notable line break—and one that shows up again in your newest book, *Here and Now*. In "To My Doppelganger," which closes the volume, you write, "to go forward, I feel, / is to go together now. There's a place / I'd like to arrive by nightfall." Can you comment on this new emphasis on the emotional?

SD: Well, I may have suppressed that verb somewhat over the years, but it seems to me I've always been trying to find out what I feel and think. What I "know" I'd like to think is propositional, something always on the verge of being replaced. I feel my way into thinking, and I often think my way into feeling. Both seem like achievements when they occur. I hold to them for as long as I can. But something always seems to happen which confounds what I think I know or feel. That said, if I knew what I felt in advance, there'd be nothing to pursue, and if we're lucky our poems instruct us in ways we couldn't have anticipated. Then, of course, in "To My Doppelganger," it's entirely possible that "I feel" is where it is for no particular feeling I had at all, but because of the pleasure—for me at least—of the near rhyme with "nightfall."

LM: In the title poem "Here and Now" there are just two regular folk, a couple—"making a small case for themselves," and some head-on frank talk about marriage, and the gutsy, "For you and me / it's *here and now* from here on in." You write, "nothing can save us," but then parry, "nor do we wish to be saved." Can you speak to these lines?

SD: Well, the poem begins, "There are words / I've had to save myself from," and goes on to cite religious phrases that I had said but never meant. So the poem represents a kind of cleaning up of one's life, an evolution toward the genuine, away from inherited and unfelt language, away from heavenly nonsense, and toward earthly sufficiencies with someone else who also knows that's all there is.

LM: That poem is dedicated to your wife, Barbara. Would you say the new poems have more emotional range? They seem to let in more emotional texture and are more frank.

SD: No, I don't think so. I would like to think, whatever their subject is, they sustain a sense of veracity with perhaps more authority. But for "frankness" and "emotional texture," I'd rather substitute words like "phrasing" and "pacing." Almost thirty years ago, I concluded a poem called "Essay on the Personal" with this language:

> We return to everything
> strange, inchoate, like living
> with someone, like living alone,
> settling for the partial, the almost
> satisfactory sense of it.

I'm still inclined to stand by it, not because of its frankness per se, but because I found rhythms that seem to authenticate its assertions. At any rate, I tend to distrust people who are frank. They go around saying what they're thinking.

LM: A bit earlier, you mentioned your growing attention to sonics. Two examples come to mind from *Here and Now*, the opening of "Love" and the end of "After Ecstasy":

> Found dead in an alley
> of words: *awesome*,
> no hope for it, and *share*,
> which must have fallen
> trying to get by on its own,
> and near the trash cans,
> almost totally exhausted,
> the barely breathing *cool*.

> He'd call her up
> and say things like *Holy shit*,
> which she understood
> to be accurate.

In both cases, the love of language and what love might really be are woven together in a strangely inevitable way that seems to be realized with subtle sonic choices. In what way has the sound of a poem become more a part of your working process? Can you talk about another poem in *Here and Now* in which this was important to the poem's realization?

SD: In all of them, really. But maybe in particular "Landscape with Friends" [p. 332], in that I never once thought about sound as I was composing it. Each word kept finding its sonic companions. This seemed to testify to my ear making unconscious choices, and those choices gelling with sense. Very satisfying.

LM: Your new book takes me back to your long poem "Loves," from *Landscape at the End of the Century*, published in 1991. So many of those "loved things" appear in the new poems—paradox and ideas, but also so much of the corporeal world: dogs, food, friendship, women, the physical body. Time was also a big element in "Loves." Can you talk about how age and mortality inform the poems in *Here and Now*?

SD: Oh, in a few ways, I'm sure. But because of the early deaths in my family (both my parents died in their late fifties), I've always lived as if I didn't have long to live, have always written as if there wasn't a lot of time to write. There are a few new poems, like "Final Bow" and "A Great Celebration" [p. 326], that may suggest a greater sense of urgency about things coming to an end, but mostly I suspect I was, as usual, finding occasions to explore . . . dare I say this? . . . my various engagements with the human condition. [laughter]

LM: Yes, the new book is elegant and also has a kind of grace. I'm thinking particularly of the poems in section IV, but since you've written (I paraphrase) "I want no one to suspect that what I reveal is my way of withholding," I wonder what's still held close to your chest?

SD: Almost everything. In that sense my life is like my poetry. I'm inclined to tell you only as much as I think is useful for you to hear, or for the poem to accommodate. If I do it well, you will think I'm being honest, maybe even vulnerable, though I hate that word. My poems are not occasions for the reader and me to become buddies. I am a rather closed person. Intimacy, true intimacy between people, occurs when one or the other is given permission to cross strongly held boundaries. In the best of poems, I suspect, the door between personal disclosure and necessary invention is opened just far enough. The best readers step in, expecting to find only the words that have been chosen for them. They don't expect to find the person. They can be sure that I'm elsewhere.

LM: "To My Doppelganger" suggests you're still quarrelling with yourself, yet there's also the suggestion of some kind of reconciliation. What happens when heart and mind are in collusion, finally?

SD: It's time to doubt the collusion.

Biography

Works by Stephen Dunn

Selected Secondary Sources

Contributors

Index

Biography

Stephen Dunn was born in Forest Hills, New York, in 1939, and earned his BA in history from Hofstra University in 1962. He attended the New School 1964 to 1966 and received his Master of Arts in Creative Writing from Syracuse University in 1970. He's the author of over twenty books of poetry and prose, including *Different Hours*, which won the 2001 Pulitzer Prize for poetry. He has taught at the Richard Stockton College of New Jersey since 1974, and he is Distinguished Professor of Creative Writing there. He has won many awards including fellowships from the National Endowment for the Arts, the Guggenheim Foundation, and the New Jersey State Council on the Arts, the James Wright Prize, and an Academy Award for Literature. He lived in Port Republic, NJ, for many years, where he and his first wife raised two daughters. He now lives in western Maryland with his wife, the writer Barbara Hurd.

Résumé Notes

Williamsport Billies, Williamsport, PA, professional basketball player, 1962–63; National Biscuit Co., New York, NY, copywriter, 1963–66; Ziff-Davis Publishing Co., New York, NY, assistant editor, 1967–68; Southwestern State University, Marshall, MN, assistant professor of creative writing, 1970–73; Syracuse University, Syracuse, NY, lecturer in poetry, 1973–74; Richard Stockton College, Pomona, NJ, professor of creative writing, 1974–; University of Washington, visiting professor, 1980; director of Associated Writing Programs Poetry Series, 1980–82; Columbia University, adjunct professor, 1983–87; University of Michigan, adjunct professor, 2000.

Works by Stephen Dunn

Books of Poetry

Five Impersonations (Marsall, MN: Ox Head Press, 1971).
Looking for Holes in the Ceiling (Amherst: University of Massachusetts Press, 1974).
Full of Lust and Good Usage (Pittsburgh: Carnegie-Mellon University Press, 1976).
A Circus of Needs (Pittsburgh: Carnegie-Mellon University Press, 1978).
Work and Love (Pittsburgh: Carnegie-Mellon University Press, 1981).
Not Dancing (Pittsburgh: Carnegie-Mellon University Press, 1984).
Local Time (New York: Quill/Morrow, 1986). A National Poetry Series selection.
Between Angels (New York: Norton, 1989).
Landscape at the End of the Century (New York: Norton, 1991).
New and Selected Poems: 1974–1994 (New York: Norton, 1994).
Loosestrife (New York: Norton, 1996). National Book Critics Circle Award finalist.
Winter at the Caspian Sea, chapbook with Lawrence Raab (Aiken, SC: Palanquin Press, 1999).
Different Hours (New York: Norton, 2000). Pulitzer Prize.
Beyond Hammonton, chapbook with Michael McGarvey (Port Republic, NJ: Port Press, 2002).
Local Visitations (New York: Norton, 2003).
The Insistence of Beauty (New York: Norton, 2004).
Everything Else in the World (New York: Norton, 2006).
What Goes On: Selected and New Poems 1995–2009 (New York: Norton, 2009). Chosen as one of the notable books of the year by ALA (American Library Association). Only two were chosen in the poetry category.
Here and Now (New York: Norton, 2011).
Falling Backwards Into the World (New York: Jane Street Press, 2012). Limited edition chapbook.
Lines of Defense (New York: Norton, 2013).

Books of Prose

Walking Light: Essays and Memoirs (New York: Norton, 1993).

Walking Light: Essays and Memoirs, revised and expanded edition, (Rochester, NY), BOA Editions 2001.

(Author of foreword) Juanita Tobin, *Ransom Street Quartet: Poems and Stories* (Boone, NC: Parkway), 1995.

Riffs and Reciprocities: Prose Pairs (New York: Norton, 1998).

Books Edited

An Alibi of Gifts, A Cat of Wind: A Handbook and Anthology of poems by children, published by The New Jersey State Council on the Arts, 1977.

Silence Has a Rough, Crazy Weather: Poems by Deaf Children, NJ State Council on the Arts, 1979.

Nightsun (guest editor), published by Frostburg State University, 2005.

Sound Recordings

Stephen Dunn, New Letters (Kansas City, MO), 1980.

Stephen Dunn Reads His Poetry and Is Interviewed by Grace Cavalieri, recorded at the Library of Congress, Washington, DC, for broadcast on *The Poet and the Poem* radio program, 1994.

Marilyn Nelson Waniek and Stephen Dunn Reading Their Poems, sponsored by the Gertrude Clarke Whittall Poetry and Literature Fund, Library of Congress (Washington, DC), 1994.

Selected Secondary Sources

Note: Dunn, Stephen (1939–),
Collection, 1947–Current 21 c.f.
Special Collections Department/ University Archives
http://www.hofstra.edu/Libraries/SpecialCollections

Description: The Stephen Dunn Collection at Hofstra University consists of the personal and professional papers of Dunn, including various publications in which he appeared in throughout his career. Correspondence with other poets, friends, and colleagues regarding the poetry of Stephen Dunn reside here. In addition to correspondence, fan mail is available. The uncollected and early versions of collected poetry by Stephen Dunn are in the collection, including handwritten versions. Memorabilia from the Pulitzer Prize celebration has also been donated, including a scrapbook of the event.

Dacey, Philip. 2000. "Interview with Stephen Dunn." *Cortland Review*. March 2000. http://www.cortlandreview.com/features/00/03/index.html.

Dunn, Stephen. 1991. "Complaint, Complicity, Outrage, and Composition." *Crazyhorse* 41: 71–93.

———. 2005. "One Summer: Musings about Avoidance, Temperament, and the Poem Becoming a Poem." *Georgia Review* 59, no. 4: 817–21.

———. 2009. "The Poem, Its Buried Subject, and the Revisionist Reader: Behind 'The Guardian Angel.'" *Midwest Studies in Philosophy* 33, no. 1: 5–10.

———. 2012. "For Love of the Sentence and Thin Ice: An Interview with Stephen Dunn by Laura McCullough." *Green Mountains Review* 25, no. 1: 77–83.

Elliott, David L. 1995. "Precarious Balances: A Conversation with Stephen Dunn." *Mid-American Review* 15, no. 1–2: 6–17.

Farnsworth, Elizabeth. 2001. "Interview with Stephen Dunn." *PBS*. April 2006, 2001. http://www.pbs.org/newshour/bb/media/jan-june01/dunn_04-26.html.

Kitchen, Judith, and Stan Sanvel Rubin. 1987. "Only the Personal Matters": A Conversation with Stephen Dunn." *Literary Review* 30, no. 4: 559–70.

Kitchen, Judith. 1995. "Fourteen Ways of Looking at Selecteds." *Georgia Review* 49, no. 2: 501–22.

Looney, George. 1986. "*Local Time* by Stephen Dunn." *Mid-American Review* 7, no. 1: 194–203.

McCullough, Laura. 2010. "An Integrity of Aloneness." *American Poetry Review* 39, no. 2: 31–34.

———. 2010. "Seriously Funny: The Strangeness and Inevitability of Stephen Dunn's Poems." *Green Mountains Review* 23, no. 2: 33–45.

———. 2011. "Between Worlds, Refuge: Stephen Dunn and the Creative Writing Workshop." *Georgia Review* 65, no. 2: 353–63.

———. 2011. "The Poem, Its Buried Subject, and the Revisionist Reader: Behind 'The Guardian Angel.'" *Lit from Within: Contemporary Masters On the Art and Craft of Writing*, edited by Kevin Haworth and Dinty W. Moore. Athens: Ohio University Press. 118–27.

Nelson, Jeanne-Andrée. 2002. "Of Sand and Storm in the Poetry of Stephen Dunn." *Southern Humanities Review* 36, no. 3: 229–39.

Nightsun, editors of. 2000. "Poet of Restraint and Extravagance: A Conversation with Stephen Dunn." *Nightsun* 20. http://faculty.frostburg.edu/phil/forum/SDunn.htm.

Osel, Joseph D. 2009. "A Conversation with the Pulitzer Prize Winner Stephen Dunn." *Commonline Journal.* September 2009. http://www.commonlinejournal.com/2009/09/commonline-interview-pulitzer-prize.html.

Pinsker, Sanford. 1983. "Acts of Clarifications: A Conversation with Stephen Dunn about Process and Poetry." *Missouri Review* 7, no. 1: 59–68.

Smith, Dave. 1995. "Can We Talk? The Welcome Poetries of Dunn and Dobyns." *New England Review* 17, no. 2: 147–66.

Snell, N. Colwell. 2007. "The Mysteries of the Ordinary: A Conversation with Stephen Dunn." *Weber Studies* 23, no. 3: 2–11.

Tracy, Kristen. 1999. "Interview with Stephen Dunn (September 25, 1997, Moscow, Idaho)." *Green Mountains Review* 12, no. 1: 24–31.

Wald, Elissa. 2004. "An Interview with the Poet Stephen Dunn." *Poets and Writers*. August 19, 2004. http://www.pw.org/content/interview_poet_stephen_dunn.

Whitney, Joel. 2004. "The Hard-to-Say." *Guernica: A Magazine of Art and Politics*. October 27, 2004. http://www.guernicamag.com/interviews/stephen_dunn_on_why_he_writes/.

Wojahn, David. 1989. "Four from Prospero." *Georgia Review* 43, no. 3: 589–601.

Contributors

R. Dwayne Betts is a the author of the memoir *A Question of Freedom* (Avery/Penguin) and the collection of poetry *Shahid Reads His Own Palm* (Alice James Books). Betts has been awarded fellowships from the Radcliffe Institute for Advanced Studies, the Open Society Institute, Bread Loaf Writers' Conference, and Warren Wilson College. As a poet, essayist, and national spokesperson for the Campaign for Youth Justice, Betts writes and lectures about the impact of mass incarceration on American society.

Michael Broek's essays and articles have appeared in many periodicals, including the *American Poetry Review*, *Journal of American Studies* (UK), *American Literature Compass*, and *European Journal of American Studies*. His chapbook of poems, *The Logic of Yoo*, was published by *Beloit Poetry Journal*. He holds a PhD in American literature.

Kurt Brown founded the Aspen Writers' Conference, and Writers' Conferences and Centers. He is the author of six chapbooks and six full-length collections of poetry, including his newest *Time-Bound* (Tiger Bark Press, 2013). He is currently an editor for the online journal *MEAD: The Magazine of Literature and Libations* and has edited ten anthologies of poetry, including his newest (with Harold Schechter), *Killer Verse: Poems about Murder and Mayhem*. He has published a memoir, *Lost Sheep: A Portrait of Aspen in the '70s* (Conundrum Press 2012). He taught for many years at Sarah Lawrence College in New York.

Wendy Cannella earned her MFA from Vermont College and completed her doctoral degree at Boston College. Her work has appeared in *Free Lunch*, *Phoebe*, and *Southern Indiana Review*. She lives in Maine with her husband and two daughters where she is working on her first collection of poems.

Stephen Corey has published nine collections of poems, most recently *There Is No Finished World* (White Pine Press, 2003), as well as individual poems and essays in a wide range of periodicals and anthologies. He is the editor of the *Georgia Review*, with which he has worked since 1983.

Philip Dacey's latest of eleven books are *Mosquito Operas: New and Selected Short Poems* (Rain Mountain Press, 2010) and *Vertebrae Rosaries: Fifty Sonnets* (Red Dragonfly Press, 2009). Winner of three Pushcart Prizes, he has written collections of poems about Gerard Manley Hopkins, Thomas Eakins, and New York City.

Gregory Djanikian has published five collections of poetry with Carnegie Mellon University Press, the last of which is *So I Will Till the Ground* (2007). His next book, *Dear Gravity*, will appear next year. His poems have appeared in many journals including the *American Poetry Review*, *American Scholar*, *Boulevard*, *Georgia Review*, *Iowa Review*, *Poetry*, *Poetry Northwest*, *Southern Review*, *Shenandoah*, and *TriQuarterly*, and they have been featured on *News Hour with Jim Lehrer*. He directs the undergraduate creative writing program at the University of Pennsylvania.

Kathleen Graber is the author of two collections of poetry, *The Eternal City* (Princeton University Press, 2010) and *Correspondence* (Saturnalia Books, 2006). She teaches in the creative writing program at Virginia Commonwealth University.

Tony Hoagland has published four collections of poems. His recognitions include the Jackson Poetry Prize, the O. B. Hardisson Award for teaching, and the Mark Twain Award. His essays about poetry appear widely. He teaches in the writing program at the University of Houston.

Andrea Hollander is the author of four full-length poetry collections. Her honors include the Nicholas Roerich Poetry Prize, the D. H. Lawrence Fellowship, a Pushcart Prize, and two poetry fellowships from the National Endowment for the Arts. The writer-in-residence at Lyon College for twenty-two years, she lives in Portland, Oregon.

James Hollis, PhD, is a Jungian analyst in private practice in Houston, Texas, where he is also a professor of analytic psychology for Saybrook University, author of thirteen books, and friend of Stephen Dunn.

Lisa Honaker is professor of literature at the Richard Stockton College of New Jersey, where she teaches courses in Victorian through contemporary British literature. She has published on late Victorian fiction and currently writes about contemporary British fiction at http://www.readingthebookers.com. In 2010, she curated the manuscript exhibit *Stephen Dunn: A Retrospective.*

Pam Houston is the author of five books of prose, including *Contents May Have Shifted* and *Cowboys Are My Weakness.* She is the director of creative writing at UC-Davis and teaches in the Pacific low-residency MFA program. In her next life, she wants to come back as a poet.

David Jauss has published two collections of poetry, two collections of fiction, a collection of essays on the craft of fiction, and three anthologies. He teaches at the University of Arkansas at Little Rock and in the low-residency MFA program at Vermont College of Fine Arts.

Judith Kitchen is the author of three collections of personal essays; the latest is *Half in Shade: Family, Photography, Fate* (Coffee House Press, 2012). She has edited three collections of short nonfiction (*In Short*, *In Brief*, and *Short Takes*) for W. W. Norton. Her novel, *The House on Eccles Road*, won the S. Mariella Gable Award from Graywolf Press. Her awards include an NEA fellowship and two Pushcart Prizes. Kitchen is an advisory and contributing editor for the *Georgia Review* where she is a regular reviewer of poetry. She lives in Port Townsend, WA, and serves as co-director of the Rainier Writing Workshop Low-Residency MFA at Pacific Lutheran University.

Ilyse Kusnetz received her MA in creative writing from Syracuse University and her PhD from the University of Edinburgh in contemporary feminist and postcolonial British literature. She teaches English and creative writing at Valencia College in Florida. Her poetry and reviews have appeared in many journals, and she is the author of a chapbook, *The Gravity of Falling* (La Vita Poetica Press, 2006). She is the book reviews editor at the *Florida Review.*

Timothy Leyrson is a graduate student at Missouri State University pursuing an MA in English (creative writing poetry emphasis.) His work has appeared in *Midwestern Gothic* and forthcoming in *Atticus Review.*

George Looney's sixth poetry collection is *Monks Beginning to Waltz*; his fifth is *A Short Bestiary of Love and Madness.* He is also the author of the novella *Hymn of Ash.* He chairs the BFA in creative writing program at Penn State–Erie, where he edits *Lake Effect* and co-directs the Chautauqua Writers' Festival.

Fred Marchant is the author of *Tipping Point*, winner of the 1993 Washington Prize, *Full Moon Boat*, *House on Water, House in Air*, and *The Looking House.* He is the editor of *Another World Instead: The Early Poems of William Stafford, 1937-1947*, and the co-translator of *From a Corner of My Yard*, by Tran Dang Khoa. Winner of the 2009 May Sarton Award from the New England Poetry Club, he teaches at Suffolk University in Boston, where he is founder and co-director of the Poetry Center and the Creative Writing Program.

James Davis May earned his PhD in English at Georgia State University. His poetry has appeared in *Five Points*, *New Republic*, *New England Review*, and *Pleiades.* Currently the writer-in-residence at Agnes Scott College, he lives in Decatur, Georgia.

Laura McCullough's most recent books of poetry include *Rigger Death and Hoist Another* (Black Lawrence Press) and *Panic* (winner of a 2009 Kinereth Gensler Award, Alice James Books and BOTYA finalist). She is the editor of two anthologies, one on Stephen Dunn and one on poetry and race (University of Georgia Press). Her essays, criticism, poems, creative nonfiction, and short fiction have appeared in the *Georgia Review*, *Birmingham Review*, *New South*, *American Poetry Review*, *Green Mountains Review*, *Painted Bride Quarterly*, and others.

Peter E. Murphy is the author of *Stubborn Child*, a finalist for the 2006 Paterson Poetry Prize, and a poetry chapbook, *Thorough and Efficient*, both from Jane Street Press, which also published *Challenges for the Delusional: Peter Murphy's Prompts and the Poems They Inspired*, edited by Christine Malvasi. His essays have appeared in the *American Book Review*, *Shakespeare Quarterly*, *Teachers and Writers Guide to Frederick Douglass*, *World Order*, and elsewhere. He directs the annual Winter Poetry and

Prose Getaway and other programs for poets, writers, and teachers in the United States and abroad.

Alicia Ostriker's most recent collection of poems is *The Book of Life: Selected Jewish Poems 1979-2011*. Her most recent collection of criticism is *Dancing at the Devil's Party: Essays on Poetry, Politics, and the Erotic*. Ostriker teaches in the Drew University Low-Residency MFA Program in poetry and poetry in translation.

Lawrence Raab is the author of seven collections of poems, including *What We Don't Know about Each Other* (winner of the National Poetry Series and a finalist for the National Book Award), *The Probable World*, and *Visible Signs: New and Selected Poems*, all published by Penguin. His latest collection is *The History of Forgetting* (Penguin, 2009). He teaches literature and writing at Williams College.

David Rigsbee is the author of *The Red Tower: New and Selected Poems* (2010), *The Pilot House* (2011), and *School of the Americas* (2012), as well as eight previous collections. He has published critical works on Carolyn Kizer (1990) and Joseph Brodsky (1999) and coedited *Invited Guest: An Anthology of Twentieth Century Southern Poetry* (2001).

Jason Schneiderman is the author of two collections of poetry, and his essays and poems have appeared widely. He directs the writing center at the Borough of Manhattan Community College.

Dave Smith was the Elliot Coleman Professor of Poetry in the writing seminars at Johns Hopkins University, where he was chairman for six years. He is now writer-in-residence and professor of English at the University of Mississippi. His most recent books are *Hawks on Wires* (poems, LSU, 2011), *Afield: Writers on Bird Dogs* (essays, edited with Robert DeMott, Skyhorse, 2010), *Hunting Men: Reflections on a Life in American Poetry* (essays, LSU, 2006), and *Little Boats, Unsalvaged* (poems, LSU, 2005). He has held fellowships from the National Endowment for the Arts, the John Simon Guggenheim Foundation, the Rockefeller Foundation, and the Lyndhurst Foundation, and was twice a runner-up for the Pulitzer Prize in poetry.

Gerald Stern is the author fifteen books of poetry including *This Time: New and Selected Poems*, which won the 1998 National Book Award. He has won the Ruth Lilly Prize and the Wallace Stevens Award and in early 2012 he published a kind-of memoir, called *Stealing History*. W. W. Norton will release a new book of poems, *In Beauty Bright*, in the fall of 2012.

Brian Turner is the author of *Here, Bullet* and *Phantom Noise*. His poetry and essays have been published in the *New York Times*, *National Geographic*, *Poetry Daily*, *VQR*, *Georgia Review*, and other journals. He is a coeditor of *The Strangest of Theatres: Poets Writing Across Borders* (McSweeney's, 2012) and his memoir, *My Life as a Foreign Country*, will be available in 2014. He received a USA Hillcrest Fellowship in literature, an NEA Literature Fellowship in poetry, the Amy Lowell Traveling Fellowship, a U.S.-Japan Friendship Commission Fellowship, the Poets' Prize, and a fellowship from the Lannan Foundation. His work has appeared on *National Public Radio*, *BBC*, *Newshour with Jim Lehrer*, and *Weekend America*, among others. He is the director of the low-residency MFA at Sierra Nevada College.

BJ Ward's most recent book is *Jackleg Opera* (IO Poetry Series/North Atlantic Books). His work has appeared in *Poetry*, *TriQuarterly*, *Painted Bride Quarterly*, *The Sun*, *New York Times*, and *The Pushcart Prize Anthology*. He earned an MA from Syracuse University where he served as University Distinguished Fellow.

Index